MATTHEW ARNOLD AND THE THREE CLASSES

MATTHEW ARNOLD and the THREE CLASSES

Patrick J. McCarthy

New York and London 1964

COLUMBIA UNIVERSITY PRESS

149821

To HELEN

PREFACE

In his greatest prose work, *Culture and Anarchy*, Matthew Arnold examines each of what he considers the three classes of England to determine its fitness as a center of authority and a source of light. Each class in turn is found wanting, and Arnold then suggests that the nation rise above the notion of classes to the conception of a state. The state, as the corporate and collective "best self" of England, would have the power to restrain the excesses of each class and the intelligence to direct the strength of each class toward the proper modes of "expansion," that is, liberty.

As they appear in *Culture and Anarchy*, the three classes have undergone a process of simplification and heightening and acquired a symmetry of form. Within the work each class is matched part for part with the other classes; each has its virtues and defects, each has its virtuous mean and its dangerous excess. To give the abstraction an air of reality, Arnold names each of the means and excesses after a living member of the class being described. He dubs the classes "Barbarians," "Philistines," and "Populace," for these are the classes not as they exist but as they are transformed for a literary purpose, and new creatures need new names. Of course no description of a class has reality in any absolute sense, and Arnold is concerned to give his line drawings only enough of the semblance of reality that they may serve the purposes of the work.

To this transformation, this shearing off of the temporal and the accidental in his representation of the classes, is due a measure of the permanent interest of *Culture and Anarchy*. In later editions of the work Arnold wisely sought even further to tone down personal allusions and to delete topical references. But some parts of *Culture and Anarchy* did not lend themselves to such a refining process, and they suffered in the revision. The chapter in which such references are the warp and woof, the one entitled "Our Liberal Practitioners," is the most unfamiliar to modern readers. *Friendship's Garland*, the book many Arnoldians regard as the *locus classicus* of Victorian irony and wit, suffers so much from its welter of timely references that only the specialist can enjoy it, and editing the work for modern readers has seemed a useless task.

For the most part, however, Arnold is able to keep his generalizations from slipping into unreality on the one hand, and on the other from becoming enmeshed in matters of merely passing interest. It is true that some readers object to Arnold's use of the stock notion of class at all. The notion, says Raymond Williams, "offered category feelings about human behaviour, based on a massing and simplifying of actual individuals, as an easy substitute for the difficulties of personal and immediate judgement." The strength of this objection must be allowed, but the notion of class, albeit vague, was a useful generalization. Arnold might not know where one class ended and where another began, but there was no mistaking a laborer for a commercial traveler. And yet his use of "class" as a mode of

approach to society has other drawbacks. Since Arnold is working toward a conception above and beyond class, he is forced
by his rhetoric to treat each of the classes similarly or to risk
seeming unfair. A flaw in one class must have a counterpart
in the other classes. The extremes of classes must be matched
each to each; praise must be distributed in equal measure to
the three groups. Arnold fits the pieces together with dexterity.
But the dexterity is suspicious: real things, or even ideas rooted
in reality, cannot be so neatly manipulated. Arnold's own views
of the classes—or, if one insists, of the individuals who make
up the classes—must be pared and fitted to the stringent
demands of his technique and literary purpose.

Of course Arnold's views of the three classes were not neat.
They were the complicated and changing products of his complete experience with them, and these views are rooted in
practical, specific affairs and issues. What these views were is
important not only to an understanding of *Culture and Anarchy*
but also to Arnold biography and to accurate judgments about
Arnold's integrity and consistency. After 1880, for example,
Arnold became interested in questions of practical politics and
wrote about them at some length. In the course of these essays
he expressed ideas that have been called reactionary. Whether
Arnold had turned conservative in his last years or whether
contemporary events made him overemphasize one aspect of
his many-sided views is a question on which a history of
Arnold's relationship to the classes may throw some light.

My purpose is not apologetic; I have wished to look closely
at the history of Matthew Arnold's relationship with the three
classes, perhaps to explain, certainly not to explain away, the
discomfort that *Culture and Anarchy* gives to many modern
readers. Since a good deal of what we can know about that
relationship during his mature years must be based on what

Arnold says about it himself, I have dwelt at length on his family and school background in an effort to discover the point of view from which he saw himself and his society. I have also looked at his relationship with his father, from whom he learned so much about the nature of authority, the necessity for it, and the resentment it arouses in those on whom it is imposed. Similarly, I have directed attention within the three classes to individuals with whom Arnold associated or about whom he expressed himself in a significant way.

It was Arnold's wont continually to measure the real against the ideal and to prefer things as they could be to things as they were. He was not content to praise what he knew was limited. Whenever we measure the real against the ideal, even if it is the reality of Arnold's life against a kind of ideal life, we too discover and note limitation, but at the same time we also confess ourselves his followers and debtors.

PATRICK J. McCARTHY

December, 1963

ACKNOWLEDGMENTS

No one can write a study of this kind without incurring a large debt to others, especially those who helped fix the area, if not the direction, of his ideas. My own interest in the interaction of literature and society was first stimulated by the lectures of Emery Neff and then centered on Arnold by the work of Neff's student, Lionel Trilling, whose *Matthew Arnold* is surely a classic of American literary scholarship. The footnotes and bibliography indicate as fully as possible my other debts to published works, but I should like to mention here the essays of J. Dover Wilson, Howard Mumford Jones, and William Robbins, each of which helped me to define my own attitudes. I regret that Donald Southgate's *The Passing of the Whigs* and G. Kitson Clark's *The Making of Victorian England* appeared too late for me to make use of them.

I wish to acknowledge a special debt to Jerome H. Buckley, who criticized the manuscript at every stage of the writing and helped clarify my ideas and the expression of them. Lionel Trilling first read the manuscript in an early version, and I shall always remember how he ignored my presumptuousness and encouraged me to finish the work. Other Columbia University people were helpful. David Robertson put at my disposal his close knowledge of the Victorian social world, and Susanne Howe Nobbe, Herbert Deane, and Marshall Suther offered judicious criticism.

The librarians of the Columbia University Library, the New York Public Library, the British Museum, the Bodleian Library, and the Balliol College Library have been helpful. For their assistance and for arranging countless interlibrary loans I would also like to thank the staff of the library of the University of Arizona. From the same university I received help from the Faculty Research Grants Committee for incidental expenses.

To many friends and colleagues I am grateful for help, encouragement and suggestions. Rosalie Colie smoothed the way in New York, London, and Oxford and read the entire manuscript. Lore Metzger and John Thayer transcribed materials in distant libraries. Gerald McNiece was helpful in matters of style, and with Christian Kiefer and Desmond Powell helped create an atmosphere of ideas in which it was possible to work. By the dedication I can only hint how much the book owes to my wife, who was always ready to take time from a busy career of her own to read and reread, do endless checking, and by her interest to nourish my enthusiasm for the subject.

CONTENTS

Chapter I

THE HEADMASTER
OF RUGBY

From 1827 to 1842, Rugby School was the scene of Dr. Arnold's headmastership; for his oldest son, Matthew, it was, very simply, home. The boy saw it first in the last years of the reign of George IV; he grew up there during the reign of William the Sailor and during the first years of Victoria's long sovereignty. For his family moved into the headmaster's house in the middle of his sixth year. He himself was enrolled in the school from the time he was fourteen and a half until he was nineteen. And for another eight months, until the death of his father, he addressed his letters from Oxford to his family at Rugby.

For the future poet and critic it would be an advantage to have a father who saw the way the world was tending. In 1827, Napoleon had been dead for six years, but effectively he had been dead since Waterloo, or perhaps since Peterloo, which marked the rise of a force that would defeat Napoleon's conquerors. By 1827, too, the era of reaction to Napoleon was over, and an age of political and social change had well begun. Change was to be the one consistent element in the history of the century, and though men like Lord Liverpool and Lord

Palmerston could dam the tide for a time, after Liverpool was to come the first Reform Bill, and after Palmerston the second. To be on the side of change was to be on the side of the future.

Certainly it was on the side of change that Dr. Arnold wanted to take his stand. He once told Arthur Stanley that he wished to reform things in proportion as he loved them. His contemporaries, at least those of his own class and above, came to think of him as an advocate of sweeping political and religious reforms, so much so that parents of Rugby scholars sometimes feared that they had put their sons in dangerous hands. And of course Dr. Arnold still enjoys his reputation as the man who revolutionized the public schools. But, in fact, it is easy to misrepresent him in both regards. That he did not so much radically reform the public schools as infuse the existing system with his own high moral purposes is at least arguable. And, as he himself well knew, he had two sides to his political nature—the deeper, instinctive one being conservative. He worked for certain changes only that he might conserve those parts of church and state that he loved and that stood in danger of destruction. Both sides mistrusted him. If he had had two necks, he felt that he would have been hanged twice.[1]

And yet, however carefully Dr. Arnold tried to strike the proper balance between the two sides of his nature, the balance of one age notoriously looks awry to succeeding generations. This is not to say that sons are wiser than their fathers or that fathers are wrong, but that sons who are to learn from their fathers must see things differently. We must see that Dr. Arnold played his part as a conserving reformer while he was headmaster of a public school in early Victorian England. He was himself the product of public-school and university education and a devoted son of the Establishment. Almost without making a deliberate choice, he had offered his services to the ruling segment of a class society and had staked his career and private happiness on the preservation of the ruling order. For these services he was well paid; in his last years his income exceeded £3,600, an amount equal to what one hundred teachers in lower-class schools were paid. Before his death at the age of forty-seven he had saved enough so that he could contemplate an early retirement, though only one of his nine children had finished her education. He was well aware that no man with a large family, a house, and a well-paid but dependent position could be a revolutionary.

With these considerations in mind we may well wonder not that Dr. Arnold failed to effect greater changes than he did but that he did so much. What was more, he had to work from the traditionbound position of a headmaster, that of a specialist employed to do society's will. It is true that he was elected at Rugby in part to reform the school itself, but this fact must not obscure for us the deep conservatism of the school and the society that supported it. I think it will be useful to trace Arnold's career at Rugby in order to learn something of the directions in which he *could* move and in which his temperament led him. But we should perhaps ask first of all, in the matter of school reform, what he could not do, and more, what neither he nor his son Matthew could even think of doing.

For what the public school did was to produce a state of mind that itself was not open to question. It inculcated as natural, and therefore fixed, an attitude toward the class system. It accomplished this first by offering young men from all strata of the responsible classes—in addition to an education—their first meeting ground. It brought together the son of the rising city merchant looking about for a suitable property in the country; the grandson of a cloth manufacturer and son of a baronet who trained the boy for Parliament by making him repeat the

Sunday sermons; the earl's son, accustomed to being called "my
lord" from birth and anxious to make a decent maiden speech
before his peers; the clergyman's son, least favored of all these
but also least bound, except that his career must be proper to
a gentleman. As a conservative force, operating below the level
of consciousness, binding men together for life with the perdur-
able stuff of adolescent affection, and binding them to the
society that produced them, the public school can hardly be
overestimated.

Public-school boys collectively learned to see themselves as a
class apart, a youth corps undergoing the initiation procedures
and training of an elite. They learned the habits and manners
of a ruling class and thought themselves young men of high
destiny and proud temper. It did not take much for older boys,
their self-importance swollen and their personal eccentricities
given free rein, to bristle against real or imagined wrongs and
lead an uprising against the masters. Rugby's Great Rebellion of
1797 has the distinction of being so violent and protracted that
a band of soldiers had to be called in to put it down. The
Winchester historian records five separate riots there between
1770 and 1818, the last also requiring the intervention of soldiers. At Harrow, Byron and the other leaders of a revolt re-
frained from blowing up part of the school only because some
of the rioters pleaded that their fathers' names were cut in the
sacred walls.[2]

In relation to the world outside, public-school boys knew
themselves as already belonging to the served rather than to the
servers, and like all *arrivistes* they guarded their position jeal-
ously. They took a firm line against those who seemed nearest
to trespassing on their preserve, the day scholars. Leslie Stephen
tells how he and his brother, James Fitzjames, called down on

themselves the high scorn of Eton students who suspected their day-student status and thought they might be sons of an ambitious footman at Windsor.[3] Trollope tells us how, as a grubby foundationer at Harrow, he suffered indescribable indignities from both students and masters. He joined in neither games nor lessons, and learned nothing because he was taught nothing. And yet such attitudes developed in public-school boys so unobtrusively that it was virtually impossible for them ever to examine their own unspoken assumptions. Without their noticing it, their spheres of reference shrank, and with them the denotations of common words. "Men" and "boys" came to mean "men like us" and "boys like us." Toward the end of the century an old Etonian, Spencer Walpole, could write that a Parliamentary career was always open to a man of conspicuous talent. All that a man need do was to make a reputation at Oxford or Cambridge. That talented men of the wrong class often found the doors of the universities and public schools closed to them did not occur to him. Similarly, when Tom Brown is asked by a friend why he was sent to Rugby, Tom honestly replies, "I suppose because all boys are sent to a public school in England." [4]

It need hardly be stressed, then, how far outside the pale were the workmen, dirty and ignorant enough, who did society's hard manual labor and never exchanged a pleasant word with the privileged boys. Tom Brown thought it great fun when the Rugby lads, riding home at the end of term, discharged pea shooters at men repairing the road. Even to the coachman the workers were just "a lot of Irish chaps, reg'lar roughs," fair game for sporting young gentlemen. At Harrow the game was a bit more serious. During the construction of the London and North-Western Railway the boys habitually stoned the laborers as the latter came through the town to buy food.[5]

However, the public schools had never lacked for critics, even from within the Establishment. In the first quarter of the nineteenth century Evangelical families in particular were concerned that boys were unsupervised outside of class hours, and that in the resultant anarchy bullying, drinking, and other vices flourished. Giving the older boys the status of praeposters, with the accompanying powers and privileges of quasi rulers, did little to mitigate the small-boy misery and moral evil. At the same time, it was precisely this unregulated, hard-fisted society of boys that won almost intemperate praise from many wearers of the old school tie. They felt that you may not overdiscipline a boy's spirit lest you crush it, and that in any case a young man must learn to discipline himself. They felt that you may not forbid all fighting simply because Anthony Francis Cooper, the brother of Lord Shaftesbury, was killed in a school fight after being heavily plied with liquor between rounds.

Against the abuses of the system Dr. Arnold was to exercise himself severely, but even he, within the confines of School House where he was master, met with only moderate success. And yet, though he made the various echelons of school authority more responsible, he had no desire to alter the general system even if that were possible, and he did not question the public-school concept of education as training for an elite. Quite to the contrary, by gradually eliminating the first two forms, he made it impossible for students to enter Rugby unless they had learned the rudiments of classical study elsewhere. By 1837, local students whose parents could not afford to give them such training were effectively barred, and Arnold had nullified the founder's expressed wish that his school provide free education for all children of the neighborhood.[6]

Dr. Arnold very nearly did not apply for the headmastership of Rugby, and his election there is still something of a mystery.

In 1827 there were only a few half-reasons why he should move his family from Laleham, a quiet Middlesex community beside the Thames. He had lived happily there for eight years preparing students for the university, studying and writing in all the spare moments left to him. He had gone into debt when he married, and had just about paid off the obligations. Of course his family was growing—six children were to be born before the family left Laleham—and he had begun to find living there too expensive. In addition, his Oxford friends urged him to find a wider sphere of usefulness—the headmastership of a public school, say. He had a first-class degree, he had commanding energy, experience, and moral force, and when he propounded to his friends his notions on school reform they thought him just the man to put such ideas into practice. But he was also independent and refused to contend against inviolable tradition or meddling trustees.

His friends were sure that he would make an excellent headmaster at Rugby School, which had shown a capacity for improvement earlier in the century under Thomas James. But Arnold had doubts that he and Rugby would suit one another, and in 1827, when the incumbent headmaster, Dr. John Wooll, resigned and its trustees advertised the position, he hesitated until he was almost the last to apply. When he did, it seemed unlikely that Rugby would give him an opportunity to try out his reform ideas. Among the fifty applicants, what chance had a man with his narrow reputation? Besides, one of the other candidates was strongly Tory and popular.[7]

On the face of things, a conservative would have an advantage at Rugby, since four of its trustees were to serve at one time or another as Tory members of Parliament and three others came from Tory families. Only perhaps two trustees were Whigs, though both were also to serve in Parliament. Almost to a man the twelve trustees were Warwickshire landlords, and three were peers of the realm. The leader of the more conservative element seems to have been Earl Howe, who was lord chamberlain to Queen Adelaide, the widow of William IV, and notorious for his purportedly intimate friendship with her.[8]

Rugby had not always been so favored, for like Harrow and Charterhouse it did not have a distinguished founder. Lawrence Sheriffe, its only begetter, was simply a citizen of London, and though the Heralds' College granted him a coat of arms for his support of Queen Elizabeth, his highest title was that of vice-warden of the Worshipful Company of Grocers. But in a codicil to his will Sheriffe left to Rugby a tract of land in London (it included what was to become Lamb's Conduit Street), and as the land increased in value so did the fortunes of the school. So, too, we may note, did the interest of the trustees. The first group, appointed by the Commission of Chancery in 1602 (and like most of the trustees of 1827, gentlemen of Warwickshire), were so negligent that the school almost lost its London property. Not until 1667, after two more Chancery commissions, did the litigation over property come to an end.

Shortly thereafter, as the revenue from the foundation continued to increase, the number of students who attended as foundationers, with a consequent remission of fees, decreased. In 1675, the first year anyone troubled to keep a school register, fourteen of the twenty-six students came from Rugby and environs and could thereby qualify as foundationers. In 1743, of fifty-three students then attending, just two were foundationers.

What was more, trustees had begun to take their duties seriously. After 1670 the headmaster could be required to post a bond of £500 if he refused to obey their orders or to quit his post within three months after they had directed him to. A sense of continuity, tradition, and loyalty to Rugby grew up among them. Vacancies were filled by a vote of those remaining, and it became common for a man's heir to be elected to his place. Skipwiths, Caves, Fieldings, Holbechs, Leighs, Lawleys, and Biddulphs served for generation after generation. Two branches of some families—the Caves, Fieldings, and Leighs—were represented.

No disposition to sever the Rugby connection showed itself when a family simply maintained its honored position or when it improved it. The eight baronets of the Cave family succeeded one another with impeccable regularity. And though as time went on, the head of the Fielding family became the earl of Denbigh, though the head of the Craven family also won his earldom, and one of the Leighs became Lord and then Baron Leigh, they too served the school. Despite the precariousness of its early existence, Rugby had in fact won aristocratic acceptance before the French Revolution, and thereafter it moved gradually closer to the exalted positions of Eton and Winchester.[9] Peers from families not earlier associated with Rugby came to serve as trustees, a movement culminated, we may suppose, in 1836, when the earl of Warwick, lord lieutenant of the county, joined the board.

In 1827, then, as Rugby went about the business of choosing a new headmaster, the political and social constitution of its board was no accident. Amid the insistent criticism of the public schools, however, three circumstances might have worked on the trustees to affect their decision on the choice they were making. For one thing, school enrollment was at a low point. During Dr. Wooll's long regime, numbers at one time reached almost 400, but now they had fallen to one-third of that total. For another, five trustees had been elected within two years of the retirement of Dr. Wooll. New members, eager to make their presence felt, would be disposed to think that it was time

for a change. And, further, the trustees had before them a letter
from Dr. Hawkins of Oriel predicting that one of the candidates, Thomas Arnold, would leave his mark—and by implication, theirs—on the public schools of England.

But the presence of neither newly appointed members nor a
few Whig members can be said to have disturbed very deeply
the essential conservatism of the Rugby trustees. All felt the
common, ancestral interests of Englishmen with "a stake in the
country," at a time when that phrase implied trustworthiness
and unimpeachable loyalty. Now, however, as the specter of
Napoleon faded and a threat of another kind posed itself, it
became possible to discuss the use of a weapon long grown
rusty in the armory of the propertied classes, political and social
change. The art consisted in knowing when to use the weapon
oneself, with economical efficiency, before it could fall into less
fastidious hands. Both Whigs and Tories had to be brought to
admit the necessity for change, the Whigs—possibly because
they had managed one change so gloriously in the past—somewhat less forcibly than the Tories.

In any case, change within the public school, an instrument
of ruling-class will, need give little pause to anyone. Reform
there could not sweep away a pocket borough like Beeralston,
of which trustee Earl Denbigh was soon to be deprived. But
reform there could stop the return to private tutoring, which the
Wilberforces and Thorntons had felt was necessary. Reform
would not damage the pervasive sense of class unity, fostered at
school by boyhood friendships and sealed afterward by family
intermarriages. Looking only at the Rugby trustees, we are not
surprised that several of their families—the Leighs and Town-
sends, Holbechs and Mordaunts, Marriots and Fieldings—were
related. The fifth earl of Aylesford, somewhat more restricted as
to choice, happily met and married the daughter of Earl Brooke,

the second earl of Warwick. So close-knit was a group of this kind that it is tempting to speculate on the power that inter-marriage might have given the senior Whig trustee, Grey Skipwith. In 1827 he was the son-in-law of a Rugby trustee recently deceased. His daughter was shortly to marry the son of another trustee, Henry Wise. And he was related by marriage to Evelyn John Shirley, the most recently appointed trustee.

Be that as it may, the atmosphere of reform at Rugby was at best an atmosphere of internal reform, and the choice of Dr. Arnold by these Warwickshire gentlemen begins to seem even more reasonable when we consider how safe a reformer he must have seemed to them. What could they know of his political temper except what his published writings and letters of recommendation revealed? And by 1827 neither of these sources could give accurate information on the stage of his political evolution. The written evidence included parts of a history of Rome that had appeared in the *Encyclopaedia Metropolitana* and had attracted no special attention. Work on a lexicon and an edition of Thucydides would seem innocuous, his contributions to periodicals equally so.[10] It would be unlikely, too, that his letters of recommendation from Oxford would make him look politically unreliable, for most of his days at Oxford, and particularly those at Oriel, had been days of youthful and exuberant Toryism. That he had come up to Oxford breathing the fire of Jacobinism was remembered only by old school friends like John Taylor Coleridge. Although his family were strong Tories, he had been disgusted into Jacobinism at Winchester by the public immorality of the dukes of Cumberland and York, and by the worldliness and corruption of the ecclesiastical princes. But at Corpus Christi his youth (he had entered at sixteen) and the singularity of his disruptive ideas had not been proof against the gentlemanly Toryism of the common room. He himself attests

how, before he took his degree and went on to his Oriel fellowship, he defended Toryism in the Attic Society and read Clarendon "with all the sympathy of a thorough Royalist." [11]

The appointment of Dr. Arnold was due, then, to a lucky
concatenation of those forces that occasionally conspire to put
a man in a position from which he can step into immortality.
In point of fact, the man whom the Rugby trustees had elected
already differed from the man they thought him to be.

The change had come during his ripening years at Laleham,
years crowded with prosaic tutoring duties but still the years in
which his mind took its permanent direction. In the spring of
the year he was to go to Rugby he remarked that he was daily
becoming more of a reformer. Toryism had shocked him once
again: he had heard Tory friends express views abhorrent to
Christian ideas of justice, and he knew also, from his studies of
Thucydides and Roman civilization, that such Toryism ignored
the lessons of history. It was typical of him to respond both as a
historian and as a man of religion. In the years that followed
he became a Whig and liberal of a special and curious sort,
reaching beyond his times and his position but also of course
being limited by them. They were years in which even some
Whigs thought that the Reform Bill virtually granted universal
suffrage. It was a time when the "Christian Knowledge Society,"
responding to an offer of liberal copy, asked the Doctor for
sermons that contained nothing "startling." The boldest reformer must feel restricted in so conservative a world.[12]

As he formulated his own political views Dr. Arnold could
not help but interfuse them with his firm religious convictions.
He based perhaps his most important concept on an analogy
between the history of states and man's upward struggle for
individual salvation. In his eyes both are born in the darkness of
paganism and sin; in youth both make their way by force and

cunning; only mature persons and states can recognize moral law for what it is and choose for themselves the ways of justice and virtue. To choose correctly is not easy and involves a struggle with man's indolent, selfish, and corrupt nature. But to give in to that nature, to prefer what is to what can be, is to lose the battle to evil and deny Christianity. The principle of improvement, in its perfect form Christianity itself, he called liberalism. Its loathsome enemy he called conservatism.[13]

Now headmaster of Rugby, Dr. Arnold began to draw out the implications of his broad theories and to publish them. He published a pamphlet arguing that anyone who wished to retain Roman Catholic political disabilities did not know that a state must abjure earlier injustices: the conservative view was an immoral relic of the past. He prefaced his edition of Thucydides with an outline of the distinct stages a state must go through in its upward progress. Another pamphlet attacked conservatism within the church and argued against its exclusiveness and inefficiency. Then in 1836, bursting with indignation, he wrote an article that almost ended his career at Rugby. He excoriated the Newmanites for trying to undermine the appointment of Dr. Hampden as Regius Professor of Divinity. The heart of the matter was doctrinal, but Dr. Arnold chose also to accuse the High-Church party of conspiracy. In his view they had used cunning means to obtain an unjust end. To make matters worse, an editor entitled the article "The Oxford Malignants." [14]

Few headmasters have had to stand up under the kind of storm that then broke about Dr. Arnold's head. Religious and political conservatives had been eying him with distrust since his first volume of sermons appeared in 1830, and pamphlets against him with titles like "Liberalism Unveiled" began to appear. At the same time rumors were circulated in Oxford that he was teaching radicalism and revolution to his students. But within the school his personal magnetism and force of character early began to have its effect, and by 1833 numbers had jumped from 123 to 315.[15] In that year, too, the Midland Tory newspaper, the *Northampton Herald,* began a protracted anti-Arnold campaign, in which they were soon joined by Theodore Hook's *John Bull.* They fixed on every aspect of the school not to their liking, from the expense of fees to matters of discipline to the headmaster's radical views. Dr. Arnold saw to it that they did not lack for copy. He gave a boy eighteen lashes for what he thought, incorrectly, was lying. He used his influence to have the *Herald* banned from the town reading room, and tried to keep out the *Times,* which also had criticized him. He antagonized the old Rugbeians so that they made separate arrangements for the annual Speech Day dinner.[16] Then, in what Stanley thought was a flamboyant gesture of independence, he made the two-day trip from the Lakes to Rugby in 1835 in order to cast a loud voice vote in behalf of the Radical candidate. In so doing he voted against the son of a Rugby trustee and against the prominent father of a Rugby student! [17]

Still, it required "The Oxford Malignants" to touch off the real storm. In March of 1836 the trustees had even expressed themselves satisfied with his conduct of the school. But after publication of the *Edinburgh Review* article, amid bitter attacks from the Tory press, they convened again at the request of Earl Howe and voted on his proposal to direct the activities of the headmaster. A vote in favor of the motion would be tantamount to dismissal. With only eight trustees present, however, the board divided four to four, and the matter was dropped.

The near vote of censure was not the only reverberation of this stormy period. In 1837, Edward Stanley, informed of his appointment as bishop of Norwich, asked that Dr. Arnold be permitted to deliver the address at the installation. The archbishop of Canterbury denied permission, stating as his reason that the main body of the clergy would find the choice objectionable. About this time, too, Lord Melbourne considered making Dr. Arnold a bishop, decided against it, and also decided that he could not appoint so indiscreet a man to an Oxford professorship of divinity. Arnold may not have learned about his lost chance for a bishopric, but Norwich told him about the professorship, and the news depressed him. Even the enrollment at Rugby fell off sharply in 1837–38. Recognizing the need for discretion, Arnold decided to heed the advice of John Taylor Coleridge that he avoid controversy.[18]

For the rest of the decade he wrote neither pamphlets nor articles. He had been sending letters to the *Hertfordshire Reformer* under the initials "F.H.," but from mid-August until May of the following year he wrote none. When he came to publish the second edition of his Thucydides in 1840, he struck out all the lively political allusions in the notes. He turned to the writing of his Roman history, determined to avoid partisanship in the treatment of party questions. He had learned, as he said, that "moderation and comprehensiveness of views are the greatest wisdom." On Tractarianism, the subject that had brought all his troubles to a head, he did his best to give no further offense. He wrote a careful, almost apologetic preface to his *Two Sermons on Prophecy*, published in 1839, hoping thereby to conciliate his Tractarian readers. And even in mid-1841, when he lapsed again into bitterness, his main effort had been to express the positive grounds of his opposition to the Newmanites.[19]

But years later, long after his death, Rugby conservative elements did not forget that they had had differences with their celebrated Doctor. In Van Diemen's Land, John Philip Gell, one of Dr. Arnold's most famous students, found that his plans

for religious instruction roused bitter hostility from Sir John
Eardley Wilmot, the governor. Sir John had been one of the
candidates for North Warwickshire in 1835 against whom Arnold had voted. And if we may credit a rumor that has survived
in his family, Theodore Walrond, another Arnold student,
failed to be elected headmaster of Rugby in 1869 because he was
"an Arnold man" and unacceptable to the Tory electors.

In all these squabbles, however, we must not overemphasize
the role played by political differences. Newspaper attacks,
coupled with Dr. Arnold's imperious methods and violent
temper, obscured the extent of agreement between him and his
enemies. Young Stanley was one of the few who saw how conservative he really was. Knowing that Arnold was going to
visit his parents at Alderley, he wrote to them shortly after the
general election of 1835:

*I think you at the Rectory are just the people to do him good
just now in the political way, and you might impress on Mrs.
Arnold how it is of the very utmost importance that he should
not be considered a party man or a Radical, for he is certainly
really not in the least one or the other. . . . People seem here
to be unconscious of the great proportion of his nature which
is Tory—all his reverence for law, and for antiquity, and for the
Establishment.*[20]

In his conduct of the school Arnold had in fact given his
conservative enemies no cause for fear. The main burden of his
work there was precisely what an enlightened conservative
would want. He introduced changes calculated to make the old
system work. Even on touchy political subjects he had always
been careful with the students. When his form reached the
section in Russell's *Modern Europe* that deals with the French

Revolution, he had them begin the book again rather than discuss it. He specifically excluded party politics as subjects for the Rugby Debating Society and the *Rugby Magazine*. "What he did for us," wrote Thomas Hughes, "was to make us think on the politics of Israel, and Rome, and Greece, leaving us free to apply the lessons he taught us in these, as best we could, to our own country." [21]

Under Dr. Arnold's direction, moreover, the school became a microcosmic state, a kind of test society, in which rulers-in-training learned the duties and dangers they would face in the outside world. They learned that "in school and close" they were "in training for a big fight"; that they must work for individual salvation, yes, but that the fight for the social order was part of their own fight. Clough at sixteen felt that his whole being was soaked through with the hope and effort of doing good for the school. The debating society and the school magazine existed first of all for the good of the school. And when Dr. Arnold died, Theodore Walrond, who had served as head of the school for two years, returned to Rugby for another term to minimize the damage to the school.[22]

The school came to reflect Dr. Arnold's quite special concept of the natural development of societies. He saw Rugby as resembling the "manhood" stage of civilization, the point at which nobility and commons are opposed by the nonpropertied democracy. Authority broadened down gradually from rank to rank, but the whole system depended on the praeposters, the sixth-form scholars. They were the important link in the chain of command, and the business of controlling the lower orders was left largely to them. Rugby was in no sense egalitarian, and only if the praeposters recognized their responsibilities, used their powers wisely, and identified themselves rather more with their superiors than with the younger students was a well-governed society possible. Some individual students below the sixth form would in time become praeposters, but the society always had one irreducible element, in this case the younger students, who could not think or act for themselves.

Arnold transformed the prefect system by making the school part of the moral life of the students. Younger students were not careless children; they were young men who lacked "moral thoughtfulness." He did not say that "boys will be boys" but that errant boys are sinners and that their sins have a bad effect on the school. And, further, he noted that most of the boys had the depressing habit of swimming with the stream and of going along with evil. The number of boys capable of active good were few indeed, and it was only right that the headmaster should flog and the praeposters use their sticks on the many careless and wicked. "Boys are not the highest order of beings in the universe," admitted the *Rugby Magazine*. They are like nothing so much as "men in an uncivilized state" who need among them "Committees of Public Safety." [23]

Were the social order reflected in the school a fixed, immutable order, few would deny that it was necessary to make its upper echelons responsible. Even if the school simply mirrored the world as it was, we might argue that the system was rooted in injustice and snobbery, that the reform of superficial abuses does not disturb the radical evil, that leaders of an old order often reform just enough to retain their privileges; but we should credit Dr. Arnold with doing, firmly and with courage, what he thought should be done. In point of fact, Dr. Arnold did not believe that the social order had reached its highest point of development. He regarded the ascendancy of numbers as a tendency of society, and far from regretting the fact, believed that "the popular power in a state should, in the perfection of things, be paramount to every other." He declared himself on the side of "the Advance," which worked for "taking off bonds, removing prejudices, altering what is existing." Yet he also felt that the world was corrupt and "the perfection of things" did not yet exist. Indeed, what altered the entire picture, in Arnold's mind, was his persistent fear that this same popular power was a clear and present danger to English civilization.[24]

Throughout the century the propertied classes of England, like their European brethren, were to live in fear of popular revolution. It is not enough to say that Dr. Arnold shared this fear; rather we should say that few men were more prone to alarm than he. His letters show him as a chronic "viewer-with-alarm." In 1819, Peterloo made him think daily of the Corcyrean uprising described in Thucydides, of the French Revolution, and of the warnings of history that men never heed. He envisioned the incubus of revolution rising on all sides—from the activities of the trades unions in 1834, the Tories in 1836, and the Chartists in 1839 and 1840. In part this tendency of Dr. Arnold's exhibits the workings of a zestful nature that relished the excitement of crises, but it points to something deeper in him: the feeling that movements toward liberty, which he admired so truly in theory, always in reality fell short of the ideal. They brought attendant evils, disgusted and frightened him.[25]

There were two exceptions. He approved, with reservations, the overthrow of Bourbonism in 1830, and he was pleased two years later when the English got rid of their rotten boroughs. But he abhorred the clamors of 1789, and had special distaste for "the Red Jacobins of 1794 and the White Jacobins of 1795, or of Naples in 1799." He did not applaud the spirit of 1776, and at one time expressed distaste even for the "Glorious Revolution of 1688." He saw it, and indeed the entire development of "historical liberty" since the Middle Ages, as an unprincipled, accidental phenomenon that brought in its train the age of revolt. Yet, again, when he was at Oxford shortly before his death, and wished not to appear weak before his Tory audience, he expressed himself—ever so guardedly—in favor of the Whig achievement. But he did so, as he said, rather than seem to show doubt that England's constitutional monarchy and protestant church were superior to their antecedents. And he kept his unqualified praise for what the revolution was able to preserve rather than what it changed. All in all it was an interesting performance, capped by a passage in which he regarded the question of whether restraints were better maintained or removed as one not affected by any predisposition in favor of maintenance over removal but depending entirely on whether good or ill resulted.[26]

It will not do to explain Dr. Arnold's preference for the slowest of slow change as lack of sympathy for the poor or as sneaking fondness for the status quo. We have seen that he was committed to authority, inequality, and the responsibility of certain groups to rule. And assuredly he loved a social climate in which perfect gentlemen could breed, and he wished to preserve an aristocracy of birth. But he knew that the aristocracy—and, in fact, all the upper classes, including his own—had borne down hard on the poor and ignored their distresses. He told Lord Selborne that a man had led an imperfect life who had not brought himself into close contact with them. He could not reconcile his own happiness with their need to labor painfully, and though he had no genius for easy, natural relationships with the poor, and knew it, he welcomed every opportunity, such as taking over the chapel at Rydal, to get acquainted with them. And he made repeated attempts to write and preach in a manner they would heed. Using Cobbett as a

model for style, he wrote newspaper articles and letters addressed to them, and even published his own newspaper for a
time in 1831. He urged Wordsworth to have his poems printed
in a cheap brown-paper edition that the poor could afford.
And using the *Lyrical Ballad* formula, he wrote sermons at
Laleham couched "in the language . . . of common life." [27]

Long before the Anglican Church began to think of its responsibilities to the poor as extending beyond parochial charity
he told his fellow clergymen that social improvement should
be one of the chief objects of an Establishment. They had too
long been preaching obedience to the poor; like the prophets in
Judea, they should denounce luxury and injustice and such particular evils as the game laws and high rents. Both Arnold and
Wordsworth thought that political and moral virtues flowed
from the possession of property, but Arnold thought that something should be done to restrain the accumulation of large
landed properties and to facilitate the distribution of small ones.
And though the hireling of Warwickshire landlords and in general a defender of property, he would even allow that on occasion the government might abrogate property rights for a
particular national benefit.[28]

Whatever the extent of his commitment to the status quo,
then, Dr. Arnold did not fail to see its flaws and do what he
could to correct them. And whatever his fear of popular up-
heaval, he did not fail to do what he could to ameliorate the
lot of the poor. A man in a dependent position, with a family
of nine children, simply must watch for cautionary signs. And
from what quarter did history show trouble more liable to come
than from the lower classes, the descendants of slaves, the spawn
of ignorance and poverty, the prey of delusions and demagogues? That they were now freemen made them all the more
dangerous. Could not repentance even now be coming too late?

At moments in 1831 and 1839, Dr. Arnold thought so. "We are engulfed, I believe, inevitably, and must go down the cataract"; and again:

My sense of the evils of the times, and to what prospects I am bringing up my children, is over-whelmingly bitter. All in the moral and physical world appears so exactly to announce the coming of the "great day of the Lord," i.e., a period of fearful visitation to terminate the existing state of things, whether to terminate the whole existence of the human race, neither man nor angel knows.[29]

It has been necessary here to suggest some of the conservative elements in Dr. Arnold's thinking, because his liberalism, viewed against the background of his conservative age, has commanded the attention of most commentators. I do not wish to imply that his total impact on the succeeding generation was toward reaction or even toward conservatism, but that in addition to liberal ideals, he encouraged certain attitudes reflecting more the England that was passing than the England that was to come. At heart his liberalism was overlaid with distrust for the common people, and because he exaggerated the sinfulness of both the young and lowly, he overestimated their ignorance and dangerousness. Since he favored strength and benevolence, he admired the paternal governments of his time: the Austria of Ferdinand and Metternich, the Prussia of Frederick William, and the France of Louis Philippe and Guizot.

He was careful therefore to distinguish between "liberal" principles and "popular" ones, and to regard the latter always with a suspicious eye. For him, just as most boys were bad, so most men were prone to evil, and their political activity could not but reflect the evil. Conversely, truly liberal principles, like goodness, tended to be the possession of the few rather than the many. He fell, then, into the error of many superior men who believe themselves alone capable of making proper judgments and taking proper actions. It is an error, unhappily, to which not only schoolmasters are prone.

Chapter II

THE SILENT YEARS

Alan Harris once used the expression "the unknown years" to describe the period of Matthew Arnold's life up to 1848. Now we know a good deal about that period, but since virtually none of our information comes from Arnold himself, perhaps "the silent years" would be a more exact designation for his early life. They were the years that shaped him, the years that molded the assumptions and predispositions from which he was ever after to view the social and political issues of his time.

His father exercised a preponderant influence during most of this period. The mature Matthew Arnold was to take many of his ideas from him, but the groundwork for the acceptance of those ideas was laid in "the silent years." For the son of Dr. Arnold did not so much deliberately adopt as unconsciously assume the social attitudes of his father simply by living in the society that nurtured them. The position in society that his father had to take, the extent to which Dr. Arnold was permitted to be a critic and reformer of that society, the way in which Rugby reflected Dr. Arnold's highest social ideals, are all part of his son's experience. Thereafter Oxford and Oxford friends became Matthew's *magistri vitae*, inculcating in a thousand subtle ways views of the world and society, but in total effect confirming what he had learned from the headmaster of Rugby School.

Between father and son can be traced a strain of antipathy that seems to go back almost to Matthew's infancy. Part of the trouble was a series of physical ailments and accidents that made him a difficult child. Before he was five he had spent more than two years with his legs in iron braces.[1] The braces were intended to correct the rickets that threatened to make him a cripple, but they were only partially successful. There was always something a little clumsy in his walk. In the end his parents could not stand the sight of their first-born son hobbling about. They took off the braces against the doctor's advice.

It is difficult not to spoil a sick child even when the child has shown signs of intractability. So the six-month-old baby, whom his father described as "backward and rather bad tempered," was coddled when ailing, remonstrated with when well. The pendulum seems to have swung back and forth with regularity. A year out of leg braces, Matthew suffered from a strange throat ailment that seemed again to require "cruel and barbarous" treatment—continued blistering, which almost scarred him for life. A bad fall and a phosphorus burn continued the cycle. And when Dr. Arnold engaged a drill sergeant to train Matthew out of clumsiness, the boy responded by falling into a hesitation of speech that was almost a stutter. Though Dr. Arnold engaged a specialist to come to Rugby to treat Matthew and Tom—his younger brother had been similarly affected—the hesitation did not disappear as quickly as it had appeared.[2]

Dr. Arnold's energy enabled him to do all of his writing and historical research in his leisure time and on his holidays, and he expected his children to emulate his industry. Young Arnolds took their places in the schoolroom as soon as they could walk, and by the time they were five they began a regimen that in-

cluded Latin and French. Again Matthew gave cause for concern; he did not take to work very well. No one could surpass
Dr. Arnold in his great sense of family fun; it matched, it almost
counterbalanced, the demand for serious work he made of himself and his family. But since serious work was the primary duty
and Matthew continued idle, it was decided that perhaps a
more formal school atmosphere would be good for the boy. He
was sent to Laleham, to the private school conducted there by
the husband of his Aunt Frances, the Reverend John Buckland.

Laleham was Matthew's birthplace, the school there having
been initially a joint venture, with Buckland in charge of the
lower half and Dr. Arnold in charge of the upper half. His
return there now, at the age of nine, was not an unqualified
success. Uncle and refractory nephew did not get along.[3] By
October of 1833 other arrangements had to be made.

A nephew of Southey, Henry Hill, of New College, Oxford,
came to Rugby as tutor for Matthew and Tom.[4] Though Hill
was in charge of the boys' studies for almost three years, Dr.
Arnold was not satisfied with their work. Twice he considered
sending them to a public school and then rejected the idea.
He preferred to keep them under his own eye for the surprising
reason that he was not sure that a public school would do
more good than harm. A boy, especially a lazy boy, might fall
in with a bad set and be corrupted.[5] The years of early adoles-
cence, at which Matthew and Tom had then arrived, were
crucial. During that period "it was almost impossible to find a
true and manly sense of the degradation of guilt or faults." [6]
Boys' bodies had begun to grow, yet their power of judgment
and sense of duty lagged behind. For such defective natures
flogging was the proper remedy. And if that failed, sons who
would not work properly should be banished to the colonies.
"There is no earthly thing more mean and despicable in my

mind," Dr. Arnold wrote in 1840, "than an English gentleman
destitute of all sense of his responsibilities and opportunities,
and only revelling in the luxuries of our high civilization, and
thinking himself a great person."[7]

So it was that in August, 1836, when Matthew and Tom
finally left home, Dr. Arnold wrote a prayer for them, and
Matthew wrote a poem that may be read as an admonition to
himself to try harder. In it he apostrophizes his thoughts of
home.

> Stand a barrier 'gainst all ill
> And all that seeks our thoughts of good t'allay
> Be unto us a watchword on our way
> In darkest hour of night, and in the bright noonday,
> Where'er our fancy strays be with us still.[8]

He wrote the lines in August, 1836, on the eve of his entering with his brother another stage of their education. Winchester, the scene of this trial flight, was Dr. Arnold's own
school, but the Doctor had misgivings as he sent them there.
For one thing, Matthew and Tom were to live in a house of
130 boys, too many for one master to manage, and under conditions rather too much like those of Dr. Arnold's own time, when
incredible bullying flourished. He expressed his worries to
friends and took the extraordinary step of asking George Mo-
berly and Charles Wordsworth, who were in charge of Winchester's fifth and sixth forms, to watch his sons and let him
know if they were making any undesirable friends.[9]

There is no reason to think that Matthew or Tom shared their
father's misgivings. And though outraged Wykehamists pelted
Matthew with bread pellets for complaining that the work of his
form was easy, Tom remembered the incident as amusing rather
than distressing. But Dr. Arnold's fears won out in the following

year, and in 1837 both boys entered Rugby, Matthew on June 25, Tom five months later.

Although Matthew had been a sixth-former at Winchester, he was reduced to the fifth as he entered Rugby. After a term he joined his father's own form and automatically became a praeposter. He did not work, or perhaps could not work, as his father expected him to. And though his father was not disposed to quarrel with him, he knew that in his father's eyes he was "fallow ground" and he lay "ready for all evil." Must he not have sensed or heard expressed what his father wrote to Trevenen Penrose, that the family was not at peace, and there were "evils" present that he was "powerless to quell"? [10] And he certainly knew, for it was no secret, that his father preferred Tom of all his sons and considered him the equal of his older brother in every way except in the writing of compositions. Others outside the family, like the sixth-former beside whom Matthew took his place, must have noticed that the boy acted with marked constraint toward his father. Of course withal he was still a boy and resented being reprimanded in class, so that on one occasion he delighted his form fellows by making silly faces over his father's head to show how little a punishment had bothered him.[11]

He was reticent on the subject of his father, and never alluded to his having been a difficult son or to the Doctor's having been a demanding father. The idea may never have occurred to him. More likely his father's strictness seemed the way a man of high principle would think it best to rear a son, and his own seeming defection just the measure by which most sons fail to live up to the ideals set for them. But though it is entirely clear that he loved his father, something in him prevented his doing for long periods what every schoolboy was expected to do and what Dr. Arnold demanded more than most fathers.

It is of course possible that Matthew feared failure, and by appearing diffident saved his self-esteem in advance by acting as if the game were not worth the candle. It is more probable that he knew how bright he was and that he could excel in examinations if he did the requisite hard "swotting." But may we not perhaps speculate further and conjecture that although Matthew would have liked to please, the price of pleasing Dr. Arnold was too high? That he knew in some way that his own independence, his sense of having to be himself, was at stake? For Dr. Arnold did not demand simply intelligence and hard work from those who would enter the inner circle of his favorites, a circle within the already chosen elite of the sixth form. He was not the kind of teacher who encouraged personalities or interests radically different from his own or who nourished exotic talents in others. He drew men to himself and made them something of himself. He asked that wills as well as minds conform to his own. And for the time they were with him, even in some cases long after, from men of the quality of Clough, Arthur Stanley, William Lake, and J. P. Gell he got what he asked.

But if Dr. Arnold was born to dominate and rule, Matthew Arnold was born to be his own man. During these early difficult years he developed his manner of studied casualness, of easy and witty indifference, that served to protect him at home and later became his mask before the world. Dr. Arnold was baffled by it, especially since his son was affectionate, the kind of lad his friends called "dear old Matt." Perhaps to a degree Matthew himself was deceived by his mask. Surely his subsequent career would have been less arduous had he been able to doff it at Oxford and work for a first-class degree. But then it was the mask, altered for a new purpose, that became the precious, indispensable element in his wonderful prose style. And even so

altered, it has served to disguise some things about Matthew
Arnold—how much he had become like his father, for example.

After Matthew had been in the sixth form for more than two
years, in 1840, Dr. Arnold continued to find fault with him,
now complaining that his son's gregariousness kept him from
making intimate friendships and from being alone enough to
learn anything.[12] During the long vacation of that year Matthew
and Tom were sent to Wales to read with William Charles
Lake, now a fellow at Balliol. A letter from Dr. Arnold to Lake
preceded them.

*Matt does not know what it is to work because he so little knows
what it is to think. But I am hopeful about him more than I was:
his amiableness of temper seems very great, and some of his
faults appear to me less; and he is so loving to me that it ought
to make me not only hopeful, but very patient and long-suffer-
ing towards him. Besides, I think that he is not so idle as he was,
and that there is a better prospect of his beginning to read in
earnest. Alas! that we should have to talk of prospect only, and
of no performance as yet which deserves the name of "earnest
reading."* [13]

It is important to know the standards against which the boy
was being measured. One could never guess that in the few
months before this letter was written Matthew had won the
Rugby prizes for both the English essay and the best poem.
Yet these did not qualify him as an "earnest reader." For he
was almost within a year of the age his father had reached when
he had taken his first class at Corpus Christi, and of the age his
godfather, John Keble, had been when he was elected fellow
of Oriel. In his own form two boys younger than he were ranked
higher, Theodore Walrond and John Conington, the latter
having entered the form at fourteen. Thomas Burbidge at

Cambridge and Richard Congreve at Oxford had recently
joined those who had distinguished themselves and Rugby.
Could the eldest son of Dr. Arnold do less? Dr. Arnold thought
not.

Nevertheless Matthew impressed Lake that summer as "the
ablest private pupil by far" he could recall, and in November
he came back from Wales to win the Balliol scholarship.[14]
Dr. Arnold confessed himself astonished; he had not expected
his son to be successful. He hoped that success would "act
wholesomely" on the boy, and so it did for a time.[15] In 1841
he won the Latin essay prize at Rugby, and in November went
into residence at Balliol. He had thus completed the "Social
Progress" within Dr. Arnold's ideal state. He had entered as an
upper-fifth boy, not a citizen, nor yet burdened with responsibilities of citizenship, become in the sixth form a member of the
commons privileged to work with the nobility for the common
weal, and arrived, triumphant, at the "manhood stage" of the
state. It was a progress in which ignorance was cared for but had
no voice, citizens had rights only as they performed duties,
leaders risked everything in the battle against ignorance and
sin. Perils threatened the progress on all sides, but one had
sometimes to face the immediate danger and fend it off, whatever the risk and whatever the means. Here the tendency to
panic, to act precipitately, became itself a danger.

The struggle was not unique to one's own time. It was part
of the human condition. History, read properly, as Dr. Arnold
read it first in "The Social Progress of States" and as Vico,
Niebuhr, and Coleridge had read it before him, revealed a re-
current pattern and operated according to discoverable natural
laws. States of tension between aristocracy and commons,
property and poverty, followed one another inevitably and un-
endingly. It was even difficult to know at a particular period

which was the party of progress, because the alignments shifted
and liberals of one age became the conservatives of another. So
one read Thucydides most carefully, because the state of tension
he described corresponded to England's "manhood state" since
the revolution of 1688.[16] This struggle in time and within nations reflected both as a microcosm the warfare from "the hid
battlements of eternity" between good and evil, and as a macro-
cosm the fight within each human heart to gain eternal life. It
was a struggle so pervasive and persistent that no individual
defense could shut it out. A refusal to become engaged, a
retreat behind the high walls of irony and persiflage, and the
manners of a dandy would serve for a time to keep a man un-
committed until he knew his mind, but at last he would have
to take a stand.

The story of Matthew Arnold's career at Oxford has been so
often rehearsed that it need not be repeated in detail here. As
everyone knows, he played the undergraduate dilettante to perfection and to the despair of family and friends. Not only did
he neglect his studies, but he apparently did not do any of the
things people think commendable in undergraduates. Though
the entire university, and particularly Arnold's two colleges,
Oriel and Balliol, were a maelstrom of religious ideas, he was
almost superciliously removed from it all. His conduct might
almost have been a comment on a university that had become
"a battlefield for theologians." [17] His plea of *nolo contendere*
attracted a good deal of attention, though, it is true, many of
the comments we have were recorded after he had become
famous. Max Müller, appalled in his heavy Germanic way at
the provincialism of Oxford, still found it to Arnold's discredit
that he refused to be taken *au grand sérieux*.[18] Principal Shairp
remembered only the banter and jauntiness of the "one wide-
welcomed for a father's fame." [19] The curious details that can be

gathered about his final schools indicate how spectacular a failure they were: we know that a few months before, he was studying under an average of four hours a day, that just before the examination Temple talked logic at him for twenty-two hours straight, and Jowett pre-Socratic philosophy far into the night, that afterward his examiners expressed annoyance that such a first-class mind should be ignorant of the assigned books.[20] The unsuccessful effort of the last few days was made to please his mother, who had told Clough how worried she was about his chances.[21] But he had been unwilling or unable to make the prolonged effort necessary to success.

Academic learning of course forms only a part of the education of a man, but in all important matters, as already suggested, Arnold managed to detach himself from the passionate concerns of others. That this cool, ironic temper concealed and protected a reflective poetic sensibility, none could guess. By every analogy with the lives of young romantic poets he should have been developing by throwing himself into one cause after another, absorbing influences in a fury of abandon. But the sensibilities of Rugby graduates had been sufficiently exacerbated by Dr. Arnold's moral pressures. In the heady atmosphere of those years they needed not the courage of commitment but the power of detachment if they were to preserve or discover some core of individuality. Clough's failure to get a first was a symptom of a deeper disorder, which did not right itself until after his marriage, then too late. Tom Arnold went off to New Zealand, thinking to make a fresh new world but finding instead a new religious faith, only to lose it again. Lake flirted with Newmanism but recovered in time to become the dean of Durham. Richard Congreve spun off to Comtism and a Positivist center on Lamb's Conduit Street.

When Arnold entered Balliol in November, 1841, it was

beginning to establish itself as the leading college in the university.[22] A system of competitive open scholarships had drawn to it a group of promising young men, one-third of whom in the years from 1838 to 1845 were from Rugby. The Snell Exhibitions open to Scottish students had brought to Balliol a distinguished group that included Archibald Campbell Tait (1829), John Campbell Shairp (1841), and William Young Sellar (1842). Tait had stayed on to form with Scott, of lexicon fame, and William George Ward a learned and even an exciting tutorial staff. With his personal charm and dialectical power Ward especially attracted undergraduates and made them feel, as Clough attested, "like pieces of paper sucked up a chimney." [23]

Matthew Arnold had no opportunity to study under Ward, who lost his tutorship in the spring before Arnold went up. The replacements for Ward and for Scott, who resigned that spring, were competent but not distinguished, the staff that fall consisting, in addition to Tait, of Edward Woollcombe, James G. Lonsdale, and John Andrews Dale. In the following Michaelmas term three vacancies occurred, this time to be filled by men who were to bring Balliol to the forefront of Oxford colleges: Lake (Arnold's tutor in 1840), Frederick Temple, and Jowett. Though each undergraduate was usually assigned to a single tutor for the whole period of residence, Arnold had to shift from one tutor to another, and we do not know who was his principal man: Temple's biographer assigns him to Jowett, but Jowett's biographer will take no responsibility for him. In any case, Arnold does not seem to have come under any strong tutorial influence, and we can only speculate what Ward or the mature Jowett would have made of him.

Of itself, Balliol society was not likely to alter the social and political views that young Matthew Arnold brought with him.

From 1819 to 1854 the college was ruled by Dr. Richard Jenkyns, an efficient, devoted, but narrow-minded man, who harbored the notion that no student would ever become a proper gentleman unless he came from one of two or three public schools. He therefore saw to it that Balliol commoners came from Eton, Harrow, or Rugby, and in this way he fixed and narrowed the college social level and tone. In later years Arnold expressed satisfaction that Oxford had begun to admit scholars of all classes, but the Oxford he knew welcomed only the sons of the aristocracy and the professional classes.[24]

The issues that split Oxford in the early forties were theological, and part of that great dispute took place within the walls of Balliol. Edward Walford, a contemporary of Matthew Arnold's at the college, remembers him as holding views proper to the son of Newman's chief adversary.

In his early days, when we dined at the same scholars' table, I shall never forget how, in opposition to the Tractarianism of the day, he used to say that the strict imposition of creeds had done more to break up than to unite churches, and nations, and families, and how even then, in our small and highly privileged circle, he was the apostle of religious toleration in every direction.[25]

It seems correct to deduce that for Arnold at that time "religious toleration in every direction" did not include toleration of Tractarianism. In any case, Matthew Arnold would have known of his father's intemperate language toward "The Oxford Malignants" and their Tractarian leaders. He would have known too of how the Doctor spoke of the Tractarians privately. In 1838, for example, Stanley had taken Ward to Rugby to discuss with Dr. Arnold the ideas that were drawing the Balliol tutor toward Newmanism. The Doctor "used the most savage phrases about Newmanism that he could invent," and Stanley was pained to note that though he was kind to Ward he was not cordial.[26] Three years later, after Dr. Arnold's inaugural lecture at Oxford, the two men met again in the Balliol common room. For Dr. Arnold, Ward's having entered within the orbit of Newman now made even kindness impossible, and there were "some passages of arms between them." [27]

At Balliol, Matthew Arnold would also have seen an example of the kind of narrow temperament that in 1845 was to strip Ward of his degrees, condemn Tract XC, and virtually force Newman to leave Oxford. For the master of Balliol, Richard Jenkyns, was a Tory and churchman of the "high-and-dry" school, who wanted things left much as they were. In 1838, Jenkyns had suspected that Stanley might be tainted with Newmanism and did not support the latter's candidacy for a Balliol fellowship. With great reluctance Stanley stood at University College, where he was promptly elected. Then in 1841, W. G. Ward published two pamphlets in favor of Tract XC, and Jenkyns, yielding to pressure from Tait, one of the Four Tutors who touched off the storm against Tract XC, removed Ward from his lectureships. And at the special convocation in 1845, Jenkyns was the first after the vice-chancellor to cast a vote of "degraded" against Ward.[28] It should perhaps also be noted here that Archbishop Whately, so much like Dr. Arnold in temperament and outlook, backed the heads of houses in their proceedings against Ward.

Within Balliol, however, a certain good will survived these disputes. Jenkyns had always liked and admired Ward, and Ward remained friendly toward Tait and Jenkyns even when he seemed intent on being the *enfant terrible* of the Tractarian movement. Outside of Balliol, however, the unfairness that proceeds from rancor as well as *odium theologicum* marked two anti-Tractarian efforts. In an extraordinary trial Dr. Pusey was convicted of preaching heresy and forbidden to preach within the university for two years. He was not allowed to appear before the tribunal, one of the judges was his original accuser, and the court decision was never formally promulgated. In the second instance, candidates for the B.D. degree who held Tractarian views suddenly found their way blocked by Dr. Hampden. Supported by the Hebdomadal Board, he used his position as Regius Professor of Divinity to turn what had always been a formal exercise into a new test of doctrine designed to harass the adherents of Newmanism.[29]

It remained for the rising generation at Oxford to view Tractarianism and even fiery W. G. Ward with the tolerance that characterized Oxford liberalism thereafter. Stanley, the leader of the group, objected throughout to the militant tactics of the Four Tutors and argued that Tract XC could be a unifying rather than a divisive force. When Ward was condemned he wrote a pamphlet labeling the action a piece of absurdity. Jowett, F. D. Maurice, and Julius Hare joined with him in protesting the persecution.

In a sense the attitudes of these young men flourished in an atmosphere that Newman himself had created. For they had come to know him not as a fierce polemicist but as "a miracle of intellectual delicacy" whom Oxonians flocked to hear on Sunday afternoons, preaching from the pulpit of St. Mary's in accents free from animus, passion, and self-interest. Matthew Arnold's famous description of him in the essay on Emerson is one of many such tributes paid by men who found Newman's doctrines abhorrent but who responded to the man with all their youthful idealism and love of beauty, their tolerance and charity. From him they derived, as Arnold wrote later to Newman himself, "a general disposition of mind rather than a particular set of ideas." [30] Stanley's first experience of Newman,

though almost dramatic, was typical. He had prepared himself
for violent antagonism before he went to hear Newman preach.
Immediately afterward he sat down and wrote penitentially to
Lake, "I will never speak against him again." [31]

It is of course true that behind the issues that divided the
Tractarians, Dr. Arnold, and Tories like Jenkyns lay political
and social concerns. All saw the rise of Dissent and the shift
of political power effected by the Reform Bill as a threat to the
Establishment. Newman and Dr. Arnold wished to set the
church on a more permanent basis and to put it above the
vagaries of party politics.[32] But since they held opposing views
on the essential nature of the church, political considerations
gave way to theological ones. In the disputes that followed, it
did not in the least matter that Newman was becoming, if anything, anticonservative, that Ward thought himself a radical,
or that the friendship of Whately and Newman foundered on
the Irish Disabilities question.[33] It is true that the immediate
occasion of the Oxford Movement, the suppression of the Irish
bishoprics, was an act of political liberalism, but it is clear that
once the movement was under way the primary enemy was religious liberalism. Goldwin Smith, an Oxford contemporary of
Matthew Arnold's, saw what he calls "Oxford Liberalism," that
is, political liberalism, emerging from the womb of the Oxford
movement but was hard put to name a half-dozen liberals at
Oxford during the years from 1841 to 1845.[34] Newman says in
the *Apologia* that the Tracts were written to combat liberalism,
and he tells specifically what he means by the term. He calls it
"the anti-dogmatic principle and its developments," and says,
"By 'liberal' I mean liberalism in religion, for questions of
politics, as such, do not come into this narrative at all." [35]

All this seems clear enough, but when we read Matthew

Arnold's version of the defeat of Newmanism the waters become muddied. As he looked back from the vantage point of 1867 he did not see a socially unified Oxford split by theological differences. Instead, he blamed the failure of the Oxford movement on outside forces, on middle-class political and economic liberalism, and on "the Dissidence of Dissent and the Protestantism of the Protestant religion," and he says that Newman himself knew that this was his enemy.[36] For the Oxford Professor of Poetry delivering his last lecture, Arnold's charge has certain advantages both rhetorical and polemical; as an account of what actually happened, the best one can say is that it is a rather special view of the facts.

But as an undergraduate Matthew Arnold had no acquaintance with the grossness and vulgarity of middle-class liberalism. Oxford was an Establishment preserve, a stronghold of conservatism. When Prince Albert was awarded a doctor's degree in June, 1841, Victoria and her consort were well received, but the Whig ministers, "individually and collectively, were hissed and hooted with all the vehemence of Oxonian Toryism." [37]

In the Oxford Union too, during the years when Matthew Arnold was a member, the tone of ultra-Toryism prevailed. Debaters who defended the liberal side of a question either for the practice or from conviction were equally unsuccessful. So rigid was the atmosphere that political subjects were not popular, for the traditional, remote academic subjects could stir up freer passions among the speakers. Lake, who was president of the Union in 1838, felt that the spirit of the Union was depressed, because to be a moderate liberal there was to become an object of suspicion.[38] After 1840 a change in emphasis is observable, but it is not marked. The appearance of subjects such as Chartism, the Maynooth Grant, or Peel's right to remain a trusted leader may be straws in the wind, but the wind indicates only the growth of a mild political interest among the members, not the presence of liberal notions.[39]

Arnold must have watched with interest the Union career of John Duke Coleridge, for the two young men had met at Laleham and were friends like their fathers before them. That Coleridge should choose in his first speech to defend Chartism seems surprising but is explainable. He had traveled the circuit with his father and observed Chartists at first hand. What could be more banal than an attack on Chartism to an audience that expects one, what more likely to attract notice than a defense, even a defense by the son of a Tory judge eager to display his declamatory powers? Thereafter he was careful to vote occasionally on the conservative side in Union matters. In another debate Coleridge won attention even in London with a thundering address against privilege. Hansard had claimed that accounts of parliamentary proceedings were exempt from the laws of libel, and in a test case a publisher was jailed. Coleridge, arguing for untrammeled reporting, was nevertheless carefully conservative: the arrest and jailing, he maintained, "were utterly subversive of the Constitution." In time Coleridge displayed enough brilliance, and carefulness, to be elected president.[40]

Whether Arnold as a student took part in any debate before the Union, we do not know. The few letters of his extant from this period are addressed to John Duke Coleridge, and in one of them he found it necessary to assure his serious friend that although he laughed too much he could still be sincere and devoted. In any case, public speaking was never one of his strong points, so that his not speaking cannot be put down as lack of interest. Not until the fiftieth-anniversary dinner in 1873 is there a record of his addressing the Union.[41]

Both Coleridge and Arnold also belonged to a small discussion group, formed in 1840, which was less formal than the Union. This group called itself the Decade and met in one another's rooms to air their minds on a previously announced topic. Membership was restricted to about twelve carefully selected members, roughly half of whom were fellows of the university.[42] To this society Coleridge gives much credit for the development of his intellectual powers.

We discussed all things human and divine—we thought we stripped things to the very bone—we believed we dragged recondite truths into the light of common day and subjected them to the scrutiny of what we were pleased to call our minds. We fought to the very stumps of our intellects.[43]

But it was Clough rather than Coleridge who was the most memorable speaker of the Decade. Shairp, Temple, Conington, and Thomas Arnold all testify to his power, "rich, penetrating, original, and convincing."[44] Unlike the Union, the Decade never held aloof from political and social questions, and it was in these that Clough was at his best. We know that he spoke in support of a resolution favoring Lord Ashley's Ten Hours Bill and in favor of the repeal of the Corn Laws. He did not worry that he might appear inconsistent in making a frontal attack on laissez-faire and the economics of supply and demand, and in prophesying that the end of the Corn Laws would inaugurate an era when manufacturers would be "the real rulers of England." [45]

These opinions Clough continued to express both in letters to friends and in the presence of the "little interior company," in which he was joined by Matthew and Thomas Arnold and Theodore Walrond. Though they had known one another at Rugby, the differences in their ages then had been too great for them to be friends. Once together at Oxford they were united by their devotion to Rugby and by the combination of sympathy and intellectual stimulation they could give one another. Walrond, the youngest of the group, won the Balliol scholarship in the tradition of Stanley, Lake, Clough, and Matthew Arnold, and after an extra term at Rugby, following Dr. Arnold's death, he had come into residence at Balliol in the fall of 1842. Thomas Arnold had also come up in that fall and entered Stanley's college, University. As time made the discrepancy in years progressively less important, what had begun with skiffing on the Cherwell and long walks in the Cumner hills was supplemented early in 1846 by regular Sunday-morning breakfasts in Clough's rooms.[46] Thomas Arnold recalls that they discussed with much spirit the leading articles of the *Spectator*, which arrived just before breakfast. He remembers the group as both idealistic and hopeful: Peel captured their imagination by disengaging himself from party trammels; hopes for a peaceful Ireland seemed to lie in the Maynooth Bill and the Colleges Act.[47] During those months they read Rintoul, the radical editor of the *Spectator*, as he attacked the Whigs for their complacency in regarding the Reform Bill as a final measure and in failing to push for free trade. The death of the Test and Corporation acts, Catholic Disabilities, and an unreformed Parliament, he maintained, had destroyed any real differences between the Whig and Tory parties, so that a realignment of the major parties was needed.[48]

We have some indication as to how far the group agreed with this radical viewpoint. Clough, it appears from his letters and from his speeches at the Decade, admired manufacturers but distrusted their economics. During this time, too, he wrote a series of letters to a short-lived weekly newspaper, the *Balance*, letters that, we may suppose, were also discussed at the Sunday

breakfasts of the "little interior company." [49] The letters show
that their speculations had led them to question accepted economic ideas. Thomas Arnold, for one, was being drawn by what
he later called "French Communism," presumably the writings
of Fourier, Saint-Simon, and Proudhon. Clough, who had taken
Carlyle's injunction to "Lower your denominator," now looked
askance at the lavish personal expenditures of Oxford gentlemen
and wealthy manufacturers. In the letters he urges them to in-
vest their excess capital in public works or lend it to emigrants.
He also toys with the notion that a scheme of price fixing might
replace the present "higgling of the market," and notes that it
would require a chamber of commerce "endowed with powers
far transcending any now thought of." But, son of a business-
man that he is, he retreats from this idea and concedes that the
doctrines of political economy are as fair and as good as England
can hope to have.

But of course Clough and his friends were not original thinkers on these subjects, and what the letters show us principally
is the probing, idealistic temper of the "little, interior company," and remind us of the moral and spiritual stresses under
which these young men had to make their way into life. The
"hungry forties" were full upon them. The Corn Laws were still
in effect. None of them had a career mapped out; none had an
income to fall back on. Carlyle had stirred them with his
fulminating, coruscating language and his charged moral im-
peratives, but though they were to read him with admiration
for some years, Clough was right to complain of his negativism
and "lack of all reality and actuality." Dr. Arnold's influence
was, if anything, stronger than ever upon them, for Stanley's
Life, published in 1844, had crystallized all that he had to say
to their generation. Less a biography than a series of introductions to his wonderful correspondence, the book reviewed for

them the history of his ideas in the rich and warm context of
his life, and together with a volume of miscellaneous works, introduced them to forgotten essays and anonymous newspaper
articles. Meanwhile the third great voice to which their generation had listened had withdrawn himself from university life.
Clough's appointment as tutor of Oriel in 1843 and Matthew's
election as fellow in 1845 may have been part of a program to
purge the college of Tractarians. To Matthew Arnold the solution that Newman found for the doubts and distractions of life
was "frankly . . . impossible," but the first to leave the "interior company," his brother, accepted the same solution before
he ended his quixotic career.[50]

After achieving two firsts at Oxford, Thomas Arnold threw
up a safe position in the Colonial Office in 1847 and went off to
farm in New Zealand. It was an act of despair, a collapse under
the pressures of his time and position, for he felt that he could
not "do good" in England and at the time had no hopes for a
better society abroad. Walrond distinguished himself in classics
and mathematics, and then decided against taking orders since
he hoped to become a statesman. But after teaching for some
seven years he entered the civil service, where he had a modest
but successful career. Clough cast around for a great work in
which to lose himself, but the best he could do in 1847, at the
height of the Irish famine, was to write a pamphlet urging the
gentlemen of Oxford to curtail their personal expenditures.
Then in a fit of Carlylean discontent, compounded by reluctance
to subscribe to the Articles, he resigned his Oriel fellowship and
took an unsuitable post at London University.

Matthew Arnold showed even less inclination than Clough to
stay on at Oriel. Besides his friend, four men remained there as
fellows after Newman's resignation, and all were to become
church dignitaries; but for only one, R. W. Church, did Arnold

ever express any regard. Edward Hawkins, the provost, was too narrow and unimaginative to command the esteem of young men. The dearest loyalties of the friends remained to each other and to the old Balliol set, who, as Arnold later wrote, "at the critical moment of opening life, were among the same influences and (more or less) sought the same things as I did myself." [51]

But however much the voices of his youth made their overly peremptory demands, Arnold remained outwardly aloof, and sought in Emerson, Béranger, and the Bhagavad Gita guides to the discovery of his passional and intuitive self. He felt as much as his brother Thomas that the world was "monstrous, dead, unprofitable," and though he felt in his "poet's feverish blood" a desire that drove him "to the world without," he felt more urgently a desire to stand apart. He did not flee from duty: apartness from the world did not imply denial of it. Solitude was the way of objectivity and knowledge.

> He who hath watch'd, not shared, the strife,
> Knows how the day hath gone.
> He only lives with the world's life,
> Who hath renounced his own.

What he fled from was the urge to "*solve* the Universe," as Clough seemed bent on doing, or the impulse to change the world that "a strong minded writer" might feel. Both lead to nothing: Clough's way is irritating and incomplete; "the strong minded writer," becoming popular, "will lose his self-knowledge, and talk of his usefulness and imagine himself a Reformer, instead of an Exhibition." [52]

Nor would Arnold join John Conington and the other Arnoldians who turned to Christian Socialism in the second half of the decade. For one thing, he had only the most qualified ad-

miration for F. D. Maurice. And he may have been put off by
the eccentric side of the movement; some Oxford members, for
example, wore curious ill-fitting trousers made by the Christian
Socialist tailor.[53]

Meanwhile Oriel gave him independence and leisure before
he would have to settle on a permanent career. As long as he
remained in England there were only a few directions in which
he could go. Of his fellow sixth-formers at Rugby all but two
who survived into maturity were to find their life's work in the
church, the military and civil services, or the law.[54] His Balliol
friends did likewise. They had been trained in a university that
was a stronghold of high-and-dry Toryism, but they had listened
to voices critical of the old order, voices that spoke to their
spirits rememberable things. Though they looked forward to a
better world, their vision was circumscribed and their modes of
thinking limited by their vocabulary and the meaning that attached to words in their society. We may look at their careers
and conclude that they were not after all very different from
their fathers. But they did differ, however slightly, and the
difference is almost always the extent to which each could follow the visionary gleam. As clergymen, Butler, Lake, Temple,
and Stanley were none of them of an old-fashioned sort. Butler
and Lake were to an extent followers of Newman; Temple contributed to *Essays and Reviews* and lived to become an archbishop; Stanley was a leader of the Latitudinarians. Lingen and
Sandford went on to careers in public education, and were
raised to the peerage for their services. Thomas Hughes devoted
his enthusiasm and great physical energy to Christian Socialism
and workers' cooperatives. John Duke Coleridge, with his
forensic power and gift for friendship, attained the highest
honor of the legal profession, the Woolsack.

Arnold completed his compulsory year of residence at Oriel

in the spring of 1846, then went off to Paris to see Rachel and to Nohant to visit George Sand. On his return his manners and dress scandalized Clough, who was practicing the abstemiousness he preached. In February, Clough was still disturbed by Arnold's Parisianism and his carelessness in going to chapel. Stanley noted that Arnold had "qualities which . . . gave much alarm to many." In March, Clough asks darkly of a correspondent, "What evil report hath come to your ears concerning Matt? Wherefore Snub?" But by that time Arnold had been appointed secretary to Lord Lansdowne, who was president of the Council and an admirer of Dr. Arnold. Tom and Clough both disapproved his taking the post, but Arnold seemed not to mind, and his mother was anxious that he have regular employment. In April he left Oxford, in his twenty-fifth year and still to all appearances moving jauntily through the disturbed air.[55]

Chapter III

AMONG
THE BARBARIANS

Arnold's position as private secretary to Lord Lansdowne was the first of a series of circumstances that were to bring him into close contact with the political and social life of his times. Unlike Clough, who did not shrink from "feverish contacts" and seemed to ignore Arnold's advice that he strive to be himself, Arnold tried to preserve a core of individuality amid the flux of contemporary developments and influences. But it was difficult to remain aloof from the furious rush of events that marked the spring of 1848. Government messengers came to Lansdowne House with the latest news from France; Chartist mobs gathered in Trafalgar Square and engaged in sporadic conflicts with the police. Even so, Arnold sought to retain a sense of objectivity. To his mother he commended Carlyle's article on Louis Philippe because it put aside "the din and whirl and brutality." He told Jane that he wished he were at Fox How, where he could seclude himself from the dizzying but meaningless excitement. For he had been caught up despite himself. He thought of doing a political article, found he had nothing profound to say, and contented himself with writing a few letters and one enthusiastic sonnet to Clough. Then the reaction set in as Arnold reminded himself that "after all man's shiftings of posture, restat vivere." A second sonnet counseled patience to the still-enthusiastic Clough, and for himself Arnold made a strict rule that he would read no more newspapers. In July, Clough wrote to Thomas Arnold, "Matt was at one time really heated to a very fervid enthusiasm, but he has become sadly cynical again of late." [1]

For Arnold, however, it was not sad cynicism but sad lucidity that saw the struggles of 1848 as part of man's "vain turmoil," "thousands of discords," and "noisy schemes." The introductory poem of his 1849 volume praises the "quiet work" of slow, eternal things to which he wished to devote himself. For this purpose the secretaryship with Lord Lansdowne had much to recommend it. The duties were not onerous. Arnold would answer only the important letters and the foreign mail; Lord Lansdowne already had a "person" to handle the routine letters and look over the accounts. The private secretary would have all the leisure he wanted for his own pursuits. [2] And the surroundings were quiet and luxurious. From Lansdowne House in Berkeley Square it was a brief stroll to Hyde Park, then a kind of upper-class preserve. It was an equally short walk to his own quarters just off Grosvenor Square, also in the fashionable Mayfair district. The young man who as a don had addressed his London letters from lodgings over a seamstress' shop had taken a large step up in the world.

What was more, he had taken a step up and into the world of the great. In that brilliant society a private secretary would find his position a trifle anomalous, but the position was that of a gentleman, and he "could expect to be asked everywhere." Since, as Arnold confessed, there was a large element of worldliness in his composition, he accepted the invitations and even became popular in society.³ Yet, as his letters to Clough and to his sister Jane continued to attest, Arnold remained obsessed with achieving some kind of permanence, ideality, and apartness. Trying to satisfy both worlds, Arnold felt his "sinews cracking under the effort to unite matter." ⁴ The immediacy and emotional force of "Empedocles," "Obermann," and "Resignation" derive in large part from this struggle.

That these tensions were ultimately resolved in Arnold's own life in favor of "the world without" was due to his having not only to live but also to make a living in the Victorian world. The nearer view of the great world that his secretaryship afforded and the attractiveness of that society also disposed Arnold in its favor. Had the Scholar Gypsy gone on his quest in a well-appointed carriage in the company of aging Regency bucks, the results would have been the same. The Scholar Gypsy found his identity by fleeing from the world; Arnold chose to seek personal stability and integration within a world of change.

Even the world of change needed a principle of stability, and it is safe to say that as Arnold entered the great world he found in the notion of an aristocracy a stabilizing principle. He had few illusions about individual aristocrats or about the wisdom or virtue of the aristocracy as then constituted. Still, he could not think of English society as other than stratified, and his strictures upon English aristocrats at that time did not add up to an attack on the social structure that supported them. Like his father, he would "enlarge the privileges and elevate the condition of the mass of the community," so that eventually "the popular power in a state should, in the perfection of things, be paramount to every other," yet not exclusive of aristocracy.⁵ Wordsworth, curiously, states a view with which Matthew Arnold at that time would most probably have agreed.

I am a lover of liberty, but know that liberty cannot exist apart from order; and the opinions in favour of aristocracy found in my works, the latter ones especially, all arise out of the consciousness I have that, in the present state of human knowledge, and its probable state for some ages, order cannot, and therefore liberty cannot be maintained, without degrees.[6]

As the Paris revolt of '48 began to stagger and fail, Wordsworth came to Arnold's mind as the one who described the kind of devious path any progress of man must take. Earlier, Arnold had given positive proof of how predisposed he was to think of an aristocracy as part of the natural order of things. On a report that the French aristocracy was in danger Arnold commented, "I think Gig-owning has received a severe, tho: please God, momentary blow: also, Gig-owning keeps better than it re-begins." [7] The incomplete disjunction in the last clause signifies his belief that whether aristocracy continues or starts afresh it still will in some way exist. Nine days later he noted to his sister, "I do not say that these people in France have much dreamed of the deepest wants of man, or are likely to enlighten the world much on the subject." [8]

Even so, a note of satisfaction entered his voice early in that turbulent March as he predicted the fall of landed privilege. "The hour of the hereditary peerage and eldest sonship and immense properties has, I am convinced, as Lamartine would say, struck." Yet at the same time he was aware that England had nowhere to turn for leadership other than to the aristocracy. He could express only consternation at George Sand's adulation of "a *people*." Nor in 1848 was Arnold willing to settle for what he called Clough's "feudal industrial class" or for Carlyle's somewhat similar "captains of industry." All classes in England were, in fact, too ignorant to supply the needs of the time, and in the

lower classes ignorance slipped into a predilection for plunder
and destruction.[9] Arnold marveled that the diffusion of modern
ideas in France was evident both in the pages of the *Revue des
deux mondes* and in the behavior of the masses, but he had no
notion how such "idea-moved" people had been developed. In
England he could see no agency for training and uplifting the
masses of the *Lumpenproletariat*. His unspoken conclusion was
that England would have to struggle along for the time being
with things much as they were, and he hoped for a gradual
amelioration of accepted institutions.

He was aware as he joined Lord Lansdowne that he brought
the prepossessions of a clergyman's son educated among the
aristocracy. He knew that though his education allowed him
to share the thoughts, feelings, and manners of the aristocracy,
he did not truly belong to that class. Yet these same advantages
cut him off from the middle classes, to which by income and
social rank he should belong. The danger was not that he would
become vulgarly servile but that he had lost "perfect mental
independence." He was apt to experience a certain intellectual
deference, a slight blunting of the judgment on matters of class
privilege.[10] In later years he used to speak of people like himself
as a class apart, the professional class, gentlemen as distinct
from the nobility. Yet distinctness did not imply independence.
"The exceptional class," as he called it, shared the cast of
aristocratic ideas and lacked a force of its own, with the result
that it was "somehow bounded and ineffective." [11] The mind
of the educated classes of England, in short, was far too deeply
interfused with aristocratic preconceptions to reach beyond to
ideas of a totally different order. In Arnold's case the nearer
view provided by his secretarial post showed him a society fallen
from its highest peak of grandeur but still impressive, cultivated,
and brilliant; a ruling caste faltering, weak, and unenlightened

but still responsible, tenacious, instinct with authority; individual leaders rising above class interests and others pandering
to class prejudices; above all, a government capable of maintain-
ing order and of lending itself to gradual reform.

It was the grandeur and elegance of Whig society that would
first catch the eye of a newcomer. Lansdowne House and its
grounds occupied the whole of one side of Berkeley Square.
From his desk Arnold looked out through two great windows
on the court in front of the house, and during his first winter
heard from the square the cries of hawkers retailing the latest
news of the French civil disturbances. Inside, the house was
cold and formal, the kind of interior that glows into life only
on social occasions of a magnificent sort. Since Lansdowne
House was, after Lord Holland's famous establishment, the
principal Whig gathering place, such evenings were not rare.
Then beribboned lords and their ladies could dance in the
grand ballroom among its sixty or eighty marble statues, or
gather to hear a concert where it was possible to doubt which
was the greater attraction, the performers or the audience. George
Ticknor recalled one concert in which the artists were three of
Europe's finest singers—Malibran, Grisi, and Rubini. On another occasion James Lacaita, an Italian patriot, carefully noted
the number of distinguished guests, among them Princess Mary,
the queen of Holland, and Madame Castiglione, the mistress of
Louis Napoleon. Whig nobility had of course its own comple-
ment of distinguished ladies in the duchess of Gloucester, Lady
Dufferin, the duchess of Beaufort, the duchess of Cambridge,
and Lady Ashburton; and in the duchess of Sutherland, Mrs.
Norton, and Lady Waldegrave, its famous beauties. At these
gatherings of the talented and the famous, Lansdowne House
could accommodate over 2,000 people.

"The Emperor," as Tom called his older brother, was never

one to be deceived by mere surface glitter, but as we have noted, he accepted invitations and generally made himself agreeable. He may even have joined a club popular with fashionable young men.[12] Yet the more obvious faults of the privileged exasperated him from the outset. He wrote to Jane that as they strolled in the park they were splendid-looking people, but their handsomeness was not proof against stupidity, pride, and hardness of heart. The women seemed frozen in conceit or only half-alive with dullness. He was soon able to show that the glitter of the great world had not touched his deeper loyalties. In 1849, when Jane was recovering from an illness, she came to London with their mother for a holiday. Arnold, solicitous, contrived to spend part of every day with them. Mrs. Arnold was delighted to find him so unspoiled.

Generations of marital interweaving had created the richly brocaded fabric of Whig society. As a ruling clique, the Whigs could form governments and change governments without letting any of the major offices get outside a few select families. Lord John Russell's first cabinet, which was in office all during Arnold's secretaryship to Lord Lansdowne, supplied places to two of Lord Russell's cousins, two of his sons-in-law, and his father-in-law. Lord Lansdowne, who was lord president of the Council, was a cousin of Lord Holland and thus was related to another large wing of the Whig hierarchy. In addition, he had studied at Edinburgh under Dugald Stewart, and there had formed friendships with Palmerston, Brougham, Jeffrey, Cockburn, Horner, and Sydney Smith. Through one branch of his family Lord Lansdowne had inherited broad acres in Wiltshire and the famous house at Bowood; through another he owned extensive lands in Kerry and held subordinate honors in the Irish peerage as the earl of Shelburne and the earl of Kerry. Once in office, he played the game of taking care of other Whigs and of his protégés. Lord Frederick Hamilton described their London society as "a sort of enlarged family party," and Sir Robert Peel had ample cause to exclaim, "Damn the Whigs! They're all cousins." [13]

Yet whatever his consanguinity to the great, Lord Lansdowne would need other qualities to impress his irreverent young secretary. Such qualities Lansdowne had in abundance, to a degree, in fact, that any other prominent aristocrat of the day would find difficult to equal. Most obviously he was a man of fashion, a familiar sight in Hyde Park with his striking demeanor, blue coat, and "voluminous white neck investment." But he was also a man of broad and generous culture, a connoisseur of the fine arts, a liberal host to men of literature and science, a wide reader of intelligence and judgment, a gentleman of perfect, unpretentious manners. In short, he was one of those men who bridge the gap between the aristocracy and the intellectual world.[14]

Since 1834 he had served as a trustee of the National Gallery, not only because he was a rich collector but also because he had become something of an arbiter of taste. Waagen, the director of the Royal Gallery of Berlin, thought he had few equals as a connoisseur, and at Lansdowne House and Bowood he had gathered perhaps the finest private collection in England. He bought recognized masterpieces of course, and also the work of contemporary artists, among them Roberts, Collins, Wilkie, Rankley, and Millais. In all, he purchased some 160 paintings and added to the impressive collection of statuary bequeathed by the first marquis.[15]

He had been so much struck by Macaulay's articles on Mill that in 1830 he proposed that Macaulay enter Parliament as member for Calne, the family borough. Macaulay frequently attended Lansdowne social affairs, as did Thackeray, but none was more favored than Thomas Moore, who had a cottage three miles south of Bowood. At Lansdowne House, Charles Kemble, Doherty, and the inevitable Samuel Rogers came to dinner, and there are accounts of breakfasts attended by Mérimée, Milnes, and De Tocqueville. Nor was the Whig lord unknown to literary women. Harriet Martineau, it is true, refused to be lionized by him; but Anna Jameson, for example, dined at the London establishment and stayed at Bowood. Even more surprisingly, he sought the company of Owen, Brewster, Wheatstone, and Murchison—all men of science; and for Charles Lyell, the distinguished geologist, who was also a Bowood visitor, he succeeded in getting a knighthood.[16]

Dr. Johnson would have found Lansdowne an easy, "clubbable" man. At the Athenaeum, which he had helped to found, he was the center of a conversational group of whom Abraham Hayward is best known. He was active in The Club, Milnes' Philobiblon Society, and the Statistical Society. Ticknor dismissed his cultured talk as a superficial display of *esprit* in Continental political style. But all other indications and opinions were that it sprang from a resilient and informed mind. His general knowledge of all literary subjects was enough to enable him to lead the conversation, except of course when a specialist was present.[17] His letters could be charming, unmannered, and witty. Greville praised his skill as an extemporaneous speaker; as government leader in the Lords he answered questions from the floor with urbane and articulate ease, and was capable of "a very pretty and dexterous flourish." Matthew Arnold singled him out as "a man with an open intelligence" amid a society largely inaccessible to ideas.[18]

Lansdowne had used the opportunities his rank afforded him to become one of the most respected leaders of his party. He had been in political life since 1803 and had attained his first

cabinet post at the age of twenty-six. Since 1830 he had been
lord president of the Council whenever the Whigs were in
power—by 1847, a total of twelve years. He had played a part
in great events: at the death of William IV it had been his
duty officially to inform the princess of Saxe-Coburg that she
was queen of England. Now, when Arnold joined him, Lord
Lansdowne was, at sixty-seven, the cohesive force in the Whig
party, the tactful reconciler of dissentient elements, the planner
of parliamentary strategy. Someone had dubbed him "the Nestor
of the Whigs," and the name had stuck.[19] For himself he was
almost pathologically unwilling to take the highest office. Twice
the queen was to send for him to form a government when it
was within his power to do so, and twice he was to refuse. His
position nevertheless was such that those who did lead could not
do so without his support. "He sought to be honoured and
esteemed," said Guizot, "rather than to act and rule." He was
content to operate from the position he filled with ease, and
unwilling to risk it for an ambition he did not feel. From his
birth, education, and rank he drew great reserves of temperate-
ness and calm, which exasperated one associate into calling him
"Mother Elizabeth" but drew from Greville the admiring observation that "all their blows . . . fall on the soft, non-resisting
cushion of Lansdowne's evasive urbanity." [20]

Arnold's secretaryship under Lord Lansdowne extended from
April, 1847, to June, 1851, and allowed him to observe at first
hand the inner workings of a Whig ministry. The period was
one that exerted to the fullest what Cavour called the English
aristocracy's "sense of the possible." The Reform Bill and the
repeal of the Corn Laws had begun to break the traditional ruling parties on the wheel of history. The composition of Parliament remained overwhelmingly aristocratic, for most of the new
electorate was content to allow its sovereignty to be exercised

by proxy. But thereafter neither the old Tories nor the Whigs were able by themselves to muster a majority in the House. The Tories were unable to resolve their differences over protection, and the Whigs, under John Russell, ruled with the half-hearted assent of the Peelites, assorted kinds of radicals, a few Chartists, and the Irish Brigade. To confuse matters further, within the major parties themselves there was a blurring of lines that reflected the shadowy and fluid character of nineteenth-century class boundaries.[21] And perhaps worst of all, personal animosities infected the relations of political leaders. Within so close-knit a faction as the Whigs, Lansdowne had frequently to mediate between the touchiness of Russell and the breezy jauntiness of Palmerston. So confused and personality-ridden were the issues that even the sovereign and her consort could take a hand in finding governments.

For all the petty squabbling and confusion that attended this era of minority rule, enough remained of Whig practical sagacity and public spirit to make Whig rule effective in one important direction. Russell's government took up those causes for which the Whigs, aided by Evangelicals and reforming radicals, had fought from 1832 to 1835, and succeeded again in effecting a series of social improvements. It reorganized the administration of the Poor Law, introduced public-health and prison-reform measures, assisted the passage of the long-delayed Ten Hours Bill, and set up a system of apprentice training for teachers. Thus a government that owed its existence to the triumph of the laissez-faire free traders increased state intervention in public affairs. Believers in untrammeled, individual action decried these measures as interference with the "normal" development of society and as self-interested paternalism. But these germs of the modern, responsible state nonetheless continued to grow and flourish.

In many respects Lord Lansdowne was a typical member of his caste: a staunch defender of liberty, toleration, and justice, a proponent of ameliorative legislation, but in no sense a "leveler" or believer in equality. His distinction lay in his ability to see the proper modes for the realization of his ideals and in his astuteness in managing the details of government. He supported the removal of political disabilities for both Catholics and Jews, urged reform of the Irish Church, and opposed tyranny to minorities abroad. He was far from being one of the "comfortable moles" of whom Arnold wrote in 1848, for these beliefs involved the taking of actions that invited criticism. In 1848, Lansdowne took responsibility for a bill to establish regular diplomatic relations between the pope and the British government, and in the following year he received Francis Pulszty, the Hungarian refugee and revolutionary, at Bowood. But in matters of parliamentary reform Lansdowne and Palmerston were the true "finality" Whigs. They fought a continual rearguard action against reform and blocked Russell's repeated attempts to have his name associated again with a franchise bill.[22] Lansdowne in a sense was also behind the slashing attacks that Robert Lowe made on the reform proposals of the mid-sixties, for Lansdowne had invited Lowe to sit for Calne in 1852, and he and Lowe were in close accord on the reform question. To Lansdowne, as to Palmerston, both the House and the Lords, as constituted after the first Reform Bill, adequately represented their concept of "the sovereign people."

It was in his work for primary education that Lansdowne gave his most valuable hostages to the future. Voluntary groups had been unequal to the task of educating the rapidly growing and turbulent masses. To protect itself the state had to take a hand. In 1839 the Whigs bypassed parliamentary discussion by using an Order in Council to set up the Committee of Council on Education. Immediately the committee began to supervise the disbursement of grants that had been made since 1833 for the building of new schools. Whereas other and more direct methods of solving the problem collapsed under fierce sectarian opposition, by 1846 the educational committee had established both an inspectorate and a pupil-teacher system, and had monopolized the time of most of the Privy Council staff. Lord Lansdowne supervised this nascent educational system and assumed full cabinet responsibility for the reforming measures adopted by the dedicated and imaginative James Kay-Shuttleworth, who had been appointed the first secretary of the committee. At the beginning Lansdowne himself had not been sanguine about the chances for success of the experimental committee, but he encouraged the heroic zeal and competency that Kay-Shuttleworth soon evidenced. Arnold paid tribute on several occasions to Lansdowne's wisdom and open-mindedness in seeing the benefits that Kay-Shuttleworth's administrative powers would work.[23] That Lansdowne recognized Kay-Shuttleworth and supported him was the more remarkable because of Kay-Shuttleworth's personality. He was neither an easy man nor a gracious one, and both clergy and the sects distrusted him. "It needed a statesman," commented Arnold, "to see his value." [24] Time and again when its budget came up for approval the education committee felt the force of sectarian pressures and made concessions to them, yet the committee gradually increased its scope and influence. In education, attested Harriet Martineau, "Government . . . originally, and always meant chiefly, Lord Lansdowne." [25]

Arnold's admiration for Lansdowne's "open intelligence" and culture did not blind him to Lansdowne's lack of "youth, faith, and commanding energy." In these latter qualities the sickly John Russell was immensely Lansdowne's superior. What was

more, Russell also supported public education, and in his attitude toward electoral reform he moved, although slowly, beyond
his fellow Whigs. Arnold complained on one occasion of Russell's penchant for plain speaking in diplomatic affairs, but by
and large he admired Lord John's "decision and good sense."
When discussing England's handling of the Schleswig-Holstein
question or its participation in the Crimean War Arnold did
not mention, as modern historians do, Russell's consistent
wrongheadedness. Perhaps personal relationships played a part
here. From 1865 on, Arnold was friendly with the Russell family,
especially with Odo Russell, the distinguished diplomat, and
later with the duke of Bedford, the head of the clan.[26] From
1870 to 1885 we hear often of his going to the family seat,
Chenies, in Buckinghamshire, for the fishing. Lord John himself had won the regard of the Arnold family in 1854 by speaking kindly of Dr. Arnold in the course of an address at a Lake
Country school, and afterward, having been introduced to the
Doctor's widow, accepting an invitation to lunch at Fox How.
When Lord John died in 1878, Arnold wrote of him publicly as
"a man whom we all admired." [27]

Of Palmerston, the stormy Irish petrel of the Whigs, and
still, in his seventies, the *enfant terrible* of the party, Arnold
would have heard a good deal at Lansdowne House. For although Lansdowne and Palmerston agreed in their opposition
to electoral reform, Palmerston's conduct in the Foreign Office
caused Lansdowne constant anxiety and frequent embarrassment. In May, 1848, the Spanish government had expelled the
English ambassador, Sir Henry Bulwer, because that gentleman
had caused to be published a dispatch from Palmerston urging
the queen to change her government. Palmerston had sent the
dispatch even though Russell had objected to it. As leader of the
party in the Lords, kept ignorant of all details, Lansdowne was

reduced to making feeble shifts in the face of slashing attacks from Stanley and Aberdeen. Indignant and disgusted, Lansdowne insisted to Russell that such an incident must not recur. Three months later, close questioning in the Lords about Palmerston's interventional moves in Sicily made it clear again that Lansdowne was either unwilling or unable to give the facts. The Don Pacifico affair of 1850 ended of course with a brilliant victory for Palmerston in the Commons, but not before Lord Lansdowne and John Russell, both totally in the dark about the doings of their gaily adventurous foreign minister, weakly offered equivocations and patent sophistries to their respective houses, nor before Stanley had moved and carried an antigovernment resolution in the Lords. When in the following year Palmerston overstepped even his wide bounds in approving Napoleon's *coup d'état* after the cabinet had agreed to remain neutral, Russell finally dismissed the foreign minister with full cabinet approval.

Yet we must not exaggerate the extent of the disagreement between Lansdowne and Palmerston. For Palmerston exercised a strange fascination over his brother Whigs and could expect a large measure of forbearance from Lansdowne, with whom he had served under three sovereigns. During the furor following Palmerston's unsuccessful attempt, and conversely, Guizot's successful attempt to pick husbands for the Spanish queen and the infanta, Lansdowne and Russell strongly supported Palmerston. It mattered not under the circumstances that traditional Whig friendship for France had been set at nought, that Lansdowne believed that Louis Philippe was indispensable to France, that he admired Guizot and was an intimate friend of the Duc de Broglie.[28] Palmerston thereafter patched up an old quarrel with Thiers, Guizot's political enemy, and bent English foreign policy to give Guizot the kind of tit-for-tat that he was soon

able to give Russell. Lansdowne might be disgruntled, but he
knew the direction in which duty lay, and 1852 found him
successfully coaxing both Russell and Palmerston to join Aberdeen's cabinet; and in 1855, Lansdowne was pleased himself to
serve under Palmerston.

Alone of the major Whig leaders whom Arnold observed at
first hand from 1847 to 1851, Palmerston has the dubious distinction of being signaled out for individual dispraise. Arnold
was not surprised after Palmerston's death in 1865 that any
reasonable assessment of his career was drowned in a flood of
post-mortem panegyric. The old English habit of not seeing
"ourselves as others see us," Arnold told his mother, was at
work. Palmerston had found his nation the first power in the
world and left her the third or possibly the fourth. But any
minister, Arnold concluded, who governs as Palmerston did, by
heeding the loud voice of middle-class public opinion, must so
fumble and bluster and fail.[29] A modern liberal historian like
Maccoby and a conservative like Algernon Cecil both adduce
similar reasons for Palmerston's tactical blunders. Even Louis
Napoleon knew that English politicians were slaves to public
opinion.[30] The aristocracy merely administered; it did not rule.
Who could blame it for clinging to the remnants of its power?
Arnold certainly would not.

In 1851, Lansdowne's secretary had availed himself of an
offer from the Whig leader and joined the school inspectorate
of the education committee. Though he told his bride that he
hoped soon to become interested in the work, as late as 1856,
Arnold complained that he could not throw himself whole-
heartedly into inspecting. "I am inclined to think," he wrote,
"it would have been the same with any active line of life on
which I had found myself engaged—even with politics." Arnold
had yet to find a worldly activity to rival the charms of poetic

contemplation, yet the fact that he mentions politics, if only to reject it, is significant; the years with Lansdowne had whetted his appetite for the world of public affairs. To Clough he had confided a desire for political life, though he knew he was not fitted for it. And to his wife he had expressed a longing to live abroad on a diplomatic appointment. Political gossip became a standard item in his correspondence, and he kept in touch with John F. B. Blackett, who was M.P. for Newcastle, and with Wyndham Slade, whose brother Frederick had political ambitions. We may be sure that Arnold took pleasure in telling Blackett's sister what the duke of Argyll and "all the Ministerial people" said at a dinner of Lord Granville's to which he had been invited.[31]

The opportunity to impress Whig leaders with his reliability as an interpreter of foreign affairs came unexpectedly in the summer of 1859. He had accepted an appointment as assistant foreign commissioner of the duke of Newcastle's commission to report on the state of popular education in France. Arnold still had no special interest in public education, but he could not turn down the chance to escape from the drudgery of routine inspecting. The commission had been formed in the last days of Palmerston's first administration, and consequently Arnold went off to France armed with introductions from Granville, lord president of the Council, and—to judge by the people Arnold visited—from Lansdowne.[32] His first official call, to see Guizot, then minister of education, brought him the news that France had rejected an English offer to mediate between France and Austria on the subject of Austria's ultimatum to Piedmont. Two days later, on April 29, Austria declared war, and Napoleon retorted with a declaration that France would fight to free Italy "from the Alps to the Adriatic." The ensuing hostilities lasted something under three months and did not settle "the Italian

question." Throughout, England watched events warily, knowing that the conflict threatened to embroil Prussia and to upset
the balance of European power. Visiting schools in Paris and
then in the south of France, Arnold studied public reactions to
the war and to Louis Napoleon, and compared these reactions
to what he heard from Lord Cowley, the English ambassador at
Paris, from Guizot, and from pro-Orleanist English society in
Paris. In less than a month he had formulated the ideas that
form the basis of his pamphlet "England and the Italian
Question." [33]

As Arnold told Clough, he wanted to approach his Whig
friends "on an accessible side." Lansdowne was much interested
in Piedmont, and though Arnold cared little either for Italians
or for European republicans, he knew that Whig libertarian
sympathies lay in those directions.[34] When Arnold first conceived the notion of writing on the subject, English public
opinion by and large, and the sentiments of the Tory government especially, were pro-Austrian. Arnold accordingly decided
to adopt a simple controlling scheme that would reflect this fact.
He said he was writing to clear up three misconceptions that led
"the English aristocracy" to oppose the Italian war: first, that
Italy never could be an independent nation; second, that the
principle of nationality on which claims for Italian independence rested was chimerical; third, that Napoleon sought to rule
Italy himself. It was an unfortunate beginning. As Fitzjames
Stephen immediately pointed out, the English aristocracy
formed no notions on the war peculiar to themselves, nor did
they or any other respectable body of English opinion ever deny
that domination of one nation by another was a calamity.
Arnold's inaccurate generalizations had laid him open to these
home thrusts. Then, too, his treatment of English aristocratic
opinion as unanimous and static dated the pamphlet very

rapidly. For official English opinion, followed by popular opinion, and to an extent by Conservative opinion, shifted quickly
in the rapid tide of events. By the time the pamphlet appeared
Napoleon had concluded the abortive peace of Villafranca, and
three important members of the Whig government that took
office in June were strongly in sympathy with Piedmont and
(we know now) increasingly disposed to work with but not to
trust Napoleon.[35] At the end of the pamphlet Arnold appended
a tribute to Palmerston's program for Italy, but he allowed the
initial generalizations to stand.

Arnold's defense of Napoleon's motives throughout the conduct of the affair was a more serious matter. Naturally Arnold
did not know that Napoleon and Cavour had secretly planned
the war against Austria at Plombières in July, 1858. Napoleon
had a sentimental interest in Italian nationalism, but he had
hatched the plot with Cavour for personal and dynastic ends.
The subsequent appeal of the two plotters to international
morality was a piece of pure cynicism. Even Napoleon was worried for a time when it appeared that a European congress might
remove any grounds for dispute, but Austria's demand that
Piedmont disarm unilaterally gave him precisely the excuse he
needed. Arnold might suspect no machinations, but hard-
headed government leaders watched Napoleon with a wary eye.
For them Napoleon was a mystery wrapped up in an enigma,
who might be a man of good will but who also was building up
a navy to rival England's. Palmerston, who was disposed more
than most to work with Napoleon, had no intention of letting
him dominate Italy or weaken Austria to the point that France
and Russia could "shake hands across Germany." For his part,
Arnold seems to have been so impressed by the trust that the
French people reposed in their emperor that he was ready to
believe that Napoleon's motives were thoroughly honorable. In

Paris his views were doubtless confirmed during one of his long chats with Lord Cowley. For Cowley was wont to tell visitors that Napoleon was a man to be trusted and that he, Cowley, had found the emperor always true to his word. After the war Cowley impressed these views on Cobden when the latter was negotiating a trade treaty with France.[36] By that time Arnold himself was back in London and busily drilling with the Queen's Westminster Rifle Volunteers, which had formed to repel an expected Napoleonic invasion.

Though Arnold's pamphlet was in part dated and ingenuous, what he wanted principally to say had important and lasting implications. Arnold felt that Louis Napoleon had just missed being the indispensable man of his time. Napoleon had achieved this near approach to greatness because he had attracted to himself the newly released forces of modern France—the peasantry, first of all, and the commercial classes—and because he had offered these industrious classes an orderly government free from both anarchy and feudalism. Arnold wished to teach what he himself had only just learned, that the age of "the people and ideas" had replaced the era of "aristocracy and character," and that the new age needed strong leaders who could take into account the ideas of 1789. Since Arnold wrote to his "great Whig friends . . . in the earnest desire to influence them," he was in effect showing them the way of survival and continued power. He explained these ideas in a long letter to Lord Lansdowne, who seemed to be both preparing for the new age and holding it back.[37]

"Inaccessibility to ideas," which Arnold had thought of as a general English shortcoming, he now saw as peculiarly the flaw of all aristocracies.[38] Since he aimed to convince and convert, he proceeded with extreme caution: he wanted to speak of the English aristocracy "with the most unbounded respect." He

compared them favorably to the French aristocracy and praised
their prudence, their endurance, and their resistance. Ideas, on
the other hand, were "popular," rising in a class not satisfied
with things as they were, flourishing only in turbulent air. Men
like Fox and Louis Napoleon were "naturally susceptible" to
certain great ideas and were therefore exceptional men. The
present generation of aristocrats suffered only from a kind of
intellectual myopia, congenital and yet perhaps curable. But in
the coming complicated age, comprehension and application of
ideas would be necessary. As Arnold's letters show, his peroration to the pamphlet was sincerely felt.

When I consider the governing skill which the English aristocracy have displayed since 1688, and the extraordinary height of
grandeur to which they have conducted their country, I almost
doubt whether the law of nature, which seems to have given to
aristocracies the rule of the old order of things, and to have denied them that of the new, may not be destined to be reversed in
their favour. May it be so! May their inimitable prudence and
firmness have this signal reward! May they have the crowning
good fortune, as in the ancient world of force, so in the modern
world of idea, to command the respect and even the enthusiasm
of their countrymen! [39]

Arnold sent a number of copies of his pamphlet to leading
Whig and liberal leaders and did his best to learn their reactions
to it. He asked Milnes, who knew everybody, to let him know
how "the judicious" regarded it; through William Forster he
hoped to learn what Cobden and Bright thought of it. He
watched for the review in the Morning Post "because of its
connection with Lord Palmerston." Republican Clough, who
liked the pamphlet immensely himself, told Charles Eliot Norton that it was widely read. Gladstone sent a polite note of

approval, but there are no other recorded reactions from political leaders.[40] If Arnold hoped to make his way into public life by means of his pamphlet, he was disappointed. Still, he thought he had shown an aptness for pamphleteering, inherited from his father, and his essay "The Twice-Revised Code," written three years later for *Fraser's Magazine,* was published separately as a pamphlet and addressed itself to a specific public problem in much the same way. The differences in the two works, however, are more important than the similarities. For by 1862, Arnold not only was dedicated to the cause of public elementary education but also had fired off his first shot in behalf of public secondary education. With the help of Kay-Shuttleworth, copies of "The Twice-Revised Code" were sent to every member of Parliament, and Arnold took up the cause in the pages of the great middle-class organ, the *Daily News.*[41] Arnold was no longer concerned primarily to influence his "great Whig friends."

Arnold had learned in France that an agency to train and organize, control and civilize the newly emergent forces did exist —the modern state. Prepared by reading and thought for what he saw, he nevertheless experienced a kind of illumination. He saw that whereas its aristocracy of birth and culture had supplied to the English nation that "invaluable example of qualities without which no really high welfare can exist," in the future the state, "the nation in its collective and corporate character," could make men aspire to what is vast and grand.[42] Five years earlier he had accepted with regret George Sand's view that the end of the English aristocratic system must come with time. He had tried in *England and the Italian Question* to point out the way of survival to his Whig friends. Now in his report for the duke of Newcastle's commission, published as *Popular Education of France,* and in its preface, later published separately as the essay "Democracy," Arnold set aside regret, and with something of an air of bravado extolled the virtues of collective action to a nation that had made Smiles's *Self-Help* a best-seller. While carefully imputing no blame to the aristocracy, Arnold noted that the class not only was fast losing the popular acquiescence on which its rule depended but also had failed to transform itself in the democratic age. Its culture was declining, it still got preferential treatment before the law, it still bought its army commissions, it refused to establish life peerages.[43] Even the conservative Guizot recognized that an "impertinent" aristocracy could not expect to take its place in a modern free society.

The shortcomings of the aristocracy, however, were not Arnold's main concern in 1861. Thirteen years earlier he had heard its hour strike, and now he saw the way, to use Lionel Trilling's striking phrase, "to make the past of Europe march with the future." He recognized the curious phenomenon by which the aristocracy still held the reins of government, and often repeated Mirabeau's observation that "he who administers, rules"; but he knew that the phenomenon would not last and that for the most part the middle classes were the real rulers. So he was content not to attack the fundamental evils of the aristocratic system but to deal with them only insofar as they impeded the path to the future. It was true that the spectacle of a class subsisting on inherited wealth set a false ideal for the rest of the nation, that it "materialised the middle class and vulgarised the working class"; but a frontal attack in a nation so sensitive about "the rights of property" would make no converts to Arnold's view. He took an early opportunity to point out to Cobden that Bright's proposed Real Estate Intestacy Bill could not hope to effect in England what the law of succession of the French Code had achieved in France, the gradual partitioning of great estates.

The same bill provided a natural point of departure for Arnold in *Culture and Anarchy* to a consideration of stock notions on property and inheritance.[44] Similarly, practical matters like the report of the Royal Commission on Copyright and the controversy over the endowment of Emmanuel Hospital let Arnold deal with the "metaphysical phantom of property." [45] In the alliance of the Church of England with the propertied classes, and especially the Tories, Arnold sensed danger to the Establishment. So to the London clergy at Sion College he quoted Barrow against inequality and private interest, and he reminded readers of his religious essays that "the prince of this world is judged." [46]

For the most part, then, Arnold did not challenge the basis of aristocratic wealth except when the immediate occasion called for such tactics. He preferred to wait for the slow workings of time and the eventually irresistible effect of reason. Toward the close of the seventies he allowed himself more latitude, and in that comparatively quiet period he delivered and published his essay "Equality," a remarkable pronouncement for a man of his background and predilections.[47] Again, on his return from America, he ventured to suggest that members of the House of Lords be elected by provincial legislatures (he knew that United States Senators were elected by state assemblies), that titles lapse on the death of the holder, and that property be dispersed by a strict law of bequest.[48]

William Morris, for one, thought that Arnold's remedies were "rose-water" and that a proper remedy would have to come out of "disaster and misfortune of all kinds." [49] Looking back from the vantage point of the eighties, Morris could see that force, or at least the implied threat of force, had made possible every significant advance toward equality. His willingness to apply this lesson to what remained to be done made him impatient

with Arnold's nervousness before the reality of power. The concept of nonviolent resistance, had they been apprised of it,
would probably satisfy neither man. But it is absurd to condemn
Arnold for failing to subscribe to violence as a necessary mode
of social change; though Wellington's "revolution by due course
of law" may not be possible under all conditions, wisdom demands that the possibilities of peaceful change be fully ex-
plored.

Yet when we make all allowances for Arnold's fears and give
him due credit for his advanced ideas, something unexplained
remains in his treatment of the aristocracy. To a modern reader,
perhaps especially to a modern American reader, his perception
of the faults of the aristocracy is often dimmed by overpolite-
ness, by a studied unwillingness to point out the most serious
flaws. He praises with faint condemnation. Even the fault he
laid so often to their charge, which a Tory leader like Bentinck
so exquisitely demonstrated, that aristocrats were impervious
to ideas, was a euphemism for a much graver fault. An intellectual shortcoming has replaced a moral flaw. The ideas to which
they were blind were not only those subversive of their privileged
position but also those that justified their existence. Arnold attributes their failures to support public education for the middle
classes to a "natural instinct" against removing a source of
middle-class inferiority. He lays all their failures in the conduct
of foreign affairs at the door of the middle classes. He finds their
failure to enact needed regulatory legislation in domestic matters
to be no fault, but freedom from the fault of meddling.[50] This
last charge in any other context would almost certainly be
ironical, but Arnold was speaking about their superiors to an
audience of workingmen. Humorous about the aristocracy Arnold was, especially in *Friendship's Garland*. But he could only
rarely be ironical toward it, for irony is a form of condescension.

Arnold's five-part review of Curtius' *History of Greece*, written for the most part in the early seventies, shows how his habits of thought linked notions of permanence, stability, and adequacy with the preservation of an aristocracy. The true direction of Arnold's thinking is the harder to get at because he sees that government as "an aristocratic work" involves "the often blind superiorities of family, property, and office" and because he recognizes that democratic theory promises that every individual will count, that each man will be stimulated and made to feel alive. But Periclean democracy lasted at most seventy-five years, and in Arnold's reading of Curtius, Athens fell because the checks provided by the old order to the new one simply wore out. He even attributes the temporary success of Periclean Athens to the strength of the still-existing conservative influences, and he maintains that however fine the achievement of the period, its inability to last must count strongly against it.

Arnold places the democratic program and the old order in a too-strict and hence unreal opposition to one another. He represents the democratic program as seeking to remove all restraint and the old order as teaching men to respect and to obey. He juxtaposes the unlimited freedom of democracy with the steadiness and gravity of the nondemocratic system. He identifies the freedom and movement of the democracy with the teaching of the Sophists, and opposes the gospel of liberalism to the "righteousness, temperance, and self-knowledge" that Socrates enjoined. His spurious antitheses seem to lead him into that elementary kind of circular argument that develops from uncritical use of words. Democratic Athens, he says curiously, proved to be impermanent because it destroyed its permanent elements: "Pericles . . . destroyed the permanent conservative influences of the Athenian State"; "the anchor chains of the influence of family and property, and of the old institutions which made

government 'an artistocratic work'—were cut"; "the Athenian
State . . . had elements of permanence and stability; when they
were gone and democracy was left to itself, the pulverizing and
dissolving forces in it worked fully." He will not of course blame
the young aristocrats of Periclean Athens for becoming con-
spirators against the new democratic order.

*They felt that this multitude had no right to be in power, that
it had upset an old state of things which was better than its own
rule; they intrigued against it, and their intrigues produced confusion because what they had intrigued against had too little
worth and dignity to be a firm rallying-point.*[51]

A few years earlier, Arnold had planned the chapter "Barbarians, Philistines, Populace," in *Culture and Anarchy*, along
lines calculated to assure his readers that he was an objective
observer. He offers us a symmetrically balanced analysis of the
three classes, each in its turn; each with its virtuous mean, excess
and defect; each with its ordinary self having a severer and a
lighter side. Yet if we do not permit ourselves to be lulled by
the air of conscientiousness with which he dulls our critical
sense, we notice, especially in the matter of "defects," that the
graver sins of the lower classes are matched against the pecca-
dilloes of the aristocracy. Invariably he leads off by naming the
aristocratic foible, impresses us with his impartiality, and then
comes down upon the lower-class vice. All men, he tells us in
one place, have something of the barbarian and something of
the populace in them.

*Place me in one of his great fortified posts, with these seeds of a
love for field-sports sown in my nature, with all the means of
developing them, with all pleasures at my command, with most
whom I met deferring to me, every one I met smiling on me, and
with every appearance of permanence and security before me*

and behind me,—then I too might have grown, I feel, into a very passable child of the established fact, of commendable spirit and politeness, and, at the same time, a little inaccessible to ideas and light.

The spirit of the populace that inhabits every man's breast is of a different order of being. Arnold slips delicately into the first person plural as he describes it.

[We are conscious of it] every time that we snatch up a vehement opinion in ignorance and passion, every time that we long to crush an adversary by sheer violence, every time that we are envious, every time that we are brutal, every time that we adore mere power or success, every time that we add our voice to swell a blind clamour against some unpopular personage, every time that we trample savagely on the fallen.[52]

To set the following sentence of John Stuart Mill's against any sentence in *Culture and Anarchy* condemnatory of the aristocracy is to see Arnold's deep-seated reluctance to offend. "All privileged and powerful classes, as such, have used their power in the interest of their own selfishness, and have indulged their self-importance in despising, and not in lovingly caring for, those who were, in their estimation, degraded, by being under the necessity of working for their benefit." [53] Arnold's developed instincts were all against such plain speaking. He shared the viewpoint expressed by another Rugbeian, the brilliant financial expert, George Goschen, afterward first Viscount Goschen: Cobden had rebuked the young Goschen for attacking his allies in the House, Bright and Cobden himself. In reply Goschen affirmed that he had strict views on the kind of language that could be used about the relations of the classes. "Mr. Bright believes," he went on, "in a degree of selfishness

on the part of the governing classes which in my humble opinion is a libel on them, and I feel so strongly on this point that
even when we may both have the same object in view, I cannot
work towards that end without declining my share in what I
think a libel." [54]

Within a few months after *Culture and Anarchy* appeared in
book form Arnold was invited to Lord Lytton's estate in
Hertfordshire, to Sir Anthony Rothschild's country house in
Buckinghamshire, and to the duke of Bedford's fishing grounds,
also in Buckinghamshire. The editor of the Tory *Quarterly Review* forgave Arnold all his hostility toward both the review
and its editor because of "the truth and usefulness" of Arnold's
remarks on the Nonconformists. Onlookers were amused to see
two bishops introducing themselves to Arnold at the Athenaeum. Arnold was pleased that "a very charming Barbarianess,
Lady Portsmouth," expressed a desire to meet him. (He gratified
her wish and was subsequently reduced by her brother's biographer to one of the people Lady Portsmouth "gathered around
her.") [55] In short, English aristocrats knew that they were not
the primary target of Arnold's criticism and rewarded him with
their society.

In the world of ideas—to use one of Arnold's favorite distinctions—the aristocracy *was* one of his primary targets, but in the
world of practice, as he in fact stated the charges against the
upper classes, so much mitigation and palliation crept in that
there is no question which of the three classes Arnold preferred.
Whatever intellectual convictions Arnold had about the aristocracy, it was the class he knew next best to his own level of
society, and it was the class to which his fellow "gentleman
intellectuals" aspired to belong. He knew it from youth as the
class above, the class one was eager to rise into. The nearer view
of the aristocracy provided by the Lansdowne years did not dis-

enchant him. When he was listing the positive merits of classes, the virtues of the Whig aristocracy were what came most easily to mind: their power of manners and power of beauty, their ability and pertinacity as administrators, their generous dealing with subordinates, their goodness despite the falseness of their position.[56] The members of this class, he told an audience of workingmen, "have plenty of faults and imperfections, but as a whole they are the best, the most energetic, the most capable, the honestest upper class which the world has ever seen." To attack such a class acrimoniously was to play the Philistine.[57]

As Arnold's reputation widened so did his circle of friends and acquaintances in that astounding English upper-class society that might be impervious to ideas but that could still charm wild prophets like Carlyle and dark poets like Tennyson. Despite the small leisure time left Arnold after inspecting and writing, he engaged to a remarkable extent in country-house visiting.[58] Just seeing and dining with successful old school friends and associates like Lord John Duke Coleridge, Lord Carlingford, Lord Lingen, Lord Iddesleigh, the dean of Durham, the dean of Westminster, and the bishop of London—to give each his designation of honor—meant meeting other luminaries in the great world.[59] Stanley, so well connected himself, had married Lady Augusta Bruce, a hostess and friend to royalty, and she invited Arnold on at least three occasions to meet young members of royal families.[60] He learned that "Vicky," princess of Prussia, had read all his books and that Princess Alice of Hesse had memorized long passages of *Culture and Anarchy*. Years later, the crown prince and princess of Prussia received him warmly in Berlin. Their example was followed a few weeks later in Dresden by the emperor of Germany.[61]

Mountstuart Grant Duff used to remark that in any country other than England Matthew Arnold would have been minister of education. For himself Arnold did not aspire so high; the appointments he sought, albeit unsuccessfully, were not honorific but were desirable only in that they could supply him with a modest competence and allow him more time for his own work. Gladstone's offer of a pension in 1883 Arnold accepted with some hesitation even though he was a man constantly worried about money, especially about meeting the payments of a large insurance he wished to leave his family.[62] He told Coleridge that he was somewhat abashed when he entered the grand house that his old friend took after he became lord chancellor. The nearest approach Arnold ever made to the fashionable Mayfair from which he started his public life was renting a house in Manchester Square, which was close but on the wrong side of Oxford Street. As far as it had been possible to him, he had been a disinterested critic of the great Victorian world; he had been neither carping nor sycophantic. That world had drawn him out of himself and provided him with a touchstone by which he could judge other contemporary civilizations: it was (he loved to italicize the word) *interesting*.

Chapter IV

THE POPULACE

Writing to Clough in 1848, Arnold reveals an important attitude. "For my soul I cannot *understand* this violent praise of the people. I praise a fagot where-of the several twigs are nought: but a *people?*" What Victorian young man, bright, sensitive, dandified, and temporarily at least, well-placed as secretary to a Whig lord, would romanticize the people? Certainly Matthew Arnold did not, nor did he approve any such curious extravagance, even when indulged in by an author whom he deeply admired, George Sand. He had liked her *Lettres au peuple* at first, but her enthusiasm had clearly been wasted on an unworthy subject.[1] Who indeed were the people? Tinkers, hawkers, servants, laborers, street sweepers—the great, faceless *vulgus profanum* that formed the underside of all civilizations. Of course the English people, if one thought of them at all, were better than most, dreary in a more solid way perhaps, respectful, reliable, *sound*. But there were levels among the people; one usually distinguished between the artisan and the common laborer, but the latter term embraced a multitude of gradations until one reached the depths of society. Here, too, were the people, "the poor"; Mayhew was to divide them into *Those That Will Work*, *Those That Cannot Work*, and *Those That Will Not Work*.[2] Tennyson had his farmer state that

"the poor in a loomp is bad." And with their ugly poverty, amid
the pestilential rookeries, the gin shops, and street brawling, the
poor indeed looked in the mass like some ill-favored lesser breed
just barely within the law.

This disdain for people in the mass, however, was only one
of a whole congeries of notions Arnold entertained about the
lowest class of English society. For the people were also, under
one aspect, "the oppressed," and since Byron and Shelley no
man of education could hear that term without stirrings of the
heart. Three of the important voices of Arnold's own youth
had spoken of the victims of tyranny and of the duty of freeing
them from bondage.

Dr. Arnold had nervously objected to the tone of Cobbett's
complaints in behalf of the poor, but even in so doing he recognized that what Cobbett said about their degradation was true.
"The puissant voice of Carlyle," sounding through the Oxford
air, had declaimed against the cupidity of the *ancien régime* that
drove the poor of Paris to seek in revolution surcease of misery.[3]
Above all, George Sand spoke to Arnold rememberable things
about the poor and oppressed. To the titanic gloom enveloping
the children of the age she brought light, hope, beauty, and
joy—joy that for fullness must be in commonalty spread. One
of Arnold's first references to her is a quotation from memory
of a letter from Indiana to Raymon.

*Believe me, if a Being so vast deigned to take any Part in our
miserable Interests, it would be to raise up the weak, and to beat
down the strong:—it would be to pass his heavy hand over our
heads, and to level them like the waters of the Sea:—to say to
the Slave, "Throw away thy chain," and to the Strong, "Bear
thy Brother's burden: for I have given him strength and wisdom,
and thou shalt oppress him no longer."*[4]

Further, the general notion of "the people" embraced the lonely and individual poor, the sick cottager, the Cumberland beggar, the hungry child—all the objects of a warm and responsive charity. Toward these Matthew Arnold was a true son of his father and a disciple of Wordsworth. If the revolution of 1848 was being fought for these, he told Clough, for "the armies of the homeless and unfed . . . /Then am I yours." [5] Whatever changes the years brought, the current of Arnold's feeling for the misery and sufferings of the poor never failed.

As he walked through the streets of London he was not blind to extremes of luxury and wretchedness; he thought of Sallust's Rome with its *publice egestas, privatim opulentia,* and wondered at the pretentiousness that called the builders of such a city "children of God." For a time his work as school inspector took him to East London, to Bethnal Green, and the silk-weaving district of Spitalfields. Surely, he thought, the misery of the poor living on the Aventine could not have equaled that of the poor of London. The Romans, at least, did not have to contend with London winters, particularly winters like that of 1867, when a record snowfall occurred during a strike of workmen. In the midst of such misery Arnold found examples of virtue and spirit: the clergyman William Tyler cheered by thoughts of Christ as he went about his work, the ragged woman in the West End begging only from workers and scorning to ask from rich passers-by.

"There are men . . . ," Arnold quoted from Senancour, "who cannot be happy except among men who are contented; who feel in their own persons all the enjoyment and suffering they witness, and who cannot be satisfied with themselves except they contribute to the order of the world and to man's welfare." [6] Arnold surely was one of these. It was not for him to throw himself into work directly for the poor, but his educational work did aim to "contribute to the order of the world and to man's welfare." To convince the middle classes that they must reorganize their secondary education, to effect thereby an enlargement and enrichment of the lives of middle-class people, to give the masses an ideal toward which they would wish to move—this was what he conceived his immediate and practical purpose to be.[7] His writings, then, are not a storehouse of observations of the degradation of the poor; he did not wish to insist on stories of misery and poverty. When he pointed out that Cobbett called the ugly, blackened towns of Lancashire "Hell-holes," Arnold wished to get at the reasons behind the existence of Bolton, Wigan, and St. Helen's. The remedy he sought for such evils was radical and not palliative. He aimed to expose the greed and shortsightedness of capital, and urged that the poor be given assistance in preventing this "perpetually swelling" multitude from gathering in "festering masses." It was good, he further noted, that free trade had made bread cheaper but bad that free trade had also increased the number of paupers to eat it. "Either do not bring men into existence"—he quoted from Senancour again—"or, if you do, give them an existence which is human." [8]

One last element present in the young Arnold's view of the populace needs to be mentioned. It is the fear that a popular revolt would drench the nation in blood. We have already noted the existence of this terror among the propertied classes, and among Arnold's own friends and associates the current of fear also ran deep, but in them it mingled curiously with libertarian hopes and with their general desire to see the lot of common man improved. Thus the young Englishmen who crowded to Paris in the spring of 1848 to attend the birth of a new age of freedom were excited, enthusiastic, but they were not, as Wordsworth had been some threescore years earlier, blissful.

Revolution, the world had learned, was not a broad and easy road to the land of promise. Jowett and Stanley, with a group of fellow tutors, hurried across the Channel as soon as the spring vacation began. Arriving in Paris, they were delighted to see the tricolor flying. "It was Jowett," comments Palgrave, "who . . . expressed the feelings of the whole party, when he said, 'How absurd all fears seemed now.'" [9] They had found Paris quiet and not delivered over to the terrorists of revolt or reaction, as their imaginations had pictured it.

Such fears existed in Arnold and his friends all through the century. When he was young, Kingsley believed that the working classes were the enemy and that men of his class eventually would have to fight for both property and honor. At the end of the fifties William Forster was careful not to arm the Bradford operatives who joined his volunteer militia, and Matthew Arnold noticed that the London volunteers were all members of the upper and middle classes. Even in the last decade of the century Thomas Hughes told Rugby boys that the danger had not yet passed, and Lord Coleridge warned an American that since Anglo-Saxon respect for law sometimes yielded to sudden pressure, authorities must have swift and stern measures ready.

Yet when the alarming events of 1848 burst on western Europe, Matthew Arnold, in London as secretary to Lord Lansdowne, was busy playing the insouciant dandy. The revolutionary impulse that had overthrown Louis Philippe in February spread like a chain reaction among the capitals of Europe, and in London, by March, Chartists were rioting in Trafalgar Square. Arnold wandered among the hostile crowds, coolly noting afterward to his correspondents that the police were "needlessly rough in *manner*." [10]

As April 10 approached, the day set for the monster procession to Parliament, respectable London barricaded itself and swore in over 100,000 special constables. Wellington hid his soldiers in public buildings and prepared for the onslaught that never came. On the day itself the police sent word to Feargus O'Connor that the procession would not be permitted, and at O'Connor's word the 20,000 Chartists on Kennington Common dispersed. By a quarter to five Arnold could write to Clough that everything was quiet. The terror of the great world had seemed to him quite beyond belief. But he knew that no positive good would come of the affair; Lord Lansdowne was already referring to the Chartists as braggarts.[11]

Nor would any good come, Arnold thought, from the activities of a London mob. It was capable of kicking up a fuss but not of any concerted or lasting effort. Only from France, famed in all arts, supreme in the art of nurturing freedom, could hope come. So Arnold watched the news from across the Channel, but with the curious split vision that nourishes hope yet prepares for disaster. On one hand, he shared with Clough a glow of moral fervor in behalf of "Man's fundamental life"; he was as enthusiastic as Guizot and Michelet for a French people that lived in an atmosphere of ideas; he was pleased with the composition of Lamartine's provisional government. On the other hand, he kept his sense of humor ready for any eventuality: he said he had engaged a hansom so that he and his brother Edward could flee from the French; he made jokes about Monckton Milnes' republicanism; he addressed a letter to "Citizen Clough" at Oriel, and inspired the composition of an amusing handbill that was passed among the students. When, in June, hopes for a stable French government dissolved in anarchy and severe repression, Arnold expressed himself to Clough in a mixture of flippancy and disgust. "What a nice set of things in France. The New Gospel is adjourned for this bout.

If one had ever hoped anything from such a set of d——d grimacing liars as their prophets one would be very sick just now." [12] Thereafter he shunned republican enthusiasms; he never mentioned Mazzini or Garibaldi; Cavour did not interest him. For a time he shut himself off altogether from hearing or speaking of public affairs. France was a "madhouse . . . from whence the cry/ Afflicts grave Heaven with its long senseless roar." The day of "liberated man" would not "dawn at a human nod" or in a revolution that Arnold came to see as "ignoble." [13]

Though temporarily dashed, Arnold's hopes for a brighter, freer world survived and found expression in three poems of his 1852 volume. The music of humanity that we hear in "Revolutions," "Progress," and "The Future," is slow, somber, heavy with thought, but in its resolution not sad. Arnold looks at man as both author of his own fate and child of a destiny that determines him—man threatened with the loss of what he values and man lured on to what he has not yet achieved, man continually striving to alter his society and to regenerate himself. He is compulsive man, but he acts under the brooding spirit of the age's belief in progress, which in Arnold becomes a subtle belief, guarded, hedged with doubt and committed to the workings of slow time, but there all the same.

We know that for the first eight years of his inspectorship, which began in 1851, Arnold had no particular interest in public primary education. It was "other people's work," not his, and he could do more good, he felt then, by adhering to his own line.[14] Since he was only the third lay inspector to be appointed, his district was an enormous one, extending, as he noted years later, "from Pembroke Dock to Great Yarmouth." [15] The first inspector appointed by the education committee, H. S. Tremenheere, had been sent to a particular section of Arnold's district,

South Wales and Monmouthshire. This was the scene of John
Frost's rising in 1839, and the implications of Tremenheere's
visit were clear. Under the guidance of far-seeing men like James
Kay-Shuttleworth and Lord Lansdowne the nation was beginning to educate its future masters. Arnold reflected this view in
a letter to his wife in which he spoke of the importance of the
schools "in civilising the next generation of the lower classes,
who, as things are going, will have most of the political power
of the country in their hands." [16]

He inspected 104 schools in the first year, his wife doing most
of the traveling with him until their family began to grow. One
of their children was born in Derby in a lodging house that was
depressingly placed between a penitentiary and a workhouse. But
though the Midlands had more than its share of the uneducated
poor, Arnold found himself in those first years inspecting schools
attended mostly by children of the lower middle class. In his
first report he singled out for praise a school in South Wales
established for the children of working people employed by
an iron company. It was one of the few schools of its kind.
For the most part, managers and teachers of schools receiving
public grants were so eager to give their schools "tone" that they
excluded children of the lowest classes. By his second year
Arnold was already recommending compulsory education as the
only way to assure that the children of all classes would be
taught.[17] Within a few years, however, he was able to report his
own mild amazement at the improvement in both the schools
and the students in the mining districts of South Staffordshire.
He was also gratified to learn that teachers for the Wesleyan
schools were being trained specifically to work among the poor.
Stories about Matthew Arnold as an inspector abound, but
none is more charming than the one told about a particular
visit to a crowded and dingy metropolitan school. An urchin

who was reading aloud came to Byron's line "Alike the Armada's pride, and spoils of Trafalgar," and with great emphasis came down on the last syllable. Arnold interrupted him by calling out with great glee, "You have an ear, sir, you have an ear!" [18]

But such moments were rare, and all through the fifties Arnold did not see the routine drudgery of inspecting as anything but a soul-wearying, necessary chore. He knew that popular education was the best safeguard against revolution, but he knew also that the English system during those years reached only half of the children of school age.[19] What was more, the "watchful jealousy" of the Establishment's National Society on one hand, and the Dissenters' British and Foreign School Society on the other, delayed enlargement of the system until William Forster's education bill of 1870 achieved a compromise. Within the schools, improvements such as the pupil-teacher system had to be won by the zeal of men like Kay-Shuttleworth against powerfully entrenched prejudice. Most important of all, Arnold could not see before 1859 the place public primary education could take within a broad, integrated and well-articulated system, a system that would embrace all classes, a system that would transcend sectarian differences, and a system that could carry England forward into the modern age.

Since they enabled him to make this discovery, Arnold's six months in France in 1859 on an appointment from the Newcastle Commission became one of the great illuminating periods of his life. His years of inspecting suddenly leaped into importance for him, since they enabled him to see by contrast the workings of the French educational system and then in turn to perceive the possibilities for improvement latent in the English system. He could now relate the anomalies and shortcomings of English education to the society that had fostered it.

French public secondary training threw into sharp relief the tangled skein of English secondary education with which an intellectually anarchic people were trying to muddle through to an age of ideas and clarity.

In studying French primary education Arnold found himself having to look into an organization of church and state dating back to Napoleon's first Consulate. He was prepared to admire Napoleon's ideas on government, having read and reread Las Cases' book and having marveled at the French leader's creative genius for administration and management. Napoleon, Arnold gradually came to see, had divined the necessity for the post-feudal world of reconciling power with reason, of establishing a well-ordered, rational system of government while restraining all anarchistic tendencies. Now he confessed himself astonished as he studied in France both the Napoleonic Code and the way in which Napoleon had held the balance between the parties of both extremes while establishing his well-coordinated scheme. The English who had defeated him on the field of Waterloo were invincible in battle, yes, but compared to this man of ideas they were also invincible in ignorance.[20]

Napoleon had still another lesson to teach modern Europe.

He restored authority in France when authority was misunderstood, trodden to the ground, insulted, degraded; when authority had been made either hateful or ridiculous—sometimes both hateful and ridiculous—by the revolution. In the small group of men of his order throughout history none like Napoleon possessed as of right and exercised with such boldness the instinct and the gift of authority.[21]

These words, so like the ones Arnold was to use for both General Grant and Louis Napoleon, are those of the eminent French statesman and historian, Guizot, to whom in 1859 Arnold brought a letter of introduction from Lord Granville. Guizot had begun his career as an opponent of Napoleon, but once he himself became a government official he recognized the value of Napoleon's repressive power. Guizot knew at first hand the horror of anarchy: his father had been hanged under the reign of terror in 1794.

From his position as professor of history at the Sorbonne Guizot had moved to administrative posts during the relatively liberal administration of Louis XVIII. But this early liberalism became obscured during his ministry under Louis Philippe, when Guizot allowed corruption to enter the government, took a hand in the sleazy business of the Spanish marriages, and opposed all moves to extend the suffrage. When the revolution came in 1848 it was the shooting of a group of rioters in front of the Foreign Office, where Guizot lived, that sent men to the barricades before dawn. As a consequence he was cordially hated by the European liberals as a proponent of despotism and plutocracy. But even in his worst hour there was something admirable, almost Olympian, in the way this austere French Protestant resisted the stormy clamor of the Chamber of Deputies. "Criez, messieurs! Hurlez! Vos cris n'atteindront jamais le niveau de mon dédain!" Arnold thought that Guizot's disdain of the meanness surrounding him was justified.[22]

To Dr. Arnold the dictatorship of Louis Philippe had been "an excellent thing," and he deeply admired Guizot, whom he met at the duchess of Sutherland's in 1840. Rugby boys read Guizot's history of the English revolution; Dr. Arnold's girls read his *Civilization of France*. The latter book also served as a model for Dr. Arnold's Oxford lectures. Guizot returned Dr. Arnold's admiration in kind: when Stanley paid the Guizots a visit in 1848 he discovered Guizot's daughter reading his life of Dr. Arnold! So Matthew Arnold was prepared to learn from this eminent Frenchman, with whom he had such ties and who by 1859, under another dictator, was again in office, this time as minister of education.

During an earlier tenure in that office Guizot had reorganized the French school system along the lines laid out by Napoleon. Having drawn up a bill providing for lay, national, and universal education, Guizot sent out an army of five hundred inspectors to direct the operation of the law. Also following Napoleon's lead, he established good relations with the religious associations and offered state support to schools conducted by the three major religious groups. In return, the state demanded guarantees of competence from the teachers and supervised both curricula and teaching methods. Since Guizot believed that religious education should be more than generalized pietistic mouthings, he defended the teaching of doctrinal religion as then conducted in the congregational schools. He also made an effort to stir local interest and to make responsibility for school management at least partially a local matter. For the guidance of prefects, rectors, and inspectors, he composed a long series of circulars, bulletins, and directives—all of which Arnold seems to have devoured in an orgy of work. If Arnold's subsequent book describing the French educational system, *Popular Education of France*, can be said to have a hero, that man is François Pierre Guillaume Guizot.[23]

Popular Education of France is a well-documented, specific, and fact-filled book. The material in it was to provide sustenance for several of Arnold's essays, most notably the one with which he prefaced the volume, the essay "Democracy." The book is a classic statement of the educational ideas that have nurtured modern democratic states, and Arnold himself readily pointed out what dangerous tendencies he thought lay in those ideas. He called these tendencies "Americanising" and "Prus-

sianising." [24] We need say nothing of the first of these: Arnold
had read his De Tocqueville carefully and himself believed in
the American specter even as he raised it before his readers.
Arnold's definition of "Prussianising"—making docile, pedantic,
formal—may surprise us unless we remember the pre-Bis-
marckian land that Henry Adams regarded as a hundred years
behind the rest of Europe. Yet if there are dangerous tendencies
in Arnold's own ideas, they are precisely what we today might
term "Prussianising" tendencies. In the preface Arnold elab-
orately and interestingly defends his concept of the state as both
the agent of man's progress and the ideal by which he is motivated. But if the concept had a forbidding aspect to Arnold's
Dissenters, how much more does it give us pause who have
seen peoples strike the increasingly ludicrous poses of nationalism, and nations guided by men of good will transform themselves into huge atomic armories. We start at shadows, perhaps,
but we cannot forget that a centralized educational system such
as Guizot's would suit ideally a monolithic state, that dependent
religions have worshipped Mars more than Apollo, and that
Guizot's France was ruled by Louis Napoleon.

Since the French government was at the time well disposed
toward the religious orders, Arnold took the opportunity to visit
a few schools conducted by them, most notably the Dominican
secondary school at Sorèze. At the time, the school was under
the direction of the celebrated orator Lacordaire, who had left
Paris twenty years earlier at the height of his fame, to return five
years later as a Dominican. Much about the place and its director may have reminded Arnold of Rugby and its famed headmaster: the high moral tone and the atmosphere of work, the
emphasis on physical exercise, the privileged society of the best
and highest boys in the school, and the director who hiked with
the boys frequently and was as energetic as the strongest of

them, who gave weekly sermons in chapel, and who tempered justice with love in the conduct of the school. Arnold mentions all these things in an engaging section of A *French Eton*. As he introduces Lacordaire he draws attention first of all to a characteristic that distinguished the public career of the Dominican and gave him "the force by which he most impressed and commanded the young."

[He had a] passion for firm order, for solid government. He called our age an age 'which does not know how to obey—qui ne sait guère obéir.' It is easy to see that this is not so absolutely a matter of reproach as Lacordaire made it. . . . Still, he seized a great truth when he proclaimed the intrinsic weakness and danger of a state of anarchy. . . . He dealt vigorously with himself, and he told others that the first thing for them was to do the same.[25]

Lacordaire had been the subject of a panegyric written some years earlier by another famous Frenchman whom Arnold met during these months, Sainte-Beuve. But in the French critic's eyes Lacordaire was, at least for a time, too much a society preacher and not enough a Dominican, so that he lost much of the rigid authority of the pulpit. To Sainte-Beuve also, then, especially after Louis Napoleon's *coup d'état*, authority had its charms. He had twice refused the Legion of Honor from Louis Philippe; in the bleak days of the reign of Charles X he had hoped for a social democracy. Yet he persuaded himself that Louis Napoleon would save France by founding a welfare state on the lines laid down by Saint-Simon, and he approved mass deportations and the censorship of speech and press as necessary steps to a desirable end.[26] How much of his enthusiasm for Louis Napoleon Arnold caught from Sainte-Beuve it is difficult to say. While Arnold was in Paris, Napoleon removed some of the restrictions on the press (after eight years of rule), and Arnold remarked to his wife how well the emperor was "going on." Sainte-Beuve used his influence with the Princesse Mathilde to secure an appointment as senator. After the appointment was made in 1865, Sainte-Beuve took Arnold to meet the princesse, and a dinner invitation followed this introduction. But the society he met at the princesse's salon did not interest Arnold, and he did not take other opportunities to attend.[27]

Arnold had gone out from England to see a nation shaken by the winds of civil discontent and found instead a well-managed autocracy. The prospect did not displease him. An efficient government that brought peace and prosperity at home and won a measure of prestige abroad did not need to be a representative government to meet Arnold's approval. Yet because he was addressing *England and the Italian Question* to an English public whom he wished to trust the emperor, he made of Louis Napoleon a popular ruler whom the industrious classes had "called . . . to power" in order to save themselves from anarchy. To support this view Arnold quoted the words "which one hears so often in conversing with members of the industrious classes,—*il nous a sauvés de l'anarchie,—il nous a tirés de l'abîme.*" He represented the government of France as an "absolute government" but one that existed "by the wish of the governed." And in Louis Napoleon the French people had secured a man who "consolidated his own power" because he was peculiarly susceptible to popular ideas.[28]

Arnold's "light play of mind" here comes to mean dubious history, curious semantics, and a questionable reading of public opinion. What he sees as "a call to power" deserves its more familiar name, *coup d'état*. The term "absolute government" means just what it says, and not even a "disinterested observer" can make it mean "popular government." That Arnold should cite as evidence the opinions of the industrious classes strikes us as the least defensible part of his procedure. It is true that he struck up conversations with his traveling companions; he tells us of his chats with a naval officer and a *chef de bataillon*, the latter a man who had risen from the peasant class, but hardly typical.[29] According to Grant Duff, Arnold's friend and an authority on European affairs, "On the Continent Mr. Arnold knew very few persons save those who are naturally thrown in the way of a distinguished Englishman provided with good introductions." [30] And when we compare the people whom Arnold saw several times in Paris—Villemain, the Mohls, the Circourts, the Duc de Broglie—with the people whom Stanley and Lake visited there, we can see that Arnold spent many of his leisure hours in the company of people whom men of his class usually saw in the French capital.

Indeed, it is at least doubtful that Arnold heard the words, quoted two paragraphs earlier, that he attributed to the French working people. Early in his tour he had written to Jane, "I saw today at Arles on the Roman obelisk an inscription to Louis Napoleon with the simple words 'il vous a sauvés de l'Anarchie.' " [31] The sentence stuck in his memory, and to be useful needed only the simple but significant change of *vous* to *nous*.

Of course one does not pin Matthew Arnold writhing against a wall simply by catching him out in a careless sentence. Nevertheless, in the preparation of his essays he tended, as he himself confessed, to put his trust too strongly in divination.[32] Privately he wrote that he was not at all sure of what Napoleon III was about, and before the peace of Villafranca he was made apprehensive by the emperor's superiority in numbers and strength. Much of his partiality to the French leader in *Friendship's Garland* is due to the terms of his discourse. He wished to shake the complacency of English liberals, for whom the form of a government rather than its actions was all-important. So he had Arminius cry "Liberalism and despotism! Let us get beyond these forms and words," a cry that does not mean that under any conditions Arnold preferred an efficient despotism to muddleheaded liberalism. Bismarck, he knew, would muffle the loud ignorance of the liberals; Arnold would teach them, though teaching took time and the teacher was always resented. Eventually Louis Bonaparte, Bismarck, and the king of Prussia, having played their game in the hour of anarchy, would have to make way for the better world.[33]

In Paris, Arnold saw other literary figures besides Sainte-Beuve—Renan, Mérimée, and perhaps Michelet, whom he had met on an earlier visit. With Renan he apparently chatted about nonpolitical topics; Mérimée was private secretary to the empress and a devotee of the court; from Michelet, Arnold had a letter of introduction to George Sand, but perhaps because Sainte-Beuve told him about the Musset affair and because he would have to travel a distance to see "such a fat old Muse," he did not visit her.[34] Had he gone, he could have expressed his conversion to the sentiments of her *Lettres au peuple*, at least insofar as they applied to the peasantry. This class had become his ideal of what a lower order should be, democratic in spirit and independent. He did not mind that they were Louis Napoleon's staunchest supporters or that they doffed their hats to army officers. They were the enemies of the feudal order because each of them now had his own plot of ground, and there was no real poverty among them.[35] The idea of a happy, self-sufficient peasantry drawing sustenance, joy, and goodness from the soil enchanted Arnold all the rest of his life. His peasants did not lead idyllic lives, nor did he assume that under rough caps their intellects were to advantage dressed, but there was a kind of bucolic aura about them that Hardy's rustics

would have found uncomfortable. Under the influence of this
charm Arnold's references to the populace from 1859 to 1865
were almost unanimously favorable. He had not forgotten
1848; the reaction against "the faults and extravagances" of the
democracy was deserved.[36] He was anxious, however, to use the
years of civic peace to widen and deepen public education and
to prevent any more night drills with pikestaves on the Yorkshire moors. So it was that in 1862, when he saw that Robert
Lowe's Revised Code for education posed a threat to genuine
popular advancement, he attacked Lowe and the utilitarian provisions for "payment by results," risking his post to do so.

Arnold enjoyed Lowe's subsequent discomfiture during an
investigation into the conduct of his department, and in an
essay published in 1866 he gave this official a permanent place
among the gallery of contemporaries whom he transfixed with
his wit like so many voodoo dolls. Lowe's rhetorical habit of
praising the middle classes extravagantly exposed him to Arnold's simple but effective ridicule. Several of the passages from
Lowe that Arnold quoted against him came, however, from a
famous speech he rather admired, the first of Lowe's series
of speeches against the reform proposals made by Russell's government in 1865 and 1866.[37] Lowe, who had spent several years
in Australia and there formed unfavorable opinions on the
soundness of democratic governments, attacked the reform proposals with a vigor and brilliance that delighted the conservatives and brought defeat to his fellow liberals. One passage from
his second speech was used to uproarious effect by the Reform
League in its demonstrations in the spring and summer of 1866.

*Let any gentleman consider the constituencies he has had the
honour to be concerned with. If you want venality, if you want
ignorance, if you want drunkenness and facility to be intimi-*

dated, or if, on the other hand, you want impulsive, unreflecting,
and violent people, where do you look for them in the constitu-
encies? Do you go to the top, or to the bottom? [38]

What Arnold used to call a period of concentration had suddenly given way to a period of expansion. Several times since
the mid-fifties Russell had introduced an electoral reform measure, but Palmerstonian fireworks abroad tended to distract attention from reform both outside and inside the House. Palmerston's death in 1865 signaled the end of an era and marked the
beginning of a period of disruption and general civil uneasi-
ness. The crisis involving the trade unions, the case of General
Eyre, and the riots incident on the passage of the second Reform Bill coincide with the publication of Arnold's lectures
on the study of Celtic literature, parts of *Culture and Anarchy,*
and *Friendship's Garland.*

The trade unions seemed to pose the most lasting problem
of the three. Strikes of the growing unions in the fifties and
early sixties were met by industry-wide lockouts by employers
anxious to crush union power. The consequent disruptions of
industry made the public uneasy, and a series of outrages per-
petrated by trade clubs in Sheffield was used by a hostile press
to discredit the entire trade-union movement. In Sheffield the
practice of "rattening," that is, hiding the tools of a worker who
was behind in his dues, had long existed, and where "rattening"
failed, other lawless measures were discovered. Under the direction of such men as the ruthless trade-club secretary William
Broadhead, gunpowder explosions and shootings served to bring
uncooperative workers and masters into line. Then in February
of 1867 the legal position that Francis Place had won for the unions in 1824 was undermined by a Queen's Bench decision that
unions were illegal because they operated in restraint of trade.

From within the ranks of labor an association of trade-union leaders, headed by Robert Applegarth, William Allan, and George Odger, took the responsibility of proving before a royal commission that the great friendly trade societies tended to restrain rather than to incite aggressive action.[39] From outside the ranks of labor came friends like Frederic Harrison and Thomas Hughes to put their legal skills to work in behalf of the unions, to write letters to the press, and to serve on the royal commission. Other friends of labor came forth to help: Sir T. Fowell Buxton, who was related to Arnold by marriage; A. J. Mundella, the liberal manufacturer, later to be Arnold's superior in the Education Department. The chairman of the royal commission was Sir William Erle, whom Arnold had met when he was on circuit with his father-in-law, Justice Wightman, and with whom he had ridden, played whist, and gone sightseeing.[40]

Arnold did not care to make the distinctions between kinds of workingmen's associations possible to Harrison and Hughes, Buxton and Mundella, and the Christian Socialists like Kingsley and Maurice and J. M. Ludlow. In *Culture and Anarchy* he speaks of that part of the populace "which so much occupies the attention of philanthropists at present,—the part which gives all its energies to organising itself, through trades' unions and other means, so as to constitute, first, a great working-class power, independent of the middle and aristocratic classes, and then, by dint of numbers, give the law to them, and itself reign absolutely." A trade unionist is really a kind of Philistine whose "graver self likes rattening; the relaxed self, deputations, or hearing Mr. Odger speak." [41] We will allow that *Culture and Anarchy* gives all classes a much-needed lesson in humility, and that sweetness and light did not exude from the trade unionists. But the tone of these remarks—especially the supercilious reference to philanthropists—and the deliberate linking together of all kinds of trade unionists cannot be defended as play of mind. "I often wished," wrote Leslie Stephen, "that I too had a little sweetness and light that I might be able to say such nasty things of my enemies." [42]

The references to Frederic Harrison that dot both *Culture and Anarchy* and *Friendship's Garland* show that Arnold had a basis of respect for the young Positivist barrister. In the latter work Arnold has his clear-headed Prussian, Arminius, go off for a long period to consort with Harrison, and the picture of Harrison "in full evening costume, furbishing up a guillotine" in a Grub Street back yard is wonderfully humorous.[43] Harrison retorted with an exhilarating satire of his own, which Arnold very much enjoyed. Arnold seemed indeed to like the man but to distrust his addiction to an abstract system and to disapprove of his efforts in behalf of trade unions. Arnold was able to disparage Harrison's trade-union activities by making them of a piece with his Comtism, but there was in fact no necessary connection between the two.[44] Harrison had taken up the cause of the unions during a prolonged dispute in the builders' trade. As part of a committee of Christian Socialists and Positivists, Harrison helped draw up letters to the newspapers explaining the objections of the operatives to payment by the hour. The strike had given Harrison "a vision of a great battle going on all around and beneath us," and he vowed to do his best to see justice done.[45]

The name of Governor Eyre was in the forefront of public attention from the autumn of 1865 until a royal commission censured him strongly two years later. A committee of liberals headed by John Stuart Mill, Thomas Huxley, and Thomas Hughes had demanded the investigation into Eyre's severe repression of a Negro uprising in one county of Jamaica. Carlyle, on the contrary, had formed a committee of citizens to support

Eyre, and called Mill's group "a knot of rabid Nigger-Philan-thropists, barking furiously in the gutter." [46] What Arnold thought of Eyre's conduct may never be known; he never mentions the Eyre case directly. One previously unnoticed reference to the Eyre affair does occur in a letter of *Friendship's Garland* written when the controversy was at its height, but the reference may be interpreted variously: "In hearts we are (except when we find ourselves in India or Jamaica) very well off; but in heads there is always room for improvement." [47] More satisfactory as evidence, but still by no means conclusive, is a remark made in *Culture and Anarchy*. Culture, Arnold notes, "enjoins us to encourage and uphold the occupants of the executive power, whoever they may be, in firmly prohibiting them [riots]." In the context of the times the addition of the phrase "whoever they may be" is significant.[48]

What happened during the Hyde Park riots of July, 1866, or rather what is supposed to have happened, is a twice-told tale. The accounts in the *Times*, beginning on July 24, differ from one another. Spencer Walpole, the home secretary, was reputed to have wept when a Reform League committee went to see him; George Holyoake, a member of the committee, said this was not true. Did the rioters prise up the railings, did they push them over intentionally, or did the crush of the crowd simply topple them over along Bayswater Road on the north and Park Lane on the east? [49] Whatever the exact details are, the upper classes of London, and particularly the residents of nearby Mayfair, were given cause for alarm.

Matthew Arnold was not near Marble Arch, the center of the riots, on that Monday afternoon, but in the evening he was sitting with his wife on the balcony of their house in Chester Square, less than a mile south of the park, when a gang of roughs broke into the square and threw stones at Sir Richard

Mayne's windows. Sir Richard was the object of the crowd's
wrath because, as police commissioner since the institution of
the metropolitan force, he had developed the techniques used
by the police to control mobs. During the Kennington Common scare in 1848 he had been the man who summoned
Feargus O' Connor to the edge of the crowd and warned him
against holding a Chartist procession. Before that month was
out he had been made a Commander of the Bath. Now in 1866
he was seventy years old, but he had gone to Marble Arch on
that day astride a white horse, and when the trouble started he
had had to avoid missiles thrown at him.[50]

In Chester Square that evening the police soon drove the
rioters away, but the effect on Mrs. Arnold can well be imagined. She was a nervous woman, and for fourteen years she
had been burdened with the care of her invalid son, Thomas.
Besides, the Arnolds were well and perhaps intimately acquainted with the Maynes.[51] On Tuesday and Thursday nights
of that week Arnold went to the House of Commons to hear
what was said about the rioting. The letters to the *Pall Mall
Gazette* that were later collected under the name of *Friendship's Garland* had begun to appear, and during that week
Arnold wrote one that he entitled "Democracy." What is England doing, Arnold asked, to raise its democracy to the concept
of a nation? England feeds the people the thin pabulum of
Dissent, and "if this is not spiritual enough, as a final resource
there is rioting in the parks, and a despotism of your penny
newspapers tempered by the tears of your executive." [52]

Demonstrations by the unfranchised masses of London continued through the following year. On February 10, Arnold
wrote of "the alarmed Conservative feeling" and the "disgust
at Bright and the working class" among tradesmen and employers as well as among aristocrats. On the following day a

great crowd of workers, wearing the rosettes that symbolized their support of reform, marched from Trafalgar Square and past the Athenaeum, where Arnold used to sit and write his letters. In May the home secretary forbade an announced meeting in Hyde Park, but despite the ban, 200,000 people gathered together, heard the speakers, and left quietly.

The Hyde Park riots came to the forefront of Arnold's mind again on December 13, 1867, when a group of Fenians blew up Clerkenwell jail, killing 12 persons and injuring 120. Both events illustrated to him the government's feebleness and lack of resolution, and he wrote to his mother and sister that "a strong hand" and "a good secret police" should deal with such matters. Like France and Prussia, England needed to develop its army and a strong administrative system into "a cohesive force." [53] Since, in that same December, Arnold was writing "Doing As One Likes," the second section of *Culture and Anarchy*, these attitudes found immediate public expression.

Indeed, to read *Culture and Anarchy* in the light of these agitations is to see how Arnold's fear of physical anarchy inflects the entire argument. One of the main functions of Arnold's hypothetic best self, the state, is to repress the dangerous working classes. Whatever faint praise he gives the workers drowns under such powerfully emotional epithets as "English rough," "Hyde Park rioter," "the mob . . . bent on mischief." Disruption, he says, has become so great "that that profound sense of settled order and security, without which a society like ours cannot live and grow at all, sometimes seems to be beginning to threaten us with taking its departure." He calls the meetings and processions that preceded the passing of the second Reform Bill "demonstrations perfectly unnecessary." As is well known, Arnold excised from later editions the famous quotation from his father recommending that rioters be flogged and their leaders be hurled from the Tarpeian Rock. But his fear and willingness to resort to strong coercive measures are too deeply woven into the texture of the work to be neatly removed. En masse, he says in his conclusion, the rioter is a "playful giant," raw and rough, and against him "the lovers of culture may prize and employ fire and strength." [54]

An uninformed reader of *Culture and Anarchy* would never learn that the Hyde Park misadventure was the exception rather than the rule in the popular demonstrations of the mid-sixties, that on scores of occasions throughout England hundreds of thousands of workers, bearing the emblems of their trades, had marched in an orderly manner, frequently through the rain.[55] Arnold simply was too much out of touch with the common people to understand that the responsible union members who made up an increasingly greater proportion of these demonstrations could not be a *jacquerie*. Through his pages march only the roughs, bent on mischief, calling for blood.

Repression of one class by another, however, was never more than a temporary stopgap to Arnold; *Culture and Anarchy* looks forward to the hour when "a man feels that the power which represses him is the *State*, is *himself*." [56] It looks forward to the peaceful arrival of the last stage in his father's "Social Progress of States," when liberty and equality for all men will have found their proper balance. Through the seventies Arnold worked at removing the obstacles to this progress. He still believed that the bright day would not "dawn at a human nod," so that he reproved Bright and later Chamberlain and Gladstone for appealing to the class interests of the populace rather than working for the future by seeking to make the people rise above selfish concerns. He approved of the extension of the franchise, but only as an expedient measure and not because any hypothetical "natural rights" were involved or because the franchise would *improve* a man. Believing that morality for the masses must ever spring from religion, he continually emphasized the need for Bible reading in schools, and edited a volume of Bible selections for elementary schools. His extensive religious writing in the seventies sprang from the earnest desire to make the Established Church coextensive with the nation it purported to serve. He saw religion as one of the bulwarks against barbarism, and to Fontanès he expressed himself to this effect in spirited French: "Pour en sortir, il vous faudrait, comme à l'ancien monde romain, le déluge et les barbares!" [57]

Arnold's views on equality, which his fellow Rugbeian, R. H. Tawney, rightly praised, were enunciated in an England "still haunted by the ghost of the feudal spirit." [58] What was more, they were enunciated after a life in which the most subtle influences worked in quite other directions. As we have seen, he did not entirely escape his heritage. But he never suspected that he did not have a perfectly clear insight into the minds of the working class. What small, occasional doubts he had were easily dispelled. After his curious address before the Working Men's College, Ipswich, in which he urged his listeners to support middle-class public secondary education, he was pleased when his sister reassured him that the address was well adapted to the audience. The sister who wrote to him, however, was not Mary, who had worked with the Christian Socialists in London, but Fan who had stayed at home in Fox How.

He continued to regard urban workmen as always ready to become park rioters. Nor did he like French urban workmen, who served only to provide unpleasant material for equally unpleasant novelists like Zola. That the work of men who labored with their hands might offer "*a happiness to the maker and the user*" was an idea simply outside Arnold's ken. In

America, Arnold drew Whitman's sputtering indignation for his failure to understand "people, people, just people." [59] Chesterton, closer to Arnold, could do justice to the insight as well as the blindness in Arnold's views of the common man.

He had (what is so rare in England) the sense of the state as one thing, consisting of all its citizens, the Senatus Populusque Romanus. But he had not the feeling of familiarity with the loves and hungers of the common man, which is the essence of the egalitarian sentiment. He was a republican, but he was not a democrat.[60]

Chapter V

THE PHILISTINES

In the course of a review of Arnold's poetry Swinburne called attention to the following question:

> It will be a curious problem for the critics of another age to work at, and, if they can, to work out, this influence of men more or less imbued with the savour and spirit of Philistia upon the moral Samson who has played for our behoof the part of Agonistes or protagonist in the new Gaza where we live. From the son of his father and the pupil of his teacher [Wordsworth] none would have looked for such efficient assault and battery of the Philistine outworks. . . . A profane alien in my hearing once defined him as "David, the son of Goliath." [1]

Perhaps the beginning of a solution to the problem lies in a simple distinction. If "Philistinism" implies high purpose, dedication, belief in the gospel of work, and a hatred of moral untidiness, then both Arnolds come within the meaning of the term. Matthew Arnold, however, used the word in two quite different senses. "Philistine" could refer to a nonprofessional, middle-class person, usually a Dissenter, or disapprovingly, to coarse, narrow, or one-sided people, whatever their rank. In the latter sense Oliver Cromwell, Luther, and George III were all

Philistines. Under the force of Swinburne's jibe Arnold called himself "properly a Philistine" in *Culture and Anarchy*, implying the simple class meaning. But even in this sense he did not think the term applied to his father or himself.[2]

In practice Arnold had a valuable sense of existing outside or above ordinary class distinctions. This sense derived from his real social position as a member of the "exceptional" or professional class, and more especially from the close connections of his family with the Establishment. On his father's side, we have to go back to Arnold's great-grandfather before we find an ancestor who was middle-class in the sense that he engaged in trade. On his mother's side, the family came from people who resided almost exclusively in parsonages. Mary Penrose, his mother, was the daughter, granddaughter (on both sides), niece, sister, wife, sister-in-law, aunt, and mother of Anglican clergymen.[3]

Although to the poor all Anglican clergymen seemed to belong to a species of aristocracy, within the church itself gradations of clergy existed, extending from the bishops, with their palaces and their average stipend of £5,000 a year, to the curates and provincial clergy, with incomes frequently less than one-thirtieth that amount. Entrée to the upper echelons of this special multilevel society was usually restricted to the one-third of the Anglican clergy who were graduates of one or the other of the two major universities. All of the Penrose clergymen, like Dr. Arnold, had attended Oxford or Cambridge and had become either teachers or holders of respectable livings. They therefore belonged to a class within the clergy corresponding to no exact level of lay society, though if we had to place them somewhere, a position between the upper middle class and the lower gentry would do. Yet because they were within the Established Church, an appointment to a deanery or bishopric could lift them out of this limbo to the social level of the higher nobility.

Arnold's close associates in school and the university came from social positions similar to his own, both inside the Establishment and, to varying degrees, above the rank and file of the middle class. Clough alone came from a family engaged in trade, yet even he had two uncles who were Anglican clergymen. The antigentleman complex that he developed at Oriel rose from an antipathy to the wasteful expenditures of Oxford gentlemen at the time of the Irish famine and was similar to the dislike of middle-class extravagance he had expressed in the *Balance*. As he had in the early days of the Decade, he continued at Oriel to find in master manufacturers the natural leaders of the future. But this was a romantic, secondhand Carlylean notion that he gradually abandoned. He was still under its influence in 1849 when he made a pleasant visit to Rochdale to see the cotton mills belonging to John Bright and was invited to dine with Bright's brother and sister. But shortly thereafter he began his three years as head of University Hall in London, a period that showed him how different his world was from that of the "mercantile Unitarians." [4]

Arnold was never in sympathy with Clough's promanufacturer sentiments. "I trust in God," he wrote to his friend as Louis Philippe's government toppled, "that feudal industrial class as the French call it, you worship, will be clean trodden under." An apostolic capitalist might share his profits among his artisans, he noted a few days later, but in England a fair return on capital had come to mean what enabled the capitalist "to live like a colossal Nob." [5] Clough did not need the lesson. He also knew that English workmen did not get a just proportion of the profits and that some substitute for devil-take-the-hindmost competition would have to be found.

Since old wealth is never tolerant of new, it is more likely that Arnold found his anticapitalist views reflected rather than controverted by those of his Whig friends. Of the two major parties, the Whigs were more responsive to pressures from the middle classes and also more willing to admit them to a share in the government. A large Nonconformist element, in fact, had formed a kind of irreducible nucleus of the Whig party, just as the Tories had the squirearchy to form the irreducible nucleus of their party. Lord John Russell had been calling the attention of the House to the rise of the middle classes since 1822, and his was the first Whig Reform Bill, introduced in 1831, which proposed to enfranchise a large segment of the middle classes. One of the Russells—at first the duke of Bedford and later Lord John—was chairman in its early years of the British and Foreign School Society. Lord Lansdowne also associated himself with the work of the Dissenters' educational organization, and like Lord Holland, he contributed generously to its funds. On at least one occasion, too, Lansdowne took the chair for the annual meeting of the Protestant Society, a Dissenters' group pledged to work for religious liberty.[6] But though the Whig grandees wooed them and Macaulay called them "vast masses of property and intelligence," the middle classes occupied few places of political responsibility and honor within the party. The Russell cabinet of 1846 included only two men who were not sons of aristocrats, inheritors of baronetcies, or lawyers. The first was Macaulay and the second was the elder Henry Labouchere, scion of a great mercantile family and himself on the way into the nobility.

As is well known, Arnold became closely acquainted with the middle classes during his school inspectorate, the duties of which sent him on a twenty-year tour of England. His dealings first of all were with the managers of his "British" schools,

well-to-do, friendly people but non-Anglicans, a class apart. In
his letters home, letters in which the tone of condescension is
unmistakable, he described the hospitality of Unitarians in Birmingham, of a Dissenter named Coote in Cambridgeshire, of
Quakers in Suffolk. In Bedfordshire he lodged with another
Quaker family whom he liked but whom he found it necessary
to patronize. "The . . . grand-uncle redeemed his sins by col-
lecting a really splendid library—you know I am particular,—
which the present people have built a room for, and had cata-
logued, and the catalogue will be a great resource to me this
evening." In time he came to realize the value of meeting people
whom his friends in the Anglican community did not associate
with. And he came to admire their straightforwardness and
honest dealing. When in 1871 a change of districts relieved him
of his "British" schools and assigned him to the "National"
schools of the Establishment, he was to have misgivings as he
took up his new assignment: the clerical managers would expect
him to stretch the law in their favor. He was to remember that
the Dissenting managers had asked for nothing but absolute
fairness.[7]

Arnold had hoped that his Dissenting schools would train
children from all levels of the working class. But what he had
to deal with, especially in the early years, were schools for
children of farmers, tradesmen, and artisans. To his dismay he
soon discovered that modest success in life had made these
people bumptious and opinionated, in matters of education no
less than anything else. And what was worse, these people were
listened to. In the Wesleyan schools, for example, teachers and
managers could not ignore meddlesome parents, since the
schools depended on pupils' fees for books, furniture, and teachers' salaries—for everything, in fact, except the buildings. The
result was that it was difficult to educate the children above

the standards of their parents. Since the parents were unable
to distinguish between kindness and indulgence and did not
discipline their children at home, they thought themselves put
upon when the teachers reprimanded the children at school. It
was hard to teach children to write forthright prose when their
elders wished them to write elegant periphrases. Only a system
of public elementary and secondary education, Arnold was to
say in the sixties, could train the offspring of such parents.[8]

Some of the managers, too, merited sharp criticism from
Arnold. He was perturbed by the dirty conditions of the London school premises and mentioned the squalor in his annual
report. After his complaint the managers cleaned the schools,
but only to the limited extent they thought necessary. "The
greater the 'liberty of action' given to managers in fixing the
standard of needful school cleanliness," he remarked, "the dirt-
ier will our public schools become." For them education was
satisfactory when it was efficient and cheap. The education
Minutes of 1846 had gone far toward eliminating the much-
admired wonders of the Bell and Lancaster monitorial systems,
but the managers still resorted to other penny-saving strata-
gems. Arnold described a system developed by a Mr. Fletcher
for use in the "British" schools whereby the cost of equipment
was kept down. Of a school of 150 children, 50 were instructed
on the gallery, 50 on the floor, and 50 at desks. The groups
rotated through the day so that each child had a chance to
write at a desk. Robert Lowe's Revised Code of 1862, with its
invidious provision of "payment by results," pandered to this
same niggardliness. With his gift for phrases, Lowe assured the
members of the House that they would get full return for the
expense of education. "If it [the new system] is not cheap it
shall be efficient; if it is not efficient it shall be cheap." [9]

Referring to this period later, Arnold wrote that he felt then that "the cause of popular education was safe." But at the time the Revised Code was adopted he saw it as a dangerous retrograde step "concocted in the recesses of the Privy Council Office, with no advice asked from those practically conversant with schools." [10] Following Kay-Shuttleworth's lead, he made a spirited frontal assault on the Code and its authors in what is surely his least typical prose essay. The controversy centering on the Code is very interesting here because Arnold found himself opposed for the first time by the two elements within the middle classes that were to become his main critical targets. Lowe, the main author of the Code, derived from the old, severely pragmatic Bentham tradition, and was one of those whom Arnold was to refer to as the Millites or the Liberal secularists. Behind the bill Arnold detected also the twin figures of Edward Baines and Edward Miall, the second of whom was to lend his name to what Arnold dubbed the Mialites or the political Dissenters.[11]

Lowe had approached the question of primary education with the narrow and mechanical views typical of Bentham and the early John Stuart Mill. He made the elementary-school grant dependent on the children's passing an examination in reading, writing, and arithmetic, thus turning the school, in Arnold's eyes, into "a mere machine for teaching" and denying that it was "a living whole with complex functions, religious, moral, and intellectual." [12] Baines and Miall, as leading Voluntaryists opposed to state aid to education, could only rejoice that state influence had been substantially reduced.

Arnold and Kay-Shuttleworth were successful to the extent that the House made one-third of the school grant depend upon attendance and the kind of larger inspection that Arnold advocated. But their efforts would have availed little unless they had been supported within the House by a group interested in education, among whom William Forster, Arnold's brother-in-law, was the most prominent Liberal. Forster had read Arnold's article, was pleased by it, and decided to give the whole matter his attention. Accordingly, when Spencer Walpole introduced a set of resolutions aiming at modification of Lowe's Code, Forster joined in the debates, using arguments drawn from Arnold's pamphlet and his follow-up letter to the *Daily News*. Arnold gave full credit to Forster for his part in effecting the compromise. He praised Forster for his earnestness, honesty, and willingness to learn. The man of letters had found an ally in the world of affairs.[13]

At first glance William Forster seemed to be an unlikely ally for the elegant and Anglican Jeremiah.[14] He was a manufacturer, a Dissenter, and (to an extent) a radical—in all three regards, therefore, like Bright, who was seven years his senior, and Mundella, who was seven years his junior.[15] Like Bright and Mundella, too, he had taken an active part in workingmen's causes and openly supported many of the Chartist aims. His father and mother had been famous Quaker preachers, and he remained faithful to their peaceful ideals even though he could also be a pugnacious pacifist, capable of addressing a noisy crowd of six thousand Chartists and pushing "a strong moral force resolution down their throats, at the cost of much physical exertion." [16] In that stormiest year of the hungry forties, 1848, he took the bold step of delivering a series of addresses to Bradford operatives on pauperism and its proposed remedies. His discussions of communism and Saint-Simonism seem to have been both naïve and superficial, but his conclusions were unconventional for one of his background: the principles of political economy do not enjoin the necessity of laissez-faire, men must put a "prudential check" on the increase of population, and the state has a responsibility to feed its paupers and to educate all its citizens.[17]

In appearance tall, graceless, and hirsute, Forster looked as though he came from rough yeoman stock. But he had come from people of some station and manners, and though his education was over before he was seventeen, private tutors had put him through a strenuous classical regimen. Friendships with Robert Owen and Thomas Cooper had set the social tone of his ideas, and Stanley's life of Arnold had shown him that moral earnestness and social aims similar to his own could exist within the Established Church. Like Clough, he had listened to "the puissant voice of Carlyle," had formed a friendship with that dourest of Scotsmen, and in the end had become disenchanted. The disenchantment came during a tour of Ireland in 1849 when Carlyle exulted in Forster's hearing that the people were suffering what they deserved. Thereafter Forster allowed the friendship to dwindle away.[18]

By the year of the Revised Code controversy, 1862, he had been married for twelve years to Jane, Dr. Arnold's eldest daughter and the one closest to Matthew. The marriage had come as a surprise to the Ambleside gossips like Harriet Martineau, for Jane had been expected to marry an Anglican clergyman. On Forster's side, the wedding made automatic his formal expulsion from the Quaker body. Whatever their differences, the couple were most happily married, and Forster soon won a respected place in the Arnold family. He helped the younger Thomas Arnold and his family get settled after their return from Tasmania. In 1859 he and Jane adopted the four children of William Delafield Arnold, who had died on his way back from India. By that time the correspondence that Matthew Arnold maintained all his life with Jane had been widened to include William. In 1858 the Oxford Professor of Poetry changed an expression in *Merope* and a year later softened an expression in his Italian pamphlet in deference to Forster's views.

If Forster took an interest in Arnold's work, Arnold more than reciprocated with his interest in Forster's occasional articles for periodicals, and more especially in his political career.[19] During the fifties Forster gradually gained a reputation as a vocal defender of the interests of labor and an advocate of cooperation between the middle and lower classes. But his rooted mistrust of Palmerston's domestic policies and his advocacy of both a national system of education and manhood suffrage made him too much a radical for the Liberal organization of Leeds. That borough, the heart of the West Riding of Yorkshire, had witnessed the most imposing demonstration of Dissenters during the strong wave of anti-Establishment sentiment that swept the midlands in the thirties, and it had returned one of the first Dissenters to sit in Parliament, Edward Baines, the editor of the *Leeds Mercury*. In the late fifties Baines's son, also an Edward, held the Liberal seat as an advocate of moderate franchise reform and an opponent of public education. In 1857, Forster's popularity with the electors almost caused a split in the Liberal vote at Leeds. Four years later he was asked to stand for Bradford, was returned unopposed, and was introduced to the House by his fellow Yorkshire Liberal, Edward Baines.

As a member of Parliament, Forster again at first made the mistake of taking too strong a line. In his maiden speech he declaimed so vigorously against a proposal to recognize the Confederacy that the chair called him to order. He quickly learned not only to hold his temper but to seek moderate and possible reforms. By 1863 he had moved so much toward the

center of the party that he was mentioned prominently as the
next Liberal leader. And his temper had improved to the point
that Arnold began to identify Forster's aims with his own.

*I have never had an opportunity of saying to you how good I
thought William's speech at Leeds; so moderate that I actually
expected it to have somewhat carried the Times with it. . . . I
think in this concluding half of the century the English spirit is
destined to undergo a great transformation; or rather, perhaps I
should say, to perform a great evolution, and I know no one so
well fitted as William, by his combined intelligence and moderation, to be the parliamentary agent and organ for this movement. . . . I shall do what I can for this movement in literature;
freer perhaps in that sphere than I could be in any other, but
with the risk always before me, if I cannot charm the wild beast
of Philistinism while I am trying to convert him, of being torn
in pieces by him.[20]*

On certain subjects the two men did not share the same
views. Forster was one of England's great supporters of the
American North and a warm admirer of Lincoln. Arnold was
noncommittal about the Civil War and preferred Grant to
Lincoln. Forster claimed the friendship of Mazzini on the floor
of the House; Arnold had no time for European republican
causes.[21] But these differences did not touch the center of their
agreement: the necessity of treating political subjects with a
largeness of mind and spirit, of raising national concerns above
petty interests of party and sect, and of preparing for the future
while preserving the best of the past.

By the early sixties Arnold had begun his work as literary
"agent and organ for this movement," and it was a work that
immediately took a practical turn. For he saw that the English
middle classes were "nearly the worst educated in the world,"

that their inferior education had alienated them from the upper classes and stratified Victorian civilization along the line where the public schools met the grammar schools. With the middle classes growing daily so wealthy and powerful that they were supplanting the aristocracy as the real rulers of England, the time had come, he warned England, to *"organise your secondary instruction."* [22] Twenty years later he remarked that "the thought of the bad civilisation of the English middle class" had been "the master-thought" governing his political writing. During the interval, then, he had devoted himself to a campaign to convince the "saving remnant" within each class that curing "the bad civilisation of the middle class" was the duty of every true-born Englishman. But just as Arnold's attitudes toward the aristocarcy and the working classes reflected a whole congeries of assumptions and preconceptions toward those classes, so also the way he saw the middle classes was determined by the entire breadth of his experience. When he spoke about them he spoke with the voice of reason, one of the clearest and most resonant then to be heard. But the voice of reason speaks always with the accent of time and place, echoing sentiments that are "felt in the blood, and felt along the heart."

It is noteworthy that Arnold's first extensive attempt to "charm the wild beast of Philistinism" in the matter of public secondary education never mentions the word "Philistine." The essays that were to form the book *A French Eton* appeared serially in *Macmillan's Magazine* in late 1863 and early 1864, and therefore were written after Arnold had run across the term "Philistine" in preparing his essay on Heine. He delighted in the word. He noted that English had no term to designate the unenlightened enemies of change. It should adopt "Philistine"! But he knew that a writer who was eager to persuade should not apply such a word to the ones he wished to sway.

In *A French Eton* he took great care to excise any sharp expression that might offend; he wished more to be effective than to be thought brilliant. After the first two parts appeared he sent copies off to Sir John Pakington and Richard Cobden with notes asking them to read the work. Pakington was in Arnold's opinion "the statesman most inclined, in education matters, to take the course I want to see taken"; Cobden received his copy as a representative of the middle classes.[23]

Arnold had picked in Cobden the right man to approach. Since the repeal of the Corn Laws, Cobden had been, with Bright, the leader of the radical wing of the Liberals. He was, moreover, not only a successful calico-print manufacturer but also an Anglican. Though not well educated himself, he knew that extension of the franchise had to be linked with provisions for national education. For years he had hoped that a national system might be established on the basis of the religious school systems in existence. Arnold had met Cobden at Forster's the previous summer, and he mentioned this connection in the letter he sent with the articles.[24]

We do not have Cobden's reply, but we can deduce from Arnold's answer to it and from what we know of Cobden's experiences with education, that he urged on the school inspector the necessity of first making primary education national and compulsory. It is almost certain too—again judging from Arnold's reply—that Cobden pointed to his own experiences as showing that bitter religious sectarianism would oppose further invasions by the state into the field of education. With neither of these ideas could Arnold agree: the masses, in their present state, he argued, could never be a governing force in the country but only a *jacquerie*; the middle classes would not be able to rule effectively until their minds had been opened. As to the extent of religious opposition, Arnold had formed

convictions of his own. "I daresay the old generation of protestant dissenters are impracticable. . . . But a new generation
is beginning to show itself in this class, with new impulses
astir in them, more freedom and accessibility of spirit: it is on
them one must work—in literature, at least." [25]

Arnold's optimism would have seemed unjustified to the
veteran statesman. The old generation of Protestant Dissenters
was still very much in power, and Cobden knew how intransigent it could be. In 1847, while he was abroad, a general election had taken place, and he returned to find himself the representative of a constituency he would have declined to serve.
He had been made representative, curiously enough, for the
West Riding of Yorkshire, the home of the *Leeds Mercury*,
Edward Baines, and organized Dissent. Cobden was embar-
rassed by the election, for he knew that his views did not match
those of his constituents. He anticipated that he would be
badgered by his contentious supporters, and he was not wrong.
Baines pressed him so hard through the pages of the *Leeds
Mercury* on both electoral reform and education that Cobden
wrote a sharp letter to him pointing out that the education
issue was splitting the Liberal party and insisting that further
agitation on the subject was useless because the principle of
state education was settled.

He did not expect his advice to be taken. Baines was the
chairman of the Congregational Board of Education, the leading Voluntaryist organization opposed to governmental assistance to schools. Not only did the Congregationalists refuse to
accept state grants themselves, but certain groups within the
sect conducted an energetic and frequently bad-tempered campaign against all governmental intrusion in religion.[26] The
Leeds Mercury supported this movement against the Establishment, but the most vehement and persistent attacks on the

church appeared in the pages of the London *Nonconformist*, a newspaper founded by Edward Miall, in 1841, in order "to right Christianity." If Matthew Arnold had been asked to give an example of what he referred to in his letter to the Forsters as "the wild beast of Philistinism," he would have pointed to the *Nonconformist*.

"The primary object of the *Nonconformist*," wrote the exigent Miall for his first issue, "is to show that a national establishment of religion is essentially vicious in its constitution, philosophically, politically, and religiously." He pledged that his weekly newspaper would make public "the innumerable evils" of the Establishment and would arouse the people of England to repudiate it. He condemned the "thousand enormities" by which a priesthood and its secular aristocracy "violate every maxim of religion, degrade, insult, harass, imprison—regard nor justice nor mercy in their pursuit of pelf. . . . Let them claim what they will, but suffer them no longer to be lords in the Church of Jesus Christ." For his newspaper's motto Miall chose "The Dissidence of Dissent and the Protestantism of the Protestant Religion." [27]

R. W. Dale, the esteemed historian of Congregationalism, admired Miall's enthusiasm and style but deprecated his facility for making enemies not only among the friends of the Establishment but also among Congregational leaders. For Miall not only engaged in hot and vigorous assaults himself but also berated his fellow Dissenters, especially "the aristocracy of Dissent," for not joining in. Because of the slashing style of these attacks Miall was disliked within his own sect. When the *Eclectic Review* concurred in his extremist policies, a group of moderate Dissenters founded the *British Quarterly Review* in protest. Outside of Dissent, another feature of Miall's Non-

conformity made him distrusted among men who in the mid-
sixties shared the fears of Matthew Arnold.

During the heyday of Chartism the anti-Establishment cause
gained powerful but temporary impetus through its association
with the popular movement. At least a dozen Chartist newspapers joined the *Nonconformist* in the cry to end church tithes
and to urge state seizure of Anglican property. Miall himself
became a leader of the "Complete Suffrage" group and was
prominent enough to be one of a Chartist delegation that went
to France to congratulate Lamartine's provisional government.[28]
Later that same year he made a long tour through the West,
speaking to large Chartist crowds. By a coincidence that cannot
be regarded as entirely fortuitous, the first place at which he
spoke during the tour was Newport, the small town in South
Wales that was the scene of Frost's rising, Tremenheere's inspectorate, and subsequent visits of inspection by Matthew
Arnold.

Such formidable opposition demanded all the pains Arnold
could take with *A French Eton*. In the volume he carefully
tailored the argument in behalf of state action to Dissenting
readers. After the second part appeared in the *Cornhill Magazine*, the *Nonconformist* took notice of the book in order to
complain that "Mr. Arnold has no notion of the depth of feeling against State interference." [29] The next part contained
Arnold's antiphonal response to his objection: he did understand the feeling of the Nonconformist middle classes who
remembered their time of "suffering and injustice." Then "the
hand which smote it—the hand which did the bidding of its
High Church and prelatical enemies—was the hand of the
State." But now, he went on, the state had no disposition to
favor one religious faith over another. The state could be an

instrument of middle-class will if that class simply chose to
employ it. He praised middle-class self-reliance in a manner
that would do credit to Roebuck or Bright. The phrase "Business and Bethels" came to his mind, one of those alliterative
"telling things" he loved to use satirically, but now he dismissed
the phrase as slighting and misleading. He managed a neat
compliment to Mr. Baines and Mr. Miall and politely provided
them with excuses for not being persuaded by him. He denied
that he wished Nonconformity to take its law from unsatisfactory "actual" Anglicanism and an unsatisfactory "actual"
aristocracy. All three must be transformed in "the world that
seems to lie before us like a land of dreams." [30]

Surely this was the voice of sweet reasonableness. These were
the words, if any, that would win Nonconformists. Perhaps they
might not charm Miall and Baines, but they would not offend
them further, and they would not drive moderate Dissenters
to make common cause with their extremist brethren. Among
Congregationalists alone, men of good will like Samuel Morley,
a public benefactor to rank with Lord Shaftesbury, Robert
Vaughan, the editor of the *British Quarterly Review*, and
R. W. Dale, the brilliant Birmingham scholar, would respond
favorably. The *British Quarterly Review* did in fact respond
favorably with a review of Arnold's poems and essays that
pleased him so much that he wrote a letter thanking the editor.[31] Yet he did not persist in the ways of gentle persuasion;
in the words of John Morley, by the end of his life he had
"irritated all the nonconformists in England." [32] What made
him change so completely in this regard admits of no ready
explanation. But the stages in the change are marked and can
be most easily traced in the changes of meaning he attached to
the word "Philistine."

The installments of *A French Eton*, in which the word does

not appear, had all been published by May, 1864. The *Essays in Criticism, First Series* had come out singly by November of that year, and in book form, with a preface, in 1865. In this volume "Philistine" is a synonym for "Englishman"; the term refers to no specific class. Arnold heaps on the Philistine all the vices of *l'homme moyen sensuel,* British style: he is ignorant, ignoble, testy, and vulgar-minded; he lacks dignity, steadfastness, and ideas.[33] The lowly Philistine sets off by contrast the subjects of Arnold's essays and makes more effective their lessons in the morality of intelligence and feeling. The Philistine is the Everyman of 1865, or as a French critic pointed out, John Bull.[34]

In 1865, Arnold spent nearly seven months on the Continent, this time inspecting secondary schools for the Taunton Commission. He returned to England early in November in an altered mood. While Arnold was in Switzerland, Palmerston had died, and the European press had taken the occasion to note the decline of England under Pam's leadership. The *Times,* on the other hand, had hailed the dead premier as a fallen hero and ignored the fact of England's decline. His patriotism aroused, Arnold determined that England must be made to see itself as Europe saw it. Soon after his return he wrote to his sister that he feared England would become "a sort of greater Holland" and he must do all he could, in every way, to prevent such an eventuality. Already he saw that he must write in more than one manner if he were to make an impression on the national consciousness. In time this belief led to the abandonment of the manner of *A French Eton* and *Essays in Criticism, First Series* and the adoption of the various manners of "My Countrymen," the rest of *Friendship's Garland,* and *Culture and Anarchy.* "Sometimes, no doubt, turning oneself one way after another, one must make unsuccessful and unwise hits, and one may fail after all; but try I must, and I know that it is only by facing in every direction that one can win the day." [35]

"My Countrymen" appeared in the *Cornhill Magazine* three months after this letter and placed the blame for England's lowered prestige squarely on the middle classes. The manner of the essay, too, faced in a new direction for Arnold: using a variation of a familiar literary device, he now represented himself as the mock-humble inquirer willing to listen to what his foreign "friends" said about England. Within the first four pages he had quoted Miall ironically, glanced at middle-class education, and for the first time identified Philistinism and the middle classes.[36] With this link forged, he now could lay to the charge of the middle classes not only all the faults of John Bull but some that other observers had laid to the charge of the aristocracy.

Arnold's aim was to shake English complacency and to make the national life more rational and more beautiful; he pointed to the need for fresh, enlightened views of the questions involving secondary education, Irish land, and the Irish Establishment. But he was arguing so much for effect that he had no compunction in paring and shaping the facts of recent English history in order to make his case. Specifically he blamed the middle classes for their attitude toward the Italian war, their attitude to the American North, and the English government's conduct during the Schleswig-Holstein dispute.

It suited Arnold in these contentions to represent the *Times* as the voice of the middle classes, and middle-class opinion as a kind of Areopagus. Then he noted how the *Times* in 1859 had first declared itself against, but later in favor of, Sardinia's abrogation of its treaty with Naples. In the first instance the *Times* had refused to admit that changed circumstances might invalidate a treaty; in the second, after Sardinia had successfully broken the treaty, the *Times* commended it for recognizing that its extremities were beyond international law. Somehow, in Arnold's view, the inconsistency of the *Times*'s editorials reflected discredit solely on the judgment of the English middle classes. And yet the *Times*'s first view of the matter, for which, Arnold noted, "much may be said," was an "aristocratical" view.[37]

Arnold noted further that the middle classes had been cold toward the American North during the Civil War, and after the victory had discovered that they had always wanted the North to win. "Some people," he conceded, "will say that the aristocracy was an equal offender in this respect: very likely." What mattered was that "the behaviour of the strong middle part makes more impression than the behaviour of a weak extreme; and the more so, because from the middle class, their fellows in numberless ways, the Americans expected sympathy, while from the aristocracy they expected none." [38] Arnold, then, would have his readers apply different standards to different classes in order to blame one class and excuse another. And we almost do what he wants, for the argument is so charmingly idiosyncratic, so blandly contemptuous of logic and simple truth that to examine it closely would surely break its gossamer wings.

Will it be enough simply to note that he assumes that the middle classes could have been wiser than the rest of the nation, that he had praised, early in the war, the cohesiveness of English opinion and credited it to the aristocracy and church, that he himself, admittedly had overestimated middle-class sympathy for the North? For it was precisely the failure of the middle classes to separate themselves from the aristocracy and to judge the American Civil War for themselves that dismayed

John Bright and John Stuart Mill. On the great majority of
the nation, with a few notable exceptions, such as the Lancashire millworkers, the aristocracy had exerted its cohesive power
to unite England in favor of the South. And if the sympathies
of the middle classes moved toward the Union cause, so too,
if we may judge by brief references in his letters, did the sympathies of Matthew Arnold.[39]

It is true that the middle classes must bear their portion of
the blame for the Schleswig-Holstein debacle. They applauded
the policy that has been variously described as "bluster and
blunder" and "meddle and muddle" but that England adopted
with a cockiness reminiscent of the way Palmerston handled
the Don Pacifico affair in 1850. But the German Confederation
was not Greece, and Palmerston and John Russell could not
keep Bismarck out of Schleswig-Holstein by threats alone. With
Napoleon as an ally, England could have made a show of
strength, but Russell had rejected Napoleon's proposals for a
European congress in language that even the *Times* found
objectionable. Together, Palmerston and Russell, the two great
carry-overs from the heyday of the aristocracy, men who had
been in office since before the first Reform Bill, had failed.
Moreover, they had failed in a matter that reflected less a new
age of ideas than the ageless struggle for power. Arnold had
been wont on other occasions to say that he who administers,
governs. But in "My Countrymen" he simply placed on the
middle classes full responsibility for the Schleswig-Holstein
failure and ignored the role played by the hapless aristocratic
survivors in a world they never made.[40]

At one of Lady Stanley's fashionable gatherings several
people told Arnold how much "My Countrymen" had amused
them. Carlyle, as might be expected, admired the essay, and
Arnold went to see him about it. His mother, however, did not

like the article, nor did Lingen, who accused him of exalting
the aristocracy and using the middle classes as a whipping boy.
Arnold felt that the objection, the result of a hasty and angry
reading, had no basis in fact.[41] Still, the letters written during
that year and the next as other parts of *Friendship's Garland*
distribute the blame for England's decline more equitably than
did "My Countrymen." [42] In addition, Arnold shaped the concept of "Philistine" to apply specifically to middle-class Dissenters. Arminius, his spokesman, rages against the same *ächt-
brittische Beschränktheit* that troubled Heine, but he is wont
especially to loathe the narrowness of Dissenters. Prominent in
his enumerations of middle-class vulgarities are marriage with
a deceased wife's sister, the abolition of church rates, antipathy
to the Establishment, and opposition to Sir James Graham's
Factory Act. Mr. Bottles, Arnold's humorously drawn Reigate
manufacturer, had begun life as a "Particular Baptist," and
though Arnold tells us that at one point he had forsaken chapel
for church, he still retained his enthusiasm for Dissenters'
causes and looked forward to marrying his wife's sister.[43]
Though Mr. Bottles' son was attending public school and
would probably end up a lord, he himself was a graduate of
Lycurgus House Academy, Arnold's version of what Dickens
had represented so unforgettably as Salem House Academy. All
this is very good-tempered and humorous, but Arnold was
deadly serious about Radicals of the Manchester school like
Mr. Bottles. Manchester was for him a symbol for sharp dealing
and for making *a good thing*; it stood for the sacrosanctity of
property; it believed in coal, population, energy, wealth, rail-
roads, and liberty—all that Arnold called machinery and Carlyle old clothes. Mr. Bottles was, in fine, the Philistine, with all
his vices and prejudices confirmed by material success. What
made him so important was that he was or soon would be the

effective ruler of England. "The great thing now," Arnold told
his mother as he was writing an early chapter of *Culture and
Anarchy*, "is to try and build for the future, avoiding the faults
which have done us so much mischief." [44]

Culture and Anarchy, with its long preface, was written in
the disturbed months between May, 1867, and December, 1868.
As a defense of culture as an ideal of individual and social
perfection it is magnificent. As an evocation of the idea of a
democratic state, capable of achieving excellence itself and capable of determining correctly what its citizens may read and
how its citizens may worship, it is an astonishing testament of
faith in man's power of goodness and power of reason. As an
analysis of the classes of England it is broad, pungent, impressive, and exasperating.

Today we believe that to few men is given the power of
uniting right reason with pure, spontaneous feeling and sweetness of temper—of joining the best, let us say, of Bentham and
Wordsworth and Newman. Reason, for us, is borne, poor weak
vessel, on a sea of surging and dark emotion, and when it
arrives, as it does for some, in a quiet and peaceful harbor, it
may hope to guide others to the same haven, but it knows that
it can never compel another to follow without destroying what
it seeks most to preserve. In practice, we believe, more than
Arnold did, in what Newman called man's involvement in a
"great aboriginal calamity." Arnold believed in man's power to
know "the firm, intelligible law of things," in his duty to teach
it to others, and in the rightness of coercing those who would
not or could not be taught. Of course he did not believe that
man attained Reason. He said, quoting Bishop Wilson, "Take
care that your light be not darkness"—as if one could make
sure—but he also knew that culture consisted in the search for,

but not the attainment of, perfection, and that man must "walk staunchly by the best light one has." [45]

Modern readers turn to Matthew Arnold because he walked staunchly by his own best light, but they sometimes wish that he were somewhat less certain about the value of that particular light and somewhat more indulgent toward others' want of it. They will observe his habit of noting, at times caustically, to how great an extent real people and institutions fail to be ideal. They will wish he himself partook more of the sweetness he so strongly recommends to others.

The sweetness in the first chapter of *Culture and Anarchy*, "Sweetness and Light," is full, genuine, and free from all acridity when it deals with Arnold's Oxonian audience and with its pursuit of the ideal. The essay was his farewell lecture as Oxford Professor of Poetry. He wished to be winning and sympathetic, and he was sure afterward that he had been. He even conciliated the High-churchmen who were present by identifying his work with Newman's struggle against liberalism, a feat requiring some careful omissions and interpretations. The sweetness thins rather abruptly, however, once he turns his gaze from Oxford and its representatives of the Establishment. He couches in general terms his praise of the merits of other religions; his dispraise finds specific and forceful expression.

Do not let us deny the good and the happiness which they have accomplished; but do not let us fail to see clearly that their idea of human perfection is narrow and inadequate, and that the Dissidence of Dissent and the Protestantism of the Protestant religion will never bring humanity to its true goal. . . . Look at the life imaged in such a newspaper as the Nonconformist,—*a life of jealousy of the Establishment, disputes, tea-meetings, openings of chapels, sermons; and then think of it as an ideal of*

a human life completing itself on all sides, and aspiring with all
its organs after sweetness, light, and perfection! [46]

Consider, he tells his audience, "the hideous and grotesque
illusions of middle-class Protestantism" and know what it is not
to be part of it. Regard its trust in machinery, its lack of delicacy of perception, and want of sensitiveness; its narrowness,
one-sidedness, and incompleteness; its *"hole and corner* forms
of religion." Consider the middle-class rich.

[Consider] *their way of life, their habits, their manners, the very*
tones of their voice; look at them attentively; observe the litera-
ture they read, the things which give them pleasure, the words
which come forth out of their mouths, the thoughts which make
the furniture of their minds; would any amount of wealth be
worth having with the condition that one was to become just
like these people by having it? [47]

That the sweetness of the apostle of culture failed him when
he spoke of Dissenters, especially rich ones, is to be regretted
but not entirely to be wondered at. As J. Dover Wilson observed, what Arnold cared most about was religion. He was
deeply engaged in the formulation and articulation of his own
religious beliefs and could not see without a pang of the heart
what passed for religious practice among Dissenters. Nor could
he understand the sense of spiritual satisfaction that they drew
from the services conducted in little Bethels—the prayer meetings, hymn sings, and "pleasant Sunday afternoons." He saw
the virtue of their high moral standards and thought them well
rewarded for them, but he could not view with sympathy their
passionate clinging to this religious creed, which for them
pulsed with life, however much he thought it failed of cultural
totality. With the vituperative Mr. Murphy inflaming the mobs

of Birmingham and Manchester, Fenians blowing up Clerkenwell jail, and rioters hurling stones in Chester Square, he saw
the spiritual anarchy of Dissent deepening into physical anarchy.[48] Born in that atmosphere of contentiousness, urging its
readers to rise above emotionalism and harshness, *Culture and
Anarchy*, for all its greatness, itself partakes of what it decries
in others.

Arnold's abandonment of the conciliatory manner of *A
French Eton* is regrettable because it made him less effective
an exponent, at least immediately, of views that Dissenters
needed to hear. They needed to learn that protesting and dissenting had little to recommend them as an ideal mode of
behavior, that stock notions had little resemblance to intelligent
ideas, that "machinery" had no justification in itself. They
needed to learn the power of "returning upon oneself," which
Arnold praised in Burke and which he himself sometimes but
not always achieved.[49] We are strongly tempted to think that
Arnold's failure in sweetness resulted partially from the haste
with which he wrote. He labored painfully over *A French Eton*;
"My Countrymen," however, was written at a time when he
was deluged with other work. It was not easy for this man,
whose goodness and sweetness shine in his personal letters, to
be sympathetic to the middle classes and especially the Dissenters. When he discovered that the manner of "My Countrymen" made a stir and roused people to pay attention, even if
they did so in order strongly to disagree, he forsook the careful
manner of *A French Eton* and the best parts of *Essays in Criticism* as less effective. The charges of vulgarity and contentiousness against the Puritans, which he repeated all through his
work of the seventies, created that atmosphere of acrimony he
deplored, in which men hold more furiously than ever the non-
sense he would have had them abandon.[50] Arnold should have

remembered the words of Joubert he brought to our attention:
"Les hommes ne sont justes qu'envers ceux qu'ils aiment." [51]

The serial publication of the first parts of *Culture and Anarchy* brought down on Arnold the charge of reviewers that he
was hostile to Nonconformists, and enabled him to reply in the
latter parts of the same work. He protested his friendship for
Dissenters and claimed that he worked for their perfection. He
wished, he said, to bring them into the mainstream of human
life and to make possible their total spiritual growth by bringing
them within the Establishment. Basing his claims on a fresh
reading of history, he traced the gradual extrusion of the Pres-
byterians from the church following their failure to impose on
the parent body their own Calvinist views. But he noted that
the differences between Presbyterianism and Episcopalianism
were not an essential of religion; both forms of church discipline had existed within the Establishment before and could
again. He illustrated, too, by a sample reading of St. Paul how
Puritans interpreted in a narrow, mechanical sense terms that
the Apostle used in a connected, fluid way.[52] In these regards
Culture and Anarchy points forward to the parts of Arnold's
religious writing of the next decade by which he aimed "to
deliver the middle class out of the hand of their Dissenting
ministers." [53]

During the late sixties and early seventies Arnold also worked
to "sap the House of Commons intellectually, so far as it [was]
ruled by the Protestant Dissenters." [54] One of his methods for
achieving this end was to hold up to ridicule those hardy
perennials of Nonconformist legislative effort, the Deceased
Wife's Sister Bill and the Burials Bill. He objected to the first
of these measures as threatening one of the advances civilization has made in refining its concept of marriage and as
making this threat on the spurious ground that the Bible does

not forbid such indelicate marriages. As for the Burials Bill, which would permit Dissenters to bury their dead with their own rites in the public churchyard, Arnold feared that indecorous behavior might attend such interments, that "Ranters or Recreative Religionists or Peculiar People" would engage in all manner of unseemly behavior on hallowed ground.[55] It requires an act of the historical imagination to feel the force of Arnold's objections. He must have known, as he did in the matter of the abolition of university tests, for example, that what the Dissenters felt to be a grievance would eventually be conceded. Still, he did not understand the enormous emotional appeal that their traditions of religious liberty held for the Dissenters. Long and painful struggles had gradually freed them from major civil and political disabilities and now tended to make them resist the lesser restraints still remaining.

In a pluralistic society today our consciences are especially tender on matters of religious liberty. We recognize that there are levels of dignity and grace in the way men worship, but we know that neither right reason nor the power of law will dissuade a man from sacrificing a bull to Athena if he so desires. As a member of the church established by law, Arnold believed in religious toleration, but he could not feel the full emotional force that minority groups attach to the concept. Arnold's skepticism toward the generally received Anglican canon of belief increased his love, so it seemed, for what he conceived to be "a national society for the promotion of what is commonly called *goodness*." [56] In a letter congratulating Frederick Temple on his appointment as bishop of Exeter, Arnold noted, "In the seventeenth century I should certainly have been in orders, and I think, if I were a young man now, I would take them." [57]

Perhaps Arnold's opposition to the Dissenters' claims is best understood in the light of his partisanship toward the Establish-

ment. For in the years immediately following the second Reform Bill, Dissent gave promise not only of throwing off its
disabilities but also eventually of disestablishing the Anglican
Church. With the belated realization that the rapidly expand-
ing electorate would have to be educated came the further
realization that an important phase of the battle between
church and Dissent would be fought over the provisions of the
next education bill. In order to provoke discussion William
Forster brought forward education proposals in 1867 and 1868,
although during those sessions he was merely a private member
of the opposition. Pressure groups quickly formed to represent
the various shades of opinion: the National Education League
to support unsectarian schools, the National Education Union
to support the denominational schools, the Central Nonconformist Committee to guard the interests of Dissent. Edward
Baines was the leading spirit of the Union, Joseph Chamberlain
of the League, Edward Miall and R. W. Dale of the Nonconformist Committee.[58] At the same time, Dissent served warning
to Forster that its "watchful jealousy" was trained on him.[59]
In 1867 and 1869, Miall stood for Bradford against Forster and
the other Liberal incumbent. In neither election was he successful in unseating Forster, but in 1869 he won the second Liberal
seat for the Dissenters. One of the issues on which he cam-
paigned was that of disestablishment.

In 1870, William Forster, now vice-president of the Council
and therefore in charge of educational matters in Gladstone's
first cabinet, introduced the government's bill for elementary
education. Received quietly at first, the bill soon roused a
storm of opposition as Dissenters realized that it would work
enormously to the advantage of church schools. Dissenters
argued that its conscience clause would be swept away by local
churchmen. Further, they strongly opposed provisions whereby

school boards could hand public money over to denominational
schools. In districts where a church school already existed, the
children of Dissenters could be compelled by the local board
to attend, and the education rates would become to the Dissenters "the old church rate in another form." [60] The liberals of
the National Education League opposed the bill because it
aimed only to supplement the old voluntary system and because
the matter of compulsion was left to the discretion of the
school boards. Gladstone had wanted the state grants simply
to go to secular education, and religious education to be left
to voluntary effort. But Gladstone was too busy with details of
the Irish Land Bill to make his views felt, the cabinet went
along with Forster, and in the House the bill won the support
of Anglicans of both parties. After several emendations it
passed into law, but its passage cost Forster any chance he had
of seizing "the great prize of power and influence," the leadership of the Liberal party.[61]

Arnold, of course, watched the progress of the legislation
carefully and was eager for its passage. He praised Forster's
management of the measure and went to the House to hear
him speak in its behalf. Though he had no official connection
with the bill, people wrote and talked to him about it, to the
extent that he had difficulty getting his work done. Like Forster,
and indeed like the men of good will in all interested parties,
he was concerned primarily in getting the children of England
into schools, but he did not wish to see the Establishment
suffer in consequence. Thus he was pleased that the bill retained its most important original provisions and that Gladstone seemed to be "in a much more Anglican mood" than
formerly.[62] Mrs. Humphry Ward gives Jane much of the credit
for Forster's compromise "by which the Church schools, with
the creeds and the Church catechism, were preserved." We

need not believe, however, that either of Dr. Arnold's children influenced Forster other than indirectly. As the writer of Forster's obituary noted, the Dissenters "had calculated upon Mr. Forster's Quaker training, and had regarded him as more one of themselves than the event proved him to be." As far as they affected the church, Forster's views on education had come into correspondence with those of Matthew Arnold.[63]

Throughout the seventies Arnold's strictures on the Philistines continued to center on opponents of the Established Church. At the beginning of the decade he found one of his alliterative names for them, the Millites and the Mialites, the former embracing "an inadequate conception of the religious side of man," the latter "an inadequate conception of man's totality." [64] His religious writings of the period aimed to bring Dissenters within the Establishment and also treated the tenets of supernatural and revealed religion as illusion and poetry. The endeavor, in R. H. Hutton's view, meant that he was attacking Dissenters "on grounds which appear to mean that they were wrong only because there was nothing worth dissenting from in the creeds of the Church." Arnold himself saw his attempt to transform the Dissenters as emerging "from no desire to give their adversaries a victory and them a defeat, but . . . from hope of signal good to this whole nation if they could be turned to better account." [65]

Forster escaped the wrath of the Philistines for a time by appealing to all the electors of Bradford in the 1874 election and gaining as a consequence almost all the Tory votes. In 1875, however, when Gladstone stepped down as leader of the Liberal party, the Millites and the Mialites of the party made it clear that despite Forster's prestige they would not support him as their next head. Some indication of how much Arnold was taken into the Forsters' councils is given by an item that

appears in Chichester Fortescue's diary. In late January, Arnold
met this old Oxford friend and told him that "neither he nor
his sister at all wanted Forster to be leader." [66] On February 1,
Forster informed Granville that he would decline to be considered for leader even if the majority chose him.

Arnold's campaign against the Philistines was no simple and
generalized struggle against ignorance and narrowness. It was
nothing less than a fight in behalf of a way of life to which
he had been raised. He defended the Establishment as the
guardian and preserver of England's cultural heritage, and he
advocated a commitment to ideas as necessary to England's
greatness in a world of increasing complexity. He knew at first
hand the opponents of an Established Church and a state-
controlled system of education; he witnessed the political
struggles of William Forster—himself a reformed Dissenter—
against them and learned how intransigent and vindictive they
could be. It was a curious campaign, for he early lost patience
with those whom he wished to win over. With little belief in
the traditional doctrines of his own church, he could not sufficiently understand and sympathize with the beliefs of others.
Failure of sympathy underlies his whole treatment of the
Dissenters. We cannot avoid the impression that though he
met and observed them, he did not know them and could not
love them. He never speaks to them without condescension.
We mark the slightly uplifted eyebrow, the not-quite-suppressed
smile. And we note that he is never more maddeningly superior
than when he protests that he is a simple, straightforward
person.

And yet we cannot say, for such are the paradoxes of human
nature, that Arnold was an ineffective advocate of his own
cause. Teaching as he did, he failed to make his readers benevolent and docile as Cicero recommends, but he did make them

well attentive. Alfred Austin in the nineties made an observation that is no less true today than it was then: the middle
classes have been Arnold's best readers. Indeed—supreme irony
of all—it is difficult to conclude that had he been more sympathetic he would have been as effective as he was.

Chapter VI

GLADSTONE, IRELAND, AND A TIME OF CRISIS

It has been possible to discuss Arnold's relation to the three classes up to the 1880's as many-sided but yet roughly consistent and coherent. About the turn of the decade, however, forces were set in motion that altered that relationship and threatened Arnold's hope that England could make a peaceful, gradual transition to the age of popular rule. The major crisis of the decade did not come for six years, but by that time it seemed to Arnold that demagoguery, anarchy, and rebellion had been loosed upon the land. He called for coercion, censorship of the press, and Conservative rule as the only means of saving England from becoming part of "the immense procession of ages, . . . countless communities [which] have arisen and sunk unknown." [1]

Stated baldly in this way, Arnold's later political views seem to have taken on a reactionary cast. Certainly reasons for his becoming reactionary are not hard to find. He had always been critical of liberalism, and his phrase "Liberal of the future" has a suspicious air. De Tocqueville's dictatorship of the majority, the Chartist pikes of '39, the London mobs of '48, the reform riots of '66 had added up to a lifetime of fears and alarms. Now he preferred order above all. Years of association with "the Dissidence of Dissent," the lovers of liberty for its own sake, the upholders of "doing as one likes" had given him a taste for unity and centralized control. And so with the wonted conservatism of age he longed for a benevolent and cultured and powerful oligarchical society. But to see that Arnold's development does not fit any ready-made formula we need consider only his support of the Conservatives in 1886. The move looks reactionary, perhaps a phase of the union of the bourgeoisie and the aristocracy that Marx said the rise of the proletariat would occasion. We are not surprised that the Whigs under Hartington also left the Liberal party in 1886. But the same issue that made the Whigs bolt their party also sent the extreme left wing of the Liberals, the Radicals under Chamberlain and Bright, into the Conservative camp. That issue was Irish home rule, but about it clustered a group of cognate problems: the rise of democracy, the security of property, and the extension of state power and responsibility, the last named embracing questions of education, religion, and local government. Arnold's reaction to such an issue could hardly be simple. The Irish situation did heighten and sharpen all of his views on class as he adapted them to the handling of a specific situation. But these views did not lose their many-sidedness, and a label will not adequately describe them.

It has become a cliché to say that every age is an age of flux and then to say that the age under consideration witnessed especially important changes. The claims of the eighties to be considered especially important have already been well advanced. We can say by way of inadequate summary that it was a necessary stage for England in the development of a planned economy. The classes accommodated themselves as best they could. Six hundred noblemen still held one-fifth of the land, but they had felt the pinch of the agricultural depression especially since Disraeli, though now a landlord himself, had not come to their aid. Governments, however, were still largely aristocratic in make-up: Gladstone's cabinet of 1886 was the first administration to have fewer than seven peers or sons of peers. For the middle classes the golden age of English industrialism had come to an end as other nations tried the English industrial formula for getting rich. Germany, for example, had entrenched itself behind high protective tariff walls and had put war reparations and the money of British investors to the creation of competitive industry. To protect themselves the British middle classes formed voluntary combinations of employers and joint-stock companies, which actually violated their own sacred principles of economic individualism. But the implication of what they were doing escaped them and they continued to pay theoretical reverence to laissez-faire. Had not laissez-faire brought them out of the feudal deserts and freed them from bondage to landed wealth? Since the working classes had trailed along on this passage to prosperity, they entered the eighties in no intractable mood. The fall of prices had increased their real wages, with the result, wrote Engels to Kautsky, that they shared "the feast of England's monopoly of the world market and the colonies." [2] So, too, the father of Beatrice Webb described labor as "docile," and Matthew Arnold wrote in 1880 that the period of expansion was still to come.[3] Yet in Birmingham, Joseph Chamberlain had taught his Radicals what a well-disciplined caucus could achieve, and on the Scottish border a party leader had made an unprecedented appeal to the people as the support and authorization for his political program. Labor became gradually more conscious of its identity and power, especially after 1884 when the agricultural workers swelled the electorate by 67 percent. By the end of the decade trade unionism had experienced one of its greatest upsurges in the century.

Gladstone formed his second government in the spring of 1880, his mind preoccupied with Bulgaria, Afghanistan, the Zulus and Boers. But Ireland was a cancer from which that government was to die. After the sickness appeared in mid-1880, Ireland virtually monopolized the time of the cabinet.[4] The critical nature of the situation not only forced the solution of class problems in Ireland analogous to those in England but also laid bare the weakness of an omnium-gatherum Liberal party no longer able to satisfy its extreme elements. Writing to one another just before the eighties began, Edward Lytton and James Fitzjames Stephen agreed that the party seemed to be splitting off in two directions, conservatism and radicalism. Lytton in India rejoiced to be away from "an England full of Morleys, Chamberlains et id genus omne," and for Stephen, liberalism had come to mean "the small dissenter way of looking at all national and international affairs." [5]

But as the decade began, Arnold, who had said things about the Dissenters himself, was never more staunchly liberal. His essay "The Future of Liberalism," written just as Gladstone's second government was taking office, made it clear that whatever future storm threatened, the nation would have to depend on the Liberals to see it through. In his earlier years there had been no question that Arnold preferred the Liberal party, but his exasperation with the Liberals' lack of clear, well-ordered principles had gradually mounted, and in 1874 he had not been unhappy at the Conservative victory.[6] But now, in the essay he described as "the last of my publications about politics and social matters," he affirmed that the country had been right to return the Liberals to office.[7] For the Liberals, rather than the Conservatives, ministered to man's instinct for expansion precisely because Liberals recognized the primacy of liberty over order. "Order is a most excellent thing," Arnold noted, "and true liberty is impossible without it; but order is not in itself liberty, and an appeal to the love of order is not a direct appeal to the love of liberty, to the instinct for expansion." [8]

Arnold's proliberalism at this time even extended itself to the matter of "mechanical legislation." In "The Future of Liberalism" he recognized that the Burials Bill and the Deceased Wife's Sister Bill would have to be passed. To make this concession to such familiar objects of Arnoldian irony and Dissenters' zeal must have cost Arnold an effort. But it was also a concession to good sense. Arnold had learned, we feel, that government time spent squabbling over minor issues was time lost for major issues. He admonished the Liberal party to see the industrial slums of Bolton, Wigan, and St. Helen's for what they were and to do something about them. Cobbett, fifty years earlier, had called them "Hell-holes," and from them a miasma still arose that poisoned the air of England. Arnold had returned once more to the theme of the essay "Equality" and the maxim of St. Paul: "Choose equality and flee greed."

In Ireland inequality threatened even "more pressing and evident troubles than in England." [9] But though the condition of Ireland was a timely subject, it was not a subject that Arnold treated extensively in "The Future of Liberalism." As he was writing, new legislation for Ireland was being discussed by the House, so that the situation there might change before his article appeared. What was more, the new legislation was being sponsored by his brother-in-law, William E. Forster, whom Gladstone had made chief secretary for Ireland two months earlier. The appointment was a popular one, for the newspapers gave prominent mention to Forster's work in Ireland as an

agent for Quaker relief during the famine of 1846. Charles
Gavan Duffy, writing his book on the Young Ireland movement
in 1880, made a point of quoting from the reports Forster had
sent back to England. And to the Irish the knowledge that
Forster stood high in Liberal party circles and could have demanded a secretaryship of state made his acceptance of the
post seem more significant than in fact it was.[10]

For they concluded, naturally enough, that Gladstone
planned to deal with problems nearer home than those that
had occupied the exotic Disraeli. Certainly the distresses of
Mayo, Kerry, Sligo, and Cork could claim to be ranked in importance with those of Dulcigno, Thessaly, and Macedonia. Bad
harvests in 1878 and 1879 had compounded for Ireland the
effects of the agricultural depression of the seventies. By early
1880 an estimated 100,000 tenant farmers were in arrears with
their rent, and Ireland for once was prepared to make its grievances known. Isaac Butt, its leader in the House, and a believer
in orderly methods, had died in 1879. When Parnell thereupon
became president of the newly formed Land League and also
leader of a majority of the Irish members, Irish agrarian discontent and incipient nationalism joined hands under a vigorous
leader. A month before the new Parliament convened, the Land
League met and formulated a scheme for the temporary suspension of rent payments and a long-term plan of land purchase.
But the Liberal government was far from ready to accept such
a plan. Its heavily Whig cabinet was largely indifferent to the
seriousness of the Irish situation, and in any case frowned on
measures that threatened the security of property. Gladstone
had only a vague notion that his Land Act of 1870 would have
to be reworked. Soon Forster found himself sending reports
from Ireland of increased agrarian crime, and thought it neces-

sary to object strongly when a carry-over bill conferring special powers on the chief secretary was allowed to lapse. Gladstone, his mind on other matters, pleaded the press of business in the House.[11] Forster however was determined that something must be done to prevent further evictions of impoverished tenants, and on June 15 he was able to announce in the House that the government would propose "to enlarge the discretionary powers of the County Court Judge, so that he might . . . give compensation to tenants . . . ejected for non-payment of rent." [12]

At this juncture, then, it would be indiscreet for Arnold to speak his mind on Ireland, but the subject had interested him for years, and he had written about it with increasing discernment since 1874. He had visited Ireland only once, and then as a boy, when his entire family went to Dublin, where Whately was archbishop. The invitation had been extended even though Dr. Arnold had told Whately that Ireland, as "a distinct nation, entitled to govern itself," had every right to establish Roman Catholicism.[13] The question whether its national distinctiveness entitled Ireland to separation from the United Kingdom seems not to have occurred to Dr. Arnold. What he saw primarily was the anomaly of the Irish Church Establishment and not the anomaly of a government conducted from Dublin Castle, where the royal standard was hoisted to celebrate the anniversary of such great Orange triumphs as the battles of the Boyne and Aughrim. But he saw, as had Burke before him, that there could be no reform in Ireland as long as the English maintained a conspiracy of indifference toward it. Matthew Arnold copied Burke's observation into his notebook: "I have never known any of the successive governments in my time influenced by any passion relative to Ireland, than the wish that they should hear of it and its concerns as little as possible." Thus English rule in Ireland, concluded Matthew Arnold in 1848, consisted in "cleverly managing the details of an imposture." [14]

He was referring specifically to the rule of Lord Clarendon, who had gone to Ireland the previous winter as lord lieutenant and there had invited lay and clerical Irish leaders to the Vice-regal Lodge to discuss his liberal plans. But Ireland was in no mood for discussions. Lord Lansdowne told Arnold that one million persons would die before the famine was over.[15] Distressed by the plight of its neighbor, England offered a subscription of £200,000 from its annual income of £300 million, and its government passed a law that enabled landlords with heavily mortgaged estates to sell them to other landlords. Ungrateful Ireland nevertheless continued rioting as it entered its third winter of hunger. Clarendon asked for and received special coercive powers. He felt, a note in Greville's diary explains, that the Catholics were too disaffected toward England to make English government of Ireland possible without the aid of the Orangemen.

Arnold wrote to Clough that praise of Clarendon made him sick.

I cannot believe that the mass of people here would see much bloodshed in Ireland without asking themselves what they were shedding it to uphold. And when the answer came—1. a chimerical Theory about some possible dangerous foreign alliances with independent Ireland: 2. a body of Saxon landlords—3. a Saxon Ch.[urch] Estab[lishmen]t their consciences must smite them. I think I told you that the performance of Polyeucte suggested to me the right of large bodies of men to have what article they liked produced for them. The Irish article is not to my taste: still we have no really superiour article to offer them, which alone can justify the violence offered by a Lycurgus or a Cromwell to a foolish nation, as unto Children.[16]

Aside from the question of home rule, this statement of 1848 fairly well defines the area of Arnold's future interests in Ireland. To the statement we must add only problems of Irish education and a curiously refined view of who is responsible for England's having no "really superiour article to offer." These changes reflect the special knowledge of education and of the middle class that Arnold had acquired by the late sixties, when it became no longer possible for the English to maintain the indifference toward Ireland that Burke and Dr. Arnold had noted. Matthew Arnold by that time had written two books on education in which he blamed the inferiority of middle- and lower-class education on the middle class. So he had decided that it was almost entirely from the middle class, with its narrowness and hardness, that the Irish got their ideas of English civilization. The English aristocracy could have improved these notions, since they had a power of manners that would be an attractive article to the Irish, but, alas, "members who are connected with Ireland are generally absentees." [17]

But if Arnold was relatively soft toward the aristocracy, he saw that the middle class would control the way practical Irish problems were handled. Before he addressed himself to any particular Irish matter he tried, in his typical fashion, to work below the level of surface dispute.

Arnold's first extended public statement on Ireland, then, the lectures published under the title *On the Study of Celtic Literature*, aimed to be "functional criticism" that would establish "scientifically" a basis for Anglo-Irish sympathy. The peroration urged Oxford listeners to work to reduce the power of Philistinism; the introduction to the published form, meant for Philistines and non-Philistines alike, makes the same plea without using the pejorative epithet.[18] Arnold wanted to make converts. Today the racist claptrap that provides the rationale of the book shows us that Arnold was as ready as his fictional Celts *"to react against the despotism of fact."* Even though the book strikes us now as an embarrassing failure, it did in its own time some modest good, and at the least, the scientism of the book convinced Arnold that Irish-Anglo union was ethnological fact and not simply colonial opportunism.[19] And since the Celts still felt, as Arnold once had, that the English connection was the clever management of the details of an imposture, preservation of the Union meant that English legislation would have to be generous and large-minded.

Gladstone's first government, in office from 1868 to 1874, tried its hand at three important Irish matters—disestablishment, land, and education—but in none of the three did it win Arnold's approval. In two instances Arnold blamed the hard unintelligence of the Dissenting middle class, unsoftened by his Celtic charms. Disestablishment, first of all, clashed with what he had often advocated for education, a system of concurrent endowment. The property of the Irish Church, according to this plan, would be apportioned between the lasting and representative communions. But though nearly everyone supported reform of an Established Church that served at most one-eighth of the Irish population, concurrent endowment was never seriously proposed even when the Lords despairingly tried to use it to block Gladstone's disestablishment bill.[20] Arnold nevertheless interpreted the failure of concurrent endowment and the success of Gladstone's measure as the handiwork almost solely of middle-class Dissenters.[21] Further, he maintained that since disestablishment of the Irish Church reflected nothing so much as Nonconformist antipathy to establishments, Ireland could not be expected to be grateful for a policy that sought to serve English prejudice rather than right Irish wrong.

To be sure, Catholic Ireland would much have preferred to

have a share in the property thus released. But it was not un-grateful for the small favor and counted it the first step toward the abandonment of the Ascendancy. Nor could this breach in the Union be charged simply to Dissenters' zeal or Gladstone's ambition. It was well known that Gladstone had resigned from Peel's government in opposition to the Maynooth grant, and that in 1865, his mind now changed, he had been unseated at Oxford for speaking in favor of Irish disestablishment. But it was not known that he was moving toward that conviction as early as 1847, before Irish disestablishment became a political issue. In that year he told Arnold's friend Goldwin Smith that he could face disestablishment of any kind without alarm. The extent to which Gladstone's act of 1869 was a Dissenters' measure may be judged by the vote in its favor, a vote larger than the liberal majority in the House. Dissenters had backed the bill, but so had the Whigs, the Irish, and some independ-ents. Morley called the measure Gladstone's legislative master-piece, and Mill defended it in the *Fortnightly*. But support from this quarter could be expected. Manning's letter of con-gratulations after the passage of the bill might also be expected. But what did Arnold think of Wilberforce's refusal to vote against the bill, or worse, the enthusiasm of his Rugby and Balliol friend, then Dr. and later Bishop Frederick Temple, or the concurrence of the archbishop of Canterbury, the same Tait who had succeeded his father as headmaster of Rugby? We know only that Arnold blamed the Dissenters.

Though Arnold placed the onus for Irish disestablishment too heavily on the Dissenters, he could hardly have exagger-ated their share in the failure of the liberals to establish an Irish university acceptable to the Catholics. The conduct of unregenerate political Dissent throughout the thorny business convinced Arnold that Dissent would never choose the path of wisdom in Irish affairs. He therefore insisted time and again that its strong resistance to reason would have to be countered by a stronger resolve that reason must prevail.[22] With Dissent so narrow and firm, political leaders had a responsibility not to flatter its prejudices. Gladstone was therefore playing a dangerous game, Arnold felt, when he formulated his Irish University Bill of 1873 with his eye too closely on Nonconformist approval. Gladstone proposed to establish a Catholic university on the impossible condition that theology, history, and philosophy would not be taught there. To Arnold such a bill was "simply ridiculous." [23] Cardinal Cullen refused to accept the measure for Ireland and attacked it vigorously in a pastoral letter. The bill failed by three to get its majority, sixty-five Irish members voting against it.

It is not necessary for us to trace further the devious history of the Catholic university issue except to note that Arnold watched it closely and wrote on the subject four times in the seventies, twice at length.[24] On this matter he showed the "many-sided and penetrating vision" into Irish affairs for which Morley praised him.[25] The plan he suggested for the establishment of a Catholic yet public institution, its Catholic faculty appointed by a nonclerical official, was substantially the same as that offered by the Edwardian Liberals in 1908 and accepted by the Irish bishops. Frederick Harrison to the contrary, the man of culture in politics was not the poorest mortal alive.

But if Arnold concluded from the liberal handling of Irish disestablishment and university education that "we owe to Puritanism . . . this impracticable condition of Ireland," land legislation demonstrated that another class also, the aristocracy, would not abandon its inveterate prejudices for the sake of Ireland.[26] Forster's Compensation for Disturbances Bill passed the Commons, but not before Lord Lansdowne, the grandson of Arnold's old Whig chief, had resigned from the government and attacked the bill as unlawful revision of private contracts.[27] Thereupon the Lords, with the Whig peers true to class rather than to party, threw out the bill by a vote of 282 against 51. William Forster was left empty-handed to face a suffering and rebellious island.

Here at work were the pedantry and passion of the aristocracy, as nervous about its land as the middle class was nervous about its religion. Would these English prejudices, allied against Ireland, make the two peoples hopelessly incompatible? Arnold tried the question in a two-part essay that appeared just before and after the terms of Gladstone's 1881 Land Bill were made public. Since, as Arnold said, "The land question is the question of the moment," and land nervousness was a prejudice he must overcome, Arnold dealt with the matter of the security of property in such a way as to drive a wedge between English landlords and bad Irish landlords. "Property is sacred," he wrote, "when it has prescription in its favor; but the very point is, that in Ireland prescription has never properly arisen." Irish property had never won the prescription of the people because of its history of harshness, evictions, and rack-renting. If Irish wrong was to be redressed, bad landlords, the authors of those wrongs, must be expropriated and justice done to the people. A plan could be worked out whereby the worst landlords would be expropriated at ten years' purchase, the less bad on a less punitive scale. Only then would the Irish nation feel that its moral grievance as well as its material grievance had been removed. English landlords, he cautioned, must not be alarmed by these proposals, and although they must recognize that property has always been subservient to the interests of the state, in this case "it is proposed to expropriate only the worst, so as to found for the good ones security and prescription." [28]

Whatever Arnold's proaristocratic proclivities were—and they were considerable—he did not hesitate when the public weal was at stake to offer a plan that struck at the root of aristocratic power and prestige. The hour had come in Ireland, as it yet had not come in England, when property must serve the larger good of pacifying Ireland and winning Irish loyalties. He saw the strength of the Land Act of 1881, which an Irish historian concedes "took away the land question" from Ireland. But Arnold saw also that the Land Act by itself would not heal the long-festering wound. It could be made to work only if another matter were also accomplished—if the middle class were to transform itself, to learn to treat Catholicism with fairness, to become something other than Salem House graduates. Whatever radical measures were used to dislodge Lords Clanricarde and Lonsdale from the land they had despoiled, equally strong measures must be taken to convert the Murdstones and the Quinions from their vulgarity. Failing these, the only alternative left was a measure just as revolutionary, coercion.[29]

The refusal of the Lords in July, 1880, to offer Ireland even the temporary consolation of the Disturbances Bill brought a new wave of violence in Ireland. Forster excoriated the Lords in a blistering speech in the House, but nothing could be done immediately. Gladstone, worn out by his duties both as premier and chancellor of the Exchequer, fell ill, and Chamberlain's plan that the bill be passed in the House came to nothing. In November, Forster came back from Ireland, threatening to resign if Parliament was not at once convened and coercion and suspension of habeas corpus asked for. But when he was supported only by Spencer and Hartington, and opposed by Bright, Chamberlain, and Gladstone, the Irish secretary backed down on his demands and conceded that to break up the government would do more harm than to postpone coercion until January.[30]

If the chief secretary for Ireland was eager to control anarchy in Ireland, his brother-in-law in England showed a similar eagerness. The difference was that Arnold saw Irish disorder as part of a larger movement, part of an "immense revolution," as he called it in a letter to Jane in Ireland. England in the future would have to deal with it at home. Forster was having difficulty in getting proper coercive powers because "the proletariate," "the Radical masses of the large towns in the north," opposed any "dispositions of interference" that could later be turned on their own anarchical excesses. In the sixties Arnold had pointed out that it was the middle class that wished to protect its penchant for doing what it liked. Now in 1880 he saw that the populace wished to protect its penchant for "tumultuously" doing what it liked. And like the middle class before it, the populace now had "the complicity of the Government." [31]

Matthew Arnold's wife, Fanny Lucy, visited the Forsters in Dublin in December, 1880, and stayed with them until the opening of the parliamentary session in January. She was therefore present when Forster received the report that the outrages in the final quarter of 1880 had reached the fearful total of 717. Late that same December the queen wrote to Disraeli that Forster seemed quite overwhelmed by his office and that even the prime minister was more impressed with the danger in Ireland than she had ever seen him. Gladstone's secretary recorded that Forster had been in London during the month and had behaved at the Athenaeum "more like an inebriated or demented man than one merely who has lost his nerve." [32] Small wonder that Arnold, writing on December 17 (the year, though unspecified, was likely 1880), declined to declare himself

opposed to a crimes bill because of the importance of "the maintenance of law and order in Ireland." [33]

When the House reconvened in January, Forster introduced
a coercion bill that empowered the viceroy to lock up whom
he chose, or more precisely, anyone under "reasonable suspicion" of disturbing public order. Irish disruptive tactics
prevented the bill from coming to a vote until the speaker,
H. B. W. Brand, took the unprecedented step of moving the
question himself.[34] Forster had been persuaded that the jailing
of a few "village ruffians" would quell the disorder. Now empowered to do so, he jailed them, and discovered that the
incidence of outrages remained high. Once entered, the road
of coercion seemed to have no turning, even after the Land
Bill was passed and payment of rents was resumed. "The
odious work of repression," writes a close student of the period,
"wore down Forster's energy and warped his judgement—not
the only judgement to go awry in the summer and autumn
of 1881."

Matthew Arnold went to Ireland at least twice during that
summer and autumn, in July and September, the latter visit
lasting probably the better part of a month.[35] No surviving
letters record what he witnessed there, but Viscount Gladstone, who followed Arnold as a visitor in October, 1881,
described Dublin as "a city in Revolutionary Russia," bought
a revolver, and practiced shooting. Forster's life was continually in danger. On one occasion his would-be assassins looked
into his carriage while Jane and their adopted daughter waited
for him at Holyhead Station, on another a signal was not
given, on another the presence of his niece prevented Forster's
being slain in Phoenix Park. On May 2, 1882, for reasons
that are important only to a later part of this discussion,
Forster resigned. Four days afterward, his successor, Lord

Frederick Cavendish, and the permanent undersecretary, Mr.
T. H. Burke, a man Arnold undoubtedly knew, were slain
in Phoenix Park by a group of terrorists known as the Invin-
cibles.

If we glance briefly back we shall see more clearly the point
at which Arnold had now arrived. In his view the long history
of English misrule in Ireland had been prolonged into the
nineteenth century by the religious prejudices of middle-class
Dissent and by the land exploitation practices of the aristocracy. For continuing this "imposture" the middle class got
more than its share of the blame from Arnold, but his proposals for land reform hit at the basis of aristocratic society.
Both classes, he warned, must transform themselves because
of the coming "immense revolution." But when that revolution came it would have to be, in Wellington's phrase, "a
revolution by due course of law," the revolution by slow steps
that Burke believed possible, or else face severe repression.[36]
The radical masses at home must not be allowed to interfere
with the control of any disorder. With the memories of '66
still fresh in his mind, Arnold entered the eighties a disciple
of the revolution but an enemy of its tyranny, a position he
makes clear in a letter to Fontanès written in January, 1880.

*The old order of things had not the virtue which Burke sup-
posed. The Revolution had not the banefulness which he supposed. But neither was the Revolution the commencement, as
its friends supposed, of a reign of justice and virtue. It was much
rather, as Scherer has called it, "un déchaînement d'instincts
confus, un aveugle et immense besoin de renouvellement." An
epoch of concentration and of resistance to the crude and violent
people who were for imposing their "renouvellement" on the
rest of the world by force was natural and necessary. Burke is to*

*be conceived as the great voice of this epoch. He carried his
country with him, and was in some sort a providential person.
But he did harm as well as good, for he made concentration too
dominant an idea with us, and an idea of which the reign was
unduly prolonged. The time for expansion must come, and
Burke is of little help to us in presence of such a time. But in his
sense of the crudity and tyranny of the French revolutionists, I
do not think he was mistaken.*[37]

Thus whatever weight attaches to the revolution, once
violence enters the balance, the scale dips against it. Violence,
however, does not enter during "the time for expansion," for
which we may read, "the time when revolution by law takes
place." But, we ask, is such a time always possible? And is it
possible not only for England but also for Ireland? Even for
England one is hard pressed for examples. The political rise
of the English middle class succeeded without a red fool-fury
of the Thames, but if not force, certainly the threat of force
was accessory to the passage of both Reform bills. In Ireland, a fortiori, only agitations that convulsed society made
possible the passage of the Land Act in 1881. Gladstone admitted as much. And Parnell knew the value of the outrages,
making only the most modest claims for his parliamentary
machinations in promoting the Irish cause. In short, Arnold's
belief in revolution without revolt involves him, at least for
Ireland, in a notion that becomes an anomaly in "the world
of practice."

Much of the time, however, Arnold seeks to avoid the anomaly by drawing a distinction between Irish acts of violence or
incitements to violence and peaceful demonstrations. Thus
although in 1881 he urges the need for Ireland of "a coercion
far more stringent and effectual than that which we apply

now," in early 1882, in the preface to the Irish Essays, he can praise the arrival of the revolution "by due course of law" with appropriate quotations from the Bible and the French moralists.[38] As a feature of this revolution he adduces the single example of a group of Irish tenants agreeing together to ban hunting on their land and to give up the revenues it brought them. But under the circumstances few such courses were open, and against an occupying enemy the deeds performed by Captain Moonlight were more effective than the action taken against Captain Boycott. To his credit, for all his continual support of strong coercion, Arnold kept steadily repeating that coercion must be used not only against Irish disorder but also against crime and outrage everywhere, and that the repression of disorder must always be followed by the redressing of grievances.[39] Eventually he realized that his quotations from the Bible and the French moralists could never apply to Ireland. He decided that procedure by law was correct for England, but for Ireland he urged that bold use of administrative powers was all that was needed.[40] His language became more impassioned with time as his exasperation grew against Morley, Huxley, the *Pall Mall Gazette* editors, and the other "English pedants" who "continue[d] to believe in the divine and saving effect, under all circumstances, of right of meeting, right of speaking, right of printing." [41] In urging coercion he more than matched Forster who, Gladstone said, "leaned rather more readily than the average Liberal to the employment of force." [42] Arnold urged the Irish secretary to take steps against William O'Brien's weekly paper, *United Ireland,* two months before Forster himself saw fit to suppress it.[43] In 1887 he recommended the most severe form of coercion, the suspension of the ordinary processes of law, and the closing of the courts.[44] Then he wished also to repeat the

jailing of Parnell and Dillon and to silence the seditious Land
Leaguers, O'Brien and T. M. Healy. Of the Irish secretaries
who followed "Buckshot" Forster, the man Arnold most approved of was Arthur Balfour, who mixed for Ireland coercion
and kindness, its own form of memory and desire. The Irish
called him "Bloody" Balfour.

The volume and quality of the political writing Arnold
produced in his last two years, 1886–88, testify to his sense
of urgency. He retired from the Education Office in the spring
of 1886 and wrote to a former chief, "Literature is henceforth
my business." [45] But keeping old promises for contributions,
mostly of a nonliterary sort, was enough to occupy these new
hours of freedom. Still, there was time for other writing. Yet
instead of literary work, political writing claimed precedence.
The three literary essays he wrote in this period must be
measured against seven articles and two public letters on contemporary politics. He seemed not to care that the *ad hoc*
nature of the essays and the speed with which he wrote them
made this segment of his work the poorest. The air of thin
patience that hovers about as he tirelessly pounds home the
same arguments time and again almost justifies Chesterton's
famous dictum on his style.

He was convinced that a time of crisis had come to England.
"I suppose things looked even worse for us at the end of the
last century," he wrote in April, 1886, "but to my eye they
look extremely bad now." At the end of that year he began
an essay with the remark that "at the present moment of
crisis, I find myself drawn back to politics." A few months
later it was again "the present critical juncture" which brought
him to political writing so that he might *be of use.*" The
time to wait for education and culture to do their slow work

had passed. In effect, Arnold was doing what he had decried
in others: he had a pressing idea and felt he must "be running
out with it into the street and trying to make it rule there."
Now he must be immediately effective, even if the effort for
a man in his mid-sixties, suffering the pains of angina, meant
the end of his creative life. "As you draw near to your latter
end," he quoted from Ptolemy, "redouble your efforts to do
good." [46]

Three reasons led Arnold to this conviction that a state of
emergency existed for England. One of these is private and may
be deferred for later consideration. James Fitzjames Stephen
came close to expressing the other two in a contemporary letter
to the *Times:* "The greatest peril lay in Ireland, for Liberal
policy there contained two great dangers: that of disrupting
the unity of the empire and of promoting social revolution at
home." [47]

Stephen is referring specifically to the Irish policy of Gladstone's third cabinet, which took office in February, 1886.
What that policy was to be had been conveyed to the English
public some three months earlier, on December 17, by the
famous but unfortunate device of the "Hawarden Kite." Arnold was in Cologne on a school-inspection tour when he
learned that Gladstone favored a measure of home rule for
Ireland. "What a move is this of Gladstone's in the Irish
matter! and what apprehensions it gives me!" he wrote to
his sister Fan.[48] To another correspondent he said that he
would believe Gladstone's home rule plans only when he saw
them. In Germany he had heard Bismarck speaking three
times in the Reichsrath. He contrasted the awkward gestures
and poor delivery of this eminently successful leader with the
flowing gestures and magnificent voice of a Gladstone who

was often victorious and never successful. He would write an article, he told Fan, pointing out that the Liberals' lack of success had been put to the proof too often.

Gladstone's plan was to set up a separate Parliament with its own executive in Dublin, and to give it control of all Irish affairs except as they related to the Empire. No Irish representation would sit at Westminster. To Arnold such a plan was the halfway house to complete independence for Ireland, tantamount to creating a hostile state just across the Irish Channel. While the bill was under discussion in the House, he wrote "The Nadir of Liberalism" for Knowles. When the bill had been defeated and Gladstone appealed to the country, Arnold wrote a hurried letter to the *Times* urging that the vote be taken on the clear issue of a separate Parliament for Ireland. Given the temper of the Irish people, he contended, a separate Irish Parliament would soon be acting like a Parliament for an independent nation. Irish independence was a delusive chimera: Ireland was not in fact an independent nation and could not declare itself one without endangering England, its own future, and the Ulster minority.

Writing in favor of the Italian nationalist movement in 1859, Arnold had enunciated a "great nationality" principle by which a people, like the Italians, could claim independence because of their history and cultural achievements. He specifically noted that this principle did not apply to Poland, Hungary, or Ireland, the more so since they were conterminous with a great nationality that overshadowed their own. Not only was Irish separation therefore "unjust" in Arnold's view but it was a "crying danger," because bitterness would follow in its wake. "To be a thorn in Great Britain's side, to make alliance with its rivals, to turn against it in a crisis of danger, would be more tempting to the Irish by far . . . than a similar conduct towards the Northern

States would have been to the South." Most of all, he insisted, making Ireland separate would begin to unravel the fibers of England's greatness. As for Ireland, he had long thought the Celts woefully inept in practical matters of government, and their pretensions to self-rule more saddening than alarming. Now he remarked only that separation would mean for the country as a whole "increased contention and misery in the near future." [49] And for that part of Ireland that was "a centre of natural Englishism and loyalty," Ulster, separation would mean abandonment to a majority "full of hatred and contempt." No more could such a constellation of evils be justified by English mistreatment of Ireland than the temporary failure to supply schools to Scotland had been grounds for making her independent. Late though the hour might be, it would be irremediable folly to give way out of disunion, weariness, and despair.[50]

Readers of the later Arnold will think it incredible that he was ever seriously charged with lack of patriotism. For the note of patriotism, firm, clear, and even strident, sounds in this work. The strength that the Union afforded, to England first and to Ireland secondarily, was for Arnold its best defense. He did not minimize the extent of Irish wrong; he frequently said that Irish leaders had ample grievance for their demands. But he saw Irish demands, however justified by the greed of landlords, as a threat to the greatness of England. Of course an Englishman need not say or even think that the Union benefited the whole of Ireland. Disraeli, for example, had written that a portion of the population of Ireland "is endeavouring to sever the constitutional tie which unites it to Great Britain in that bond which has favoured the power and prosperity of both." [51] He doubtless never thought that it was not the prosperous portion of Ireland that wished to sever the English connection. W. E. H. Lecky managed the same trick beautifully in his

multivolumed *History of Ireland in the Eighteenth Century.*
That work deals only with the Anglo-Irish of the Supremacy
and gives no indication that there was a portion of the Irish
people that might support a land war and a home rule movement.

To an extent Arnold's views were penetrating and realistic.
In the matter of the Irish Protestant minority he anticipated
the famous remark of Lord Randolph, "Ulster will fight, Ulster
will be right," and recommended that Ireland have either two
or three provincial assemblies to handle local affairs.[52] For
Arnold did, in fact, support a kind of home rule, but a kind,
as he went to some pains to explain, that depended on the
retention of Irish members at Westminster. That England
should do its utmost to hold Ireland, that in fact no European
nation should set free an adjacent and vulnerable territorial
unit, was a belief that leading statesmen and political thinkers
held even before the ominous rise of Bismarck's Prussia. De
Tocqueville, no friend of centralization, had warned, "A people
which in the presence of the great military monarchies of
Europe, would proceed to break up its sovereignty would seem
to me to forswear, by this single fact, its power and perhaps its
existence and its name." In *Representative Government* (1861)
Mill had echoed Arnold's opinion that a small national group
might best be absorbed into a larger one of higher culture.[53]
And in a pamphlet written shortly after the rise of Fenianism
he had described the history of Irish wrongs in a manner that
would do credit to a Fenian, but he had argued against either
a qualified or absolute separation, urging instead the adoption
of radical land and educational measures. What worried Arnold
was that Gladstone did not understand the importance of
Ireland to England.[54] The Union gave security to the Kingdom's chances of retaining its present European position; it

gave grounds for hope of continued future greatness. Lincoln
had given his life to secure the union of the states; Bismarck
had brought France to her knees and tumbled Louis Napoleon
into oblivion with his federation of German states. Both afforded to Arnold ample proof that a gain in effectiveness was
possible to the nation that secured to itself all its components.

Mill, however, stated one condition under which English
rule of Ireland should not continue, the stipulation coming
deep from his liberal convictions: failure to rule Ireland in a
manner acceptable to the Irish.[55] A similar principle converted
Gladstone to home rule, more specifically the dawning realization that England could not govern Ireland properly as long as
Ireland remained the pawn of party politics and class interest.
No one dreaded a great organic change more than Gladstone,
but he saw that the continuance of English rule over Ireland
mocked the history of liberal sympathy to the Poles, the Italians,
the Serbians and the Greeks. Arnold would do as much as Mill
and Gladstone to win Irish accedence in English government,
but he would not give Ireland her freedom. He had not forgotten Burke's admonition to grant concessions willingly lest
later they bear the taint of bitterness. But home rule was for
Arnold not a concession but a capitulation, a leap into the
dark of an uncertain future. To an age when free men give
glad assent to the principle of self-determination, Arnold speaks
with the voice of a discredited colonialism. He had written of
the belief that "one class is capable of properly speaking for
another" as "the last left of our illusions," but there was another
illusion that he did not see.[56]

A curious form of idealism may have obscured Arnold's
view of the Irish question, his belief that in the government
of Ireland, English good sense would triumph over prejudice.
References to this good sense and to "the body of quiet,

reasonable people" who exercised it abound in his Irish essays.
He had always carried some such phrase along with him like
a solemn, thoughtful dummy ready to nod assent to whatever
point he was making. With his essay "The Zenith of Conservatism," however, the rhetorical device seemed to take on
a vitality of its own. The notion of "our best selves," which
had buttressed his concept of the state, had leaped the gap
from noumenon to phenomenon and now stood ready in large
numbers to initiate the practical measures Arnold advocated
for the pacification of Ireland. He accommodated his language to their new size: they were "the same great force of
reasonable opinion in this country which is now favourable
to Ministers," "the great body of reasonable people in England," "the real mind of the country in this matter," "whoever is not infected with the Jacobinical temper and passions."
He appealed "not to the populace only, not to Jacobins, not
to socialists, not to newspaper declaimers, not to Radical
demagogues, not to these only, but to the great body of quiet
reasonable people throughout the country." [57] The critic, "working through literature," keeping apart from immediate practice,
might hope slowly to create such a force by appealing to it. But
the world of practical politics, addicted though it is to hyper-
bole, must reckon also with the hard facts of class interests.
Arnold, though dealing with practical politics, would not be so
limited. "I agree with Mr. Labouchere that aristocracies are not,
in general, the best of guides in politics. But I . . . [do not]
believe him capable of really thinking the political Dissenters
and the Radical working men to be . . . even so good. . . . It
is on the country as a whole, and on the mind of the country,
that we must rely." [58] In effect, Arnold has dismissed the three
classes and has trusted instead to a myth of his own creation,
in practical matters a dangerous mode of procedure. For Eng-

land's class society did have another chance during the next thirty years to show its "best self," thanks to Kitty O'Shea and the retributive power of the Victorian conscience. And the consequences again were bloody, emerging in the deadly forms of Sinn Fein, Black and Tans, and civil war.

What James Fitzjames Stephen had termed the second effect of Liberal policy in Ireland, the growth of social revolution in England, gained in momentum as the home rule movement faltered. With a disgruntled Chamberlain sitting among the Liberal Unionists and Lord Randolph Churchill and his Fourth party giving the Tories a measure of popular appeal, the new electorate of 1884 seemed for a time safe from the uses of demagoguery. But Gladstone's power with the people was legendary and of course a source of concern to the Conservatives. Bagehot in 1872 had used the subject of Gladstone's popularity to introduce a famous passage on the responsibility of ministers not to "raise questions which will excite the lower orders of mankind." [59] As long as the uneasy alliance among the Whigs, moderate liberals, and the radicals lasted, Gladstone would feel no temptation to debase the pure gold with which he had won the love of the people. But there had been gradual attrition in the upper ranks of the party. Gladstone complained to the queen that Whig noblemen had been drifting to the Tories ever since the repeal of the Corn Laws, and the tendency of middle-class wealth had been to move over with them to the Tory benches. In 1886 the defections consequent upon the first Home Rule Bill stripped the party of all but a few Whigs personally loyal to Gladstone and alienated both the landed gentry and the professions. Gladstone told an audience in Liverpool in June, 1886, "It cannot be pretended that we are supported by the dukes, or by the squires, or by the established clergy, or by any other body of very respectable persons." [60] Among the middle-class intellectuals an extraordinary group opposed home rule: Tyndall, Huxley, Froude, Jowett, Goldwin Smith, Browning, and Tennyson. Only among the middle-class Dissenters did Gladstone's support remain unimpaired. The sentiment expressed by Mr. Spurgeon, the famous Nonconformist preacher, did not wane: "You do not know how those of us regard you, who feel it a joy to live when a premier believes in righteousness." [61]

Clearly the next move for the Liberal party was to look for new sources of strength in the masses. But "People's William," as Carlyle had dubbed him was never a thoroughgoing radical. When he made the remark Arnold used to quote, "All the world loves a peer," Gladstone was speaking for himself too.[62] Younger Liberals like Chamberlain and Dilke were far in advance of him, Gladstone told Sir Henry Ponsonby, and they would be pushed still further by the extreme liberalism of the masses. It was a prospect he dreaded. Whether or not Gladstone wished it, therefore, the home rule campaigns were fought on a line that grew gradually more horizontal than vertical. Arnold's comments reflect the gradual shift. In March of 1886 he writes to Fan that Gladstone relies on "the mass of middle class Liberalism"; in May he includes among Gladstone's "passionate supporters" "the Radical workmen in the great towns"; by August, Arnold has hit upon his phrase to describe the new alliance, "Cleon and his democracy," and thereafter this phrase appears in every political essay.[63]

Arnold saw that England was now in the full tide of an epoch of expansion, a period rich in its possibilities for enlarging the life of man but prone to the loss of "salutary restraints." [64] Thus Arnold applauded Forster's work for the third Reform Bill, and at the same time kept a weather eye open for any signs of anarchy, especially after the home rule question

became prominent. "The Nadir of Liberalism" mentions briefly
the Trafalgar Square riots of the previous February and the subsequent trial and acquittal of the speakers. The affair had been
a sorry spectacle all around, but it had frightened respectable
London for weeks. What had begun as a peaceful demonstration of workers to protest against the wide unemployment attracted what Engels called "hawkers, loafers, police spies, pick-
pockets." The meeting ended with a procession through Pall
Mall that the roughs turned into an excuse for window break-
ing and shop looting. The leaders had failed to control the
demonstration properly, and the police had simply stayed away.
To Arnold the whole thing heightened "yet further the impression of our impotence and disarray." [65]

When in late 1886 and early 1887 events moved slowly in
Gladstone's favor, the support of the new electorate followed.
Arnold had nourished the vain hope that the Conservatives
might take decisive and remedial action to solve the land
question. Instead they rejected Parnell's request that evictions
be forbidden and brought on themselves the so-called "Plan
of Campaign," by which tenants refused to pay rents until
the landlord agreed to a reduction. Chamberlain's declaration
that Irish rents were too high and the concerted nature of the
Irish no-rent movement won the sympathy of the workers.
What was more, the impulsive resignation of Lord Randolph
Churchill lost for the Conservatives their outstanding popular
figure and occasioned a series of conciliatory talks between
Chamberlain and the Gladstonians that continued into the
following summer. Arnold, unhappy at this turn of events,
wrote that Chamberlain was stirring things up with his "sig-
nallings to the enemy." [66] Meanwhile the local organizations
of the Liberal caucus, which had supported Gladstone over
Chamberlain throughout 1886, now invited Irish members to

address English workers in the large towns. Then in June, Gladstone made a triumphal progress through Wales, speaking to huge crowds that had given up their day's wages to hear him. Arnold's references to "Cleon and his democracy" increased as Gladstone's power waxed, until they reached their climax in the last primarily Irish essay, "From Easter to August." During these months the middle class lost for Arnold its place as the primary enemy; the "feather-brained democracy" with its insatiable appetite for "claptrap and insincerities" had begun to move.

It is important to estimate correctly the nature of the anti-democratic position at which Arnold had arrived. His primary concern was the retention of Ireland for the Empire; from this concern proceeds his strong opposition to the force that could make Gladstone's policy succeed. When he vents his spleen on the democrats as inflamed, indulgent, unrealistic, he sees that their ingenuousness, and not mere wilfulness, has made them supporters of a mischievous scheme. He does not mistake English workingmen, even in the mass, for fierce Corcyreans. Force he had always abhorred, to the point of inveighing against the mass demonstrations that so easily spilled over into casual violence. In this regard his fears overcame his judgment. Still, he saw the violence of the masses as set off by demagoguery, the masses as primarily the ready dupes of invidious leaders. Consequently he almost invariably speaks of the populace in connection with its victimizers: "The new democracy [is] inflaming itself by feeding greedily on the declamation of stump orators"; "Mr. Gladstone and his followers will ply the democracy with fiercer stimulants than ever"; "the masses are stirred, tempers are kindled, a torrent of insincere and envenomed declaration feeds the flame." [67] Explain it as we will, however, Arnold's language here is itself inflamed and gives off more heat than light. We should nevertheless notice one further fact: Arnold's language when he is speaking of Gladstone is scarcely less impassioned than his language about the masses.

We would expect Arnold's contentions that Gladstone was a political manipulator, an astute parliamentary manager, a statesman who had won minor victories but never major successes. But we are surprised by his charges that mere political ambition motivated Gladstone and that he fomented class discontent and stirred up provincial enmities to subserve personal ends. We may well suspect that personal animus infected Arnold's feelings about Cleon and his democracy. The point is worth examining.

There were adequate grounds in which such a personal antipathy could have taken root.[68] A world of belief separated the young man who yawned with boredom when Strauss's *Leben Jesu* appeared and the party leader who could interrupt a political discussion to go "off like a man possessed" when Strauss's name was mentioned.[69] But there were adequate grounds for agreement too, and these governed the relationship in the beginning. Arnold had sent the political leader copies of his early prose works and had received complimentary letters in return. With the third of these gifts, a copy of *A French Eton*, Arnold sent a compliment of his own: "In all these questions which concern the future we can none of us help turning with hope to you, in whatever capacity." [70]

When Arnold began his series of unsuccessful attempts to get an appointment that would free him from school inspecting, Gladstone seemed willing to supply him with recommendations but not with more positive help. Though Morley denies Gladstone interfered, Arnold was sure that the latter had blocked his chance to get a commissionership under the Endowed Schools Act. In 1882, Arnold applied again, this

time for a vacancy in the Charity Commission. Forster made
a strong effort in his behalf, sending not only a warm letter of
recommendation but a detailed minute in which he noted that
the burden of work facing the Charity Commission warranted
the appointment of not one but two members.[71] The attempt
failed. "Gladstone," Arnold concluded, "will never promote
the author of *Literature and Dogma.*" Following this dis-
appointment, Gladstone's offer of a pension in 1883 came as
a complete surprise. Arnold's letter to Morley to ask whether
he should accept refers to Gladstone as "Pericles" and "your
great leader." [72] Then in 1884, from America, Arnold sent
Gladstone a friendly note and a copy of a speech of Bancroft
that was warmly admiring of the Liberal leader.

Meanwhile William Forster and his wife, Matthew Arnold's
beloved sister Jane, began to develop suspicions about Gladstone that may seem to us now to have no basis whatever but
that they entertained with apparently increasing conviction and
may well have passed on to Arnold. These suspicions arose
from the role Gladstone played in the sensational events leading up to and following Forster's resignation from the Irish
Office. Forster resigned because he objected to the release
from prison of Parnell and the other Irish leaders before Ireland had been pacified. At the center of the issue was the
charge that the Liberal government had released Parnell in
return for his support, a charge to which Forster gave dramatic
substance in the House. He forced the reading of the complete
text of a letter in which Parnell expressed himself as willing "to
co-operate cordially for the future with the Liberal party." [73]
After Forster's death his biographer, T. Wemyss Reid, made
public Forster's repugnance throughout the business to negotiating with the jailed leaders of the Land League. Reid also

implied that in proceeding as he had, Gladstone had not dealt frankly, openly, and fairly with Forster. Later, Gladstone and then his son went to some pains to erase the impression that Forster had left the cabinet because of Gladstone's intriguing. But the fact simply remained, as Lord Selborne carefully noted, that Forster had lost confidence in Mr. Gladstone's conduct of Irish affairs.

Forster himself stated the essential nature of the difference between himself and Gladstone. In a speech made in 1884 condemning the government's failure to send an expedition to rescue General Gordon, Forster remarked, "I believe every one but the Prime Minister is already convinced of that danger . . . and I attribute his not being convinced to his wonderful power of persuasion. He can persuade most people of most things, and, above all, he can persuade himself of almost anything." To the bluff and honest Forster a mind like Gladstone's—subtle, cautious, indirect—was incomprehensible. Forster afterward denied that he had charged Gladstone with insincerity, but Forster's words were frequently repeated with the construction that Lord Hartington put upon them: they were "a bitter and personal and evidently highly prepared and long-reflected-over attack upon the sincerity of Mr. Gladstone." [74]

Thereafter Forster virtually dissociated himself from Irish affairs, and by the time the "Hawarden Kite" appeared in December, 1885, he had already been stricken with the illness of which he died four months later.[75] Requested to make public his views on home rule, Forster wrote a letter to the *Daily News* and *Standard* expressing unqualified opposition to the establishment of a separate Parliament in Dublin. His wife records that he wished to take part in the parliamentary debates and compel Gladstone to speak his mind straight out. She told Ellis Yarnall that Gladstone had suffered a "moral deterioration," to the extent that when he had decided on a course of action he could see or hear of no other. His Irish failure preyed on Forster's mind; he talked about Ireland when visitors like Matthew Arnold, Lord Selborne, or Goschen called. Gladstone heard a rumor that Forster might support his home rule scheme and wrote to inquire if the rumor were true. Forster replied that his views had not changed. When he died his obituary in the *Times* noted that his death had occured "in the very week which is to see the introduction of measures of which, if he were alive and well, he would be one of the most formidable opponents."

There is no reason to go to these lengths to show that Arnold thought Gladstone unpredictable and unreliable. Long before the events of the eighteen-eighties Arnold had remarked on Gladstone's tendency to shift easily.[76] Others made some of the same charges Arnold made. Morris had remarked on Gladstone's "capacity of shutting his eyes to everything that his momentary political position forbids him to see." [77] From the floor of the House, Lord Salisbury charged that Gladstone's Irish program had no other object than to keep him in office. Buckle, then editor of the *Times*, loudly swept the string of abuse against Gladstone. Nevertheless the evidence suggests that Arnold accepted Forster's view: Gladstone was not a man to be trusted, and on a subject like Ireland he was liable to pursue a crotchet of his own in defiance of the best interests of England. With his messianic delusions, Gladstone would have no compunction in marshaling the might of the masses to his own inscrutable ends. We may smile at Arnold, but the voice of caution, even long after the event, even in a writer like G. M. Young, still sounds.

Gladstone threw himself on the warm-hearted, close-thinking, hard-fighting Liberalism of the North, and told it what it wanted to hear in the accents of a great actor who has found his part at last. But the instrument with which he worked . . . was a dangerous instrument, especially for a man in whose mind the boundaries of self-conviction and self-deception were so feebly guarded.[78]

Yet on the question of home rule Gladstone was the man of vision, Arnold the short-sighted man of letters. Arnold had simply ignored his own advice to literary, intellectual liberals "not to be rushing into the arena of politics." For all his belief in pragmatic tests in morals, religion, and politics, in the end he himself had erred on the side of an impossible ideal. He had thought that a society based on wealth would sacrifice the emblems of its esteem, and that Ireland was as good a place as any to "unsettle men's notions as to the constitutive characters of property." [79] And he had believed that equality could broaden down peacefully from precedent to precedent, even in Ireland. Ideals, of course, tend to get muddied on the fields of practice, and Arnold found that his ideals of peaceful transition required the use of police truncheons and Kilmainham jail. He had in fact idealized the populace too, muttering his charm about their integrity, piety, good nature, and good humor, but at the same time wishing them other than they were.

By the late eighties Arnold was heartily sick of popular clamor. Under the changed circumstances of the England of 1859, writing to an aristocratic audience, he had praised Louis Napoleon extravagantly because the French emperor possessed *"largely and deeply interwoven in his constitution, the popular fibre,"* and because he knew how to win "not only the atten-

tion of the masses, but their enthusiasm." [80] In 1887, Arnold
was attracted to General Grant for quite other reasons. A
letter of Grant's showed that he possessed "the virtue, rare
everywhere, but more rare in America, perhaps, than anywhere
else, the virtue of being able to confront and resist popular
clamour, the *civium ardor prava jubentium*." Recalling *United
Ireland's* incendiary editorials, Arnold praised Grant's "governing instincts" for enabling him to say "I always admired the
South . . . for the boldness with which they silenced all opposition and all croaking by press or by individuals within
their control." [81] But if popular clamor sickened Arnold and
popular power frightened him, he adhered to a view of the
future beyond the conceptions of conventional political liberalism. Only a very atypical conservative would write as Arnold
did in September, 1887:

*Everywhere the propertied and satisfied classes have to face an
aspect of things which is new and unfamiliar to them; everywhere a change is preparing; everywhere the word equity is ac-
quiring a force and an extension hitherto unknown; everywhere
it becomes plainer that he who thinks it enough to say, May I
not do what I will with my own? will no longer be suffered to
have the last word.* [82]

William Morris had accused Arnold of cowardice in not
facing up to the need for force as the only way to overthrow
Whiggery. But as matters developed in England, the franchise
proved itself enough to destroy the extremities of wealth and
poverty that Arnold had deplored. In the hands of the people
it has organized secondary education, set up local governments, and partially endowed religious education—all projects
that Arnold had approved. The piety of the people has not
disestablished the church. Their good humor, perhaps, still

tolerates the House of Lords. "The stupid and noxious Tory-ism opposed to all serious improvement" that Arnold had fought even in these last distracted years, has heard its hour strike and has departed.[83] The middle classes have quite given up the liberty of doing as they like. With other Englishmen, they have seen in the time of peace the wisdom of the co-operative spirit and sense of interdependence that won the Battle of Britain. This spirit carried England through the economic crisis following the war and persists today in the philosophies of all political parties. The spirit has thrived thus far in the atmosphere of nationalism, but signs there are in number that it will yet seek, in the company of like spirits of other nations, a broader, freer air.

NOTES

Chapter I. THE HEADMASTER OF RUGBY

1. In his *Thomas Arnold*, Thomas W. Bamford disputes the too-generous claims made for Dr. Arnold as a school reformer. For Arnold on himself as a reformer, see A. P. Stanley, *Life of Thomas Arnold*, pp. 353, 391, 248.

2. During Dr. Keate's regime Eton had a placid history, perhaps because he flogged the boys with dogged regularity for twenty-five years. See Lionel Cust, *A History of Eton College* (New York, 1899), pp. 158–61; Rouse, pp. 182–86; Arthur F. Leach, *A History of Winchester College* (New York, 1899), pp. 396–400, 402–6, 419–22; P. H. Bryant, *Harrow* (London and Glasgow, 1936), p. 37.

3. L. Stephen, *Life of Sir James Fitzjames Stephen*, p. 77.

4. Anthony Trollope, *Autobiography* (Edinburgh and London, 1883), I, 16; Spencer Walpole, *The History of England from the Conclusion of the Great War in 1815* (London, 1911), I, 132; Hughes, *Tom Brown's School-Days*, p. 268.

5. Bryant, *Harrow*, p. 56.

6. Thomas W. Bamford, "Discipline at Rugby under Arnold," *Educational Review*, X (Nov., 1957), 18–28, and *Thomas Arnold*, pp. 128–54.

7. In the election Thomas Short, a High-churchman of the old-

fashioned sort and a Tory, came within one vote of Arnold's total. He was a fellow of Trinity College, Oxford, and a great favorite with his students. He is not to be confused with Thomas Vowler Short of Christ Church. See Palmer, *Memorials, Part I*, I, 116.

8. Available records indicate when a man was appointed, when he died, and only occasionally when he resigned. When no date of resignation is given, I assume that a man remained a trustee until he died. See *Rugby School Register*, I, ix.

9. Cust, *A History of Eton College*, p. 149.

10. No accurate bibliography of these is available, and Stanley's list is not reliable. See Stanley, *Life of Thomas Arnold*, p. 773.

11. *Ibid.*, pp. 11–12, 541; Wymer, pp. 35–36.

12. Stanley, *Life of Thomas Arnold*, pp. 77, 541, 281.

13. *Ibid.*, pp. 173, 249, 307, 391.

14. Thomas Arnold, *Miscellaneous Works*, pp. 5–78, 81–111, 259–338, and "The Oxford Malignants and Dr. Hampton."

15. Powell, *Liberalism Unveiled*; Stanley, *Life of Thomas Arnold*, p. 248; Oswell, I, 51.

16. Bamford, *Thomas Arnold*, pp. 51–53, 73–75, 80–84, 88–90.

17. None of the several accounts of this action is entirely correct. Arnold voted against the Tory candidate, William Stratford Dugdale, son of Dugdale Stratford Dugdale, and against John Eardley Wilmot, who described himself at the hustings as a Conservative Whig. Summarizing the election, Henry Smith listed Wilmot in the Tory column. Thus Dr. Arnold had a choice between two conservatives and Captain A. F. Gregory, who insisted that he was a moderate Radical. See the *Times*, Jan. 19 (p. 5) and Feb. 3 (p. 7), 1835, and H. S. Smith, *Parliaments of England*, II, 96. See also Prothero, I, 141.

18. A. P. Stanley, *Memoirs of Edward and Catherine Stanley*, pp. 32–66; *Greville Memoirs*, III, 267. Cf. D. Cecil, pp. 140–41. Greville's story is confirmed in Churton, II, 261–62. On the professorship of divinity, see Bamford, *Thomas Arnold*, p. 146.

19. For an example of a note excised in the second edition see

Thomas Arnold, *History of the Peloponnesian War* (1830), I, 471, n.; Stanley, *Life of Thomas Arnold*, p. 488; Thomas Arnold, *Two Sermons on the Interpretation of Prophecy in the Chapel of Rugby School* (Oxford, London, and Rugby, 1839), p. vi.

20. Prothero, I, 141.

21. Stanley, *Life of Thomas Arnold*, pp. 248–49, 342; Hughes, *Memoir of a Brother*, p. 89.

22. Hughes, *Manliness of Christ*, p. 194; Clough, *Correspondence*, I, 35; *Rugby Magazine*, I, iv; II, 16; George Granville Bradley, "Theodore Walrond" (letter signed "Rugbeiensis"), *Guardian*, XLII (July, 1887), 1030.

23. Stanley, *Life of Thomas Arnold*, pp. 94–117, 155–56; *Rugby Magazine*, II, 13; I, 10.

24. Stanley, *Life of Thomas Arnold*, pp. 536, 350.

25. *Ibid.*, pp. 44, 478, 308, 338, 429, 489–90, 495, 500, 286–87. For a comment on Arnold's exaggerated fear of town workmen, see [Francis Newman], review of *The Miscellaneous Works* of Thomas Arnold, pp. 417–18.

26. Stanley, *Life of Thomas Arnold*, pp. 235, 259, 307–8, 614, 716; Thomas Arnold, *Introductory Lectures on Modern History*, pp. 250–77.

27. Stanley, *Life of Thomas Arnold*, pp. 724–25, 536, 253, 256–57, 647, 763, 275, 208–9, 47; Palmer, *Memorials, Part I*, I, 157, and *Part II*, II, 451; W. and D. Wordsworth, II, 915.

28. Thomas Arnold, *Miscellaneous Works*, pp. 262, 480, 501; Stanley, *Life of Thomas Arnold*, pp. 242–43, 249–52, 532, 66; Thomas Arnold (the younger), *Passages in a Wandering Life*, p. 40.

29. Thomas Arnold, *Introductory Lectures on Modern History*, p. 187; Stanley, *Life of Thomas Arnold*, pp. 527–28, 532, 501–2, 267.

Chapter II. THE SILENT YEARS

1. Wymer, pp. 73–74.
2. Tom was still searching for a cure in 1846. In that year he

tried mesmerism, perhaps at the suggestion of the Arnolds' Lake
Country neighbor, Harriet Martineau, who had been "cured" of a
tumor by mesmerism. See Clough, *Correspondence*, I, 168.

3. Wymer, p. 139.

4. [Thomas Arnold, the younger], "Matthew Arnold (By One
Who Knew Him Well.)"

5. Stanley, *Life of Thomas Arnold*, p. 358.

6. Thomas Arnold, *Miscellaneous Works*, p. 368.

7. Stanley, *Life of Thomas Arnold*, p. 554.

8. Wymer, p. 141.

9. Charles Wordsworth, *Annals of My Early Life, 1806–1846*
(London, 1891), p. 270.

10. Stanley, *Life of Thomas Arnold*, p. 457.

11. Wordsworth, *Annals of My Early Life*, p. 270; W. T. Arnold,
"Thomas Arnold the Younger," p. 117; [William Gover], "Memo-
ries of Arnold and Rugby Sixty Years Ago," *Parents' Review*, VII
(April, 1896), 134; Woods, p. 9.

12. Wymer, p. 186.

13. Lake, *Memorials*, p. 161.

14. Lake, "More Oxford Memories," p. 828. Clough had felt
that of the two Rugby candidates Matthew had the better chance.
See his *Correspondence*, I, 104.

15. Wymer, p. 186.

16. Selections from *The Peloponnesian War* were read as a history text at Rugby. See Thomas Arnold, *Miscellaneous Works*, p.
346.

17. Goldwin Smith, p. 269.

18. Müller, p. 273.

19. Shairp, "Balliol Scholars," *Glen Desseray and Other Poems*,
p. 218.

20. Clough, *Correspondence*, I, 133; Sandford, *Memoirs of
Archbishop Temple*, I, 81, n.; Lake, "More Oxford Memories,"
p. 828.

21. Clough, *Correspondence*, I, 131.

22. For this section I have found useful the account by Archdeacon Edwin Palmer in Abbott and Campbell, pp. 102–7. Useful but inaccurate in details is Knickerbocker, *Creative Oxford*, pp. 79 ff.

23. Davis, p. 208.

24. Matthew Arnold, *Essays, Letters, and Reviews*, pp. 24–25.

25. Walford, p. 13, col. 3.

26. Prothero, I, 210.

27. Abbott and Campbell, I, 87.

28. Wilfred Ward, p. 344.

29. Church, pp. 320–35.

30. Matthew Arnold, *Unpublished Letters*, p. 56.

31. Lake, "Rugby and Oxford, 1830–1850," p. 668.

32. See Dr. Arnold's letter to Dr. Hawkins in Stanley, *Life of Thomas Arnold*, p. 577.

33. In 1894, Jowett regarded Newmanism as not "politically conservative." See Abbott and Campbell, I, 177.

34. Goldwin Smith, pp. 268–69.

35. Newman, *Apologia*, pp. 120, 104–5.

36. Matthew Arnold, *Culture and Anarchy*, ed. Wilson, pp. 62–63. This is the edition referred to for all citations from *Culture and Anarchy*.

37. *Greville Memoirs*, IV, 385.

38. Morrah, p. 89.

39. These subjects are mentioned in Conington, I, xxiii–iv.

40. Morrah, p. 109; E. H. Coleridge, I, 77.

41. E. H. Coleridge, I, 145–46; Morrah, p. 251. For a hint that Arnold frequently attended Union debates, see *Letters of Matthew Arnold to Arthur Hugh Clough*, p. 102.

42. The books of the Decade are lost, but a list of members can be gleaned from the scattered references to it: (besides Matthew Arnold and Coleridge) Thomas Arnold, Clough, Lake, Jowett, Stanley, Constantine Prichard, John F. B. Blackett, George Butler, John Campbell Shairp, Chichester Fortescue, John Conington,

Frederick Temple, James Riddell, R. W. Church, Theodore Walrond, Edward Goulburn, John B. Seymour, G. G. Bradley.

43. Knight, p. 412.

44. Thomas Arnold (the younger), *Passages in a Wandering Life*, p. 59.

45. Clough, *Poems and Prose Remains*, I, 31.

46. The exact dating of the breakfasts is given in that part of Matthew Arnold's obituary in the *Times* written by "one who was a constant companion throughout these years." Since Walrond and Clough were then dead, this must have been Tom. He left Oxford to go into residence at Lincoln's Inn on April 25, 1846, a date that probably served him as an *aide-mémoire*. See the *Times*, April 17, 1888, p. 10, cols. 1–3. See also the *Annual Register*, 1888, p. 142. The *Annual Register* is a comprehensive annual survey of the events of the year, especially useful for parliamentary history.

47. Thomas Arnold (the younger), "Arthur Hugh Clough: A Sketch," pp. 106–7. Editorials in support of Peel appeared in the *Spectator* for Jan. 24 and Feb. 7, 1846.

48. *Spectator*, editorials for Jan. 10 and Feb. 28, 1846.

49. Clough, letters to the *Balance*, Jan. 23, 1846, p. 26; Jan. 30, p. 34; Feb. 6, p. 42; Feb. 13, p. 50; March 6, p. 77; March 20, pp. 93–4. See also Clough, *Correspondence*, I, 126–27, 130, 243.

50. Clough, *Correspondence*, I, 106; Matthew Arnold, *Letters, 1848–1888*, I, 4 (hereafter referred to as *Letters*), and *Letters to Clough*, p. 75. On Clough's appointment, see Clough, *Correspondence*, I, 166. On Newman, see Matthew Arnold, *Discourses in America*, p. 139.

51. Matthew Arnold, *Letters*, I, 206, II, 32, and I, 326–27.

52. Matthew Arnold, "Written in Emerson's Essays," and "Obermann," *Poetical Works*, p. 3, line 1; p. 309, lines 94–95, 101–4; and *Letters to Clough*, pp. 59, 63.

53. Abbott and Campbell, I, 135–36; Matthew Arnold, *God and the Bible*, pp. 21–22.

54. A "calling-over" list of the sixth form, dated June, 1839, appears in Arbuthnot, p. 286.

55. Clough, *Correspondence*, I, 179, 181. For Stanley's remark see W. T. Arnold, "Thomas Arnold the Younger," p. 117.

Chapter III. AMONG THE BARBARIANS

1. Matthew Arnold, *Letters*, I, 4 (the article to which Arnold refers—Carlyle, "Louis-Philippe"—swirls with emotion), and *Letters to Clough*, p. 68; Clough, *Correspondence*, I, 215.

Hereafter, unless otherwise specified, all citations under "Arnold" refer to Matthew Arnold.

2. Lacaita, p. 73. James Lacaita served as secretary to Lord Lansdowne from 1857 to 1863.

3. Lacaita, p. 73; Arnold, *Letters*, I, 14; Mrs. Humphry Ward, p. 46.

4. Arnold, *Letters to Clough*, p. 111; *Letters*, I, 15–16; *Letters to Clough*, p. 65.

5. Stanley, *Life of Thomas Arnold*, pp. 536–37.

6. Note added to Barron Field's manuscript biography, quoted in Todd, p. 204.

7. Arnold, *Letters to Clough*, pp. 80, 68.

8. Arnold, *Letters*, I, 6.

9. Arnold, *Letters*, I, 4; *Letters to Clough*, pp. 77, 66; *Letters*, I, 5.

10. Arnold, *Popular Education of France*, pp. 75–76.

11. Arnold, *Mixed Essays*, pp. 44–45, 67–68, 111. Noel Annan has made special studies of the genealogy of the particular segment of the professional classes to which Arnold belonged. See his *Leslie Stephen* (Cambridge, 1952), and his chapter "The Intellectual Aristocracy," in *Studies in Social History*, ed. J. H. Plumb (London, 1955).

12. This was the Alfred Club in Albemarle Street, named after Alfred D'Orsay; Chichester Fortescue, Henry Grenfell, and Alfred Seymour were members (Fortescue, p. 15). See also *Essays in Criticism, Second Series*, pp. 326–27, where Arnold quotes with approval Amiel's description of "high society, as the Old World knows it"; Clough, *Correspondence*, I, 290.

13. Pope-Hennessy, *Monckton Milnes: The Flight of Youth*, pp. 31–32; Christie, *Transition from Aristocracy*, p. 144.

14. Escott, *Social Transformations of the Victorian Age*, pp. 3–4; Martineau, *Autobiography*, I, 271.

15. Waagen, II, 143; [anon.], "Visits to Private Galleries," *Art Union Monthly Journal*, IX (1847), 329–31, 358–60.

16. G. O. Trevelyan, *Life and Letters of Lord Macaulay* (New York, 1876), I, 135–36; Thackeray, II, 665, 685, and IV, 338; Malcolm Elwin, *Thackeray, a Personality* (London, 1933), p. 239; Lacaita, pp. 83–84; Martin, II, 178; Bosanquet, p. 61; Anna Jameson, *Letters to Ottilie Von Goethe* (London, 1939), pp. 127, 132; Charles Lyell, *Life, Letters and Journals* (London, 1881), II, 118, 135, 148.

17. T. H. S. Escott, *Club Makers and Club Members* (New York, 1914), p. 184; Humphry Ward, *History of the Athenaeum, 1824–1925* (London, 1926), p. 12; J. K. Laughton, *Memoirs of the Life of Henry Reeve* (London, 1898), II, 68, 94; Abraham Hayward, "Lord Lansdowne," *Saturday Review*, XV (Feb., 1863), 167–69; Sydney Smith, *The Letters* (Oxford, 1953), II, 784.

18. *Greville Memoirs*, VI, 400; Arnold, *Unpublished Letters*, p. 48.

19. No biography of Lord Lansdowne or even an adequate account and estimate of his career has been written. Harriet Martineau's chapter on him in *Biographical Sketches*, is the best contemporary portrait.

20. Guizot, p. 133; *Greville Memoirs*, II, 345, and VI, 148.

21. For example, in the Parliament that sat at the beginning of 1847 a member who engaged in business was almost as likely to be sitting among the Tories as among the Whigs. See Aydelotte, "The House of Commons in the 1840's."

22. *Greville Memoirs*, II, 220, 234, VI, 304, 356, and VII, 30; Bell, II, 199; Martin, II, 175, 178; Gash, p. 214; Maccoby, *English Radicalism, 1832–1852*, pp. 150, 158. According to Greville, Lans-

downe was often on the point of admitting a moderate electoral reform bill, but when the decision had to be made he always joined Palmerston against what was proposed.

23. Kay-Shuttleworth, who had been a poor-law administrator, never quite freed himself of the concept of public education as education for paupers. Arnold of course moved beyond this position, but he shared Kay-Shuttleworth's belief in the primacy of religious education, in education as an aspect of social reform, and in the enlarging and cultivating effects of proper elementary education. Kay-Shuttleworth sent the proofs of his *Memorandum on Popular Education* to Arnold, who read and approved of the work. See Arnold, *Letters*, I, 150, 161–62; Connell, pp. 203–42; Frank Smith, p. 289; Judges, pp. 104–27.

24. Arnold, "Schools," *Reign of Queen Victoria*, II, 239–40; "The Twice-Revised Code," pp. 348, 359; *Reports on Elementary Schools*, ed. Marvin, Appendix B, p. 271.

25. Martineau, *Biographical Sketches*, p. 336.

26. Arnold, *Letters*, I, 130; *Culture and Anarchy and Friendship's Garland*, p. 285; *Letters*, I, 271, 276, 277, 341, and II, 29, 57, 280.

27. Fletcher, pp. 311–12; Arnold, *Mixed Essays*, p. 103.

28. *Greville Memoirs*, II, 333, and III, 92–93; Guedalla, p. 289.

29. Arnold, *Letters*, I, 306–7; *Culture and Anarchy and Friendship's Garland*, pp. 324–26.

30. Derek Beales, "An International Crisis: The Italian Question," in Appleman, Madden, and Wolff, eds. *1859: Entering an Age of Crisis*, p. 181.

31. Arnold, *Letters*, I, 17; *Unpublished Letters*, pp. 31–32; *Letters to Clough*, p. 135; *Letters*, I, 26; *Unpublished Letters*, p. 22; *Letters*, I, 61.

32. Fitzmaurice, I, 421; Arnold, *Popular Education of France*, p. 2, and *Letters*, I, 80.

33. See the letter to Jane dated May 22, 1859, in *Unpublished Letters*, pp. 43–49. For other details about Arnold's decision to

write see M. M. Bevington's useful introduction to his edition of *England and the Italian Question.*

34. Lacaita, p. 94. To Gladstone Arnold wrote about his pamphlet: "It is . . . the greatest honour of all to be read by you with sympathy when one writes of Italy, for which you yourself, by what you have written, have done so much" (Gladstone Papers, BM, Add. MS. 44392, fol. 109).

35. Gladstone, the reluctant liberal, joined the Whigs for the first time in 1859 because of the Italian question and Conservative foreign policy in connection with it. See Morley, *Life of Gladstone,* I, 628; Beales, "An International Crisis," p. 191.

36. Arnold, *England and the Italian Question,* p. 39, and *Letters,* I, 96; Cowley, pp. 134–40; Bell, II, 236–57; Morley, *Life of Cobden,* II, 243, 255. Algernon Cecil believes that after Villafranca Napoleon was acting in good faith toward England (*British Foreign Secretaries,* p. 211).

37. Arnold, *Letters to Clough,* p. 150; *Unpublished Letters,* p. 48; *Letters,* I, 88.

38. As usual we can find a parallel notion in Dr. Arnold, in this case in Dr. Arnold's quotation from Madame de Staël: "La séparation des classes nuit à quelques égards à l'esprit proprement dit. Les nobles y ont trop peu d'idées et les gens de lettres trop peu d'habitude des affaires." See Thomas Arnold, "Early Roman History," p. 88.

39. Arnold, *England and the Italian Question,* pp. 55–56; *Unpublished Letters,* p. 48.

40. Arnold, *Letters,* I, 101–103; Clough, *Correspondence,* II, 571; Armytage, "Matthew Arnold and W. E. Gladstone," p. 218.

41. Arnold, "The 'Principle of Examination,'" *Daily News,* March 25, 1862, p. 6, col. 1. The *Daily News* was among the defenders of the Revised Code and was "unable on this subject to shake off . . . a superstitious reverence for old watchwords of . . . extreme Dissenters." See "The Twice-Revised Code," p. 365.

42. Arnold, *Mixed Essays,* p. 5.

43. Arnold, *Popular Education of France*, pp. xvii, xxiv, xxviii, 173. Lord Lansdowne, incidentally, had supported a life-peerage bill in 1856. See *Greville Memoirs*, VII, 200.

44. Armytage, "Matthew Arnold and Richard Cobden in 1864," p. 252; Arnold, *Culture and Anarchy*, pp. 174–80. For an illuminating commentary, see Trilling, pp. 284–88.

45. Arnold, *Mixed Essays*, pp. 458–85; "Endowments," *Pall Mall Gazette*, Nov. 12, 1870, p. 10 (repr. in *Essays, Letters, and Reviews*, ed. Fraser Neiman, pp. 175–78—hereafter referred to as "Neiman"); "Emmanuel Hospital."

46. Arnold, *St. Paul and Protestantism*, pp. 167, 169; *Last Essays on Church and Religion*, pp. 165–66, 168; "A First Requisite for Church Reform," *Pall Mall Gazette*, May 30, 1870, p. 3 (Neiman, pp. 169–74). For Arnold's letter to Newman on the subject and Newman's reply, see *Unpublished Letters*, pp. 57–59.

47. Arnold, *Mixed Essays*, pp. 36–72. See also *Essays in Criticism, Second Series*, pp. 296–97; "A Comment on Christmas," *Contemporary Review*, XLVII (April, 1885), 471.

48. Arnold, *Civilization in the United States*, pp. 142–47.

49. Thompson, p. 283.

50. Arnold, *Mixed Essays*, pp. 346–47; *Culture and Anarchy and Friendship's Garland*, pp. 289–90; *Civilization in the United States*, pp. 136–38; *Mixed Essays*, pp. 355–56.

51. Arnold, "Curtius's History of Greece" (unsigned reviews of the five volumes), *Pall Mall Gazette*, Oct. 12, 1868, pp. 9–10; April 28, 1871, pp. 10–11; June 4, 1872, pp. 11–12; July 22, 1872, pp. 11–12; March 25, 1876, p. 12 (Neiman, pp. 124–55).

52. Arnold, *Culture and Anarchy*, pp. 106–7.

53. Mill, *Principles of Political Economy*, II, 329.

54. *Lord Goschen and His Friends (The Goschen Letters)*, ed. Percy Colson (London, 1946), p. 20.

55. Hardinge, III, 11.

56. In "The Twice-Revised Code" Arnold praised Palmerston's punctilious consideration of his subordinates and contrasted it with

the calculated disregard shown by Robert Lowe, Arnold's superior. Arnold may have been thinking of the Spanish incident in May, 1848, involving Henry Bulwer, which caused such embarrassment to Lord Lansdowne.

57. Arnold, *Mixed Essays*, p. 374; *Culture and Anarchy and Friendship's Garland*, p. 331; *Essays in Criticism, First Series*, p. 165.

58. The following is a list of Arnold's hosts and their houses: Sir Anthony Rothschild at Aston Clinton (Bucks.), Meyer Rothschild at Mentmore (Bucks.), Lord Derby at Knowsley (Lancs.), Lord Rosebery at Durdans (Surrey), Lord Chesham at Latimer (Bucks.), Lord Cowper at Panshanger (Herts.), the duke of Bedford at Chenies (Bucks.), Lord Lytton at Knebworth (Herts.), Lord Lovelace at East Horsley (Surrey), Lord Pembroke at Wilton (Wilts.), Sir Trevor Lawrence at Dorking (Surrey), W. J. Evelyn at Wotton (Surrey), Lord Granville near Sunningdale (Berks.), Lord Iddesleigh at Pynes (Devon.), Wyndham Slade at Montys (Somerset), F. C. Lawley at Exminster (Devon.), Grant Duff at Hampton (Middx.), Lord Aberdare at Duffryn Ash (Glamorgan), Baron Carl von Canitz in Silesia, Count Redern at Carlsdorf bei Angermünde. (I have supplemented a list that appears in Chambers, p. 134.)

59. Frederick Temple did not become archbishop of Canterbury until after Arnold's death.

60. In 1874, Lady Stanley invited Arnold to meet Prince Christian and Princess Helena of Schleswig-Holstein ("Carlyle's Last Letters to Froude, IV," ed. W. H. Dunn, *Twentieth Century*, CLX [Sept., 1956], 245–46). See also *Later Letters of Lady Augusta Stanley 1864–1876* (London, 1929), p. 78; Arnold, *Letters*, II, 11, 26, 38.

61. Arnold boasted of his reception at the Dresden court and dismayed his fellow hotel guests, among them twenty-year-old Logan Pearsall Smith. Smith's account of Arnold's behavior is a lovely mock-aesthete performance, all the more delightful in that

it stresses his own priggishness and suggests that Arnold was performing for him and for a Russian family that was keen on observing characters and types. See Smith, *Unforgotten Years* (Boston, 1939), pp. 133–37.

62. Buckler, *Matthew Arnold's Books*. This collection of letters between Matthew Arnold and his publishers reveals the amusing fact that in 1870, after Arnold had created his character Mr. Bottles, Arnold received a legacy from a distant cousin of his, a brewer.

Chapter IV. THE POPULACE

1. Arnold, *Letters to Clough*, p. 77.

2. See Mayhew, *London Labour and the London Poor*.

3. Arnold, *Discourses in America*, p. 142.

4. Arnold's great tribute to the influence of George Sand is his essay on her written about a year after her death (*Mixed Essays*, pp. 236–60). See also *Letters to Clough*, pp. 58–59.

5. Arnold, "To a Republican Friend, 1848," *Poetical Works*, p. 7, lines 12, 14.

6. Arnold, review of Obermann, 1863 ed., in the *Academy*, I (Oct., 1869), 2 (Neiman, p. 160).

7. Arnold, *Mixed Essays*, p. 376; *A French Eton*, pp. 130–31. "I am convinced that nothing can be done effectively to raise this [lower] class except through the agency of a transformed middle class" (*Letters*, I, 224).

8. Arnold, *Culture and Anarchy and Friendship's Garland*, p. 338; *Mixed Essays*, pp. 389–91; *Culture and Anarchy*, pp. 194–95, 186; review of Obermann, p. 2 (Neiman, p. 160).

9. Abbott and Campbell, I, 133.

10. Arnold, *Letters*, I, 4; *Letters to Clough*, pp. 74–75.

11. Arnold, *Letters*, I, 7; *Letters to Clough*, p. 79.

12. Arnold, *Letters to Clough*, p. 84.

13. Arnold, "Sonnet to the Hungarian Nation," dated July 21, 1849, *Poetical Works*, p. 480; "To a Republican Friend, 1848

(continued)," *ibid.*, p. 7; *Essays in Criticism, First Series*, p. 278.

14. Arnold, *Letters*, I, 78; *Unpublished Letters*, pp. 31–32.

15. In an account of a speech of thanks Arnold made at a testimonial dinner given him by the teachers of the Westminster district on the occasion of his retiring, Nov. 12, 1886, in *Pall Mall Budget*, April 19, 1888, p. 9 (Neiman, p. 308).

16. Arnold, *Letters*, I, 17.

17. The National Reform League seriously considered making free, national, compulsory education part of its program in 1850 (see Cole, pp. 154–55). Arnold's suggestion, made in an official report in 1853, still came almost 50 years before primary education was made universal and compulsory in England. Just over a decade earlier Lord Melbourne had said to Queen Victoria, "I do not know why there is all this fuss about education. None of the Paget family can read or write and they do very well" (D. Cecil, p. 130).

18. *Pall Mall Budget*, April 19, 1888, p. 11.

19. "Le vrai secret pour préparer les révolutions, c'est de former des générations de Gavroches, n'est-ce pas?" (Arnold to Fontanès, *Letters*, II, 315). F. D. Maurice and the Christian Socialists generally echoed this sentiment. See Williams, p. 113; Arnold, "Schools," *Reign of Queen Victoria*, II, 265.

20. Arnold, *Popular Education of France*, pp. 40, 147, 165–66, 236–37; *Letters*, I, 10, 114; *Schools and Universities on the Continent*, pp. 115–16.

21. E. L. Woodward, *Three Studies in European Conservatism*, pp. 119–20.

22. Arnold, *Letters*, I, 6; Mrs. Humphry Ward, p. 50.

23. Arnold saw this minister again in 1865 when he made another educational tour. The *Note-Books* show Arnold to have been a lifelong reader of Guizot.

24. Arnold, *Popular Education of France*, p. 167.

25. Arnold, *A French Eton*, pp. 25–26.

26. For some months the "Causéries de Lundi" appeared in the

Moniteur and reflected the party line. See Mott, pp. 364–72, and Nicolson, p. 196.

27. Arnold, *Letters*, I, 104, 261–62. In 1869, Sainte-Beuve quarreled with his fellow senators and made a speech on behalf of free thought. Arnold noted this speech in his essay on Sainte-Beuve's death, remarking that Sainte-Beuve "would have had the same tendency to oppose the heady current of a medium where mere Liberalism reigned" (*Essays in Criticism, Third Series*, pp. 148–49).

28. Arnold, *England and the Italian Question*, pp. 22–23, 28–30.

29. Arnold, *Letters*, I, 83–84.

30. Grant Duff, "Matthew Arnold's Writings," p. 293.

31. Arnold, *Unpublished Letters*, p. 46.

32. Arnold, *Letters*, I, 304. On his essay "A Word About America," written before he had been to America, he wrote, "One had to trust a great deal to one's 'flair' " (*Letters*, II, 200).

33. Arnold, *Culture and Anarchy and Friendship's Garland*, pp. 224, 245–46, 283. John Stuart Mill, be it noted, admitted no excuse for dictatorial regimes; "Louis Napoleon was perhaps the only man Mill ever really hated" (Packe, p. 280).

34. Arnold, *Letters*, I, 103–4, 106, 111. Arnold had of course visited George Sand at Nohant in August, 1846. See *Mixed Essays*, pp. 236–38.

35. Arnold, *Letters*, I, 84, 86–87, 119.

36. Arnold, "The Twice-Revised Code," p. 355.

37. Arnold, *Culture and Anarchy and Friendship's Garland*, pp. 335–36; *Letters*, I, 252; Lowe, pp. 32–62 (the passages Arnold used may be found on pp. 40, 51–52). Arnold said he liked this speech in *Letters*, I, 262–63.

38. G. M. Trevelyan, *Life of John Bright*, p. 352.

39. Odger seems to have been the only working-class leader Arnold ever praised (*Culture and Anarchy*, p. 94).

40. Arnold, *Letters*, I, 138–41, 164–65.

41. Arnold, *Culture and Anarchy*, pp. 104–5, 107–8.

42. L. Stephen, *Studies of a Biographer*, II, 104.

43. Arnold, *Culture and Anarchy and Friendship's Garland*, pp. 271–73.

44. Harrison, "Culture: A Dialogue"; Arnold, *Letters*, I, 372; and *Culture and Anarchy*, pp. 39–41, 65–66.

45. Harrison, *Autobiographic Memoirs*, I, 250, 252–53; S. and B. Webb, pp. 245–46.

46. Carlyle, "Shooting Niagara: And After?" *Critical and Miscellaneous Essays*, III, 598.

47. Arnold, *Culture and Anarchy and Friendship's Garland*, p. 362. Arnold's remark was first published March 20, 1866. A royal commission made its report on Eyre a few weeks later.

48. George H. Ford points out this reference in his excellent article, "The Governor Eyre Case in England," pp. 232–33.

49. A judicious piecing together of all the best accounts may be found in Trilling, pp. 245–47.

50. Arnold, *Letters*, I, 335; *Greville Memoirs*, VI, 52; *Annual Register*, 1866, pp. 99–100.

51. Lady Mayne was a good enough friend of Arnold's to ask in June, 1866, for a ticket (for the Oxford Encaenia?) that he did not intend to use (*Letters*, I, 331). It is probable that the Arnolds moved to Chester Square because of the close proximity to Eaton Place where Justice Wightman lived. As one of the judges of the Court of Queen's Bench, the justice was doubtless acquainted with Sir Richard Mayne.

52. Arnold, *Culture and Anarchy and Friendship's Garland*, pp. 232, 240.

53. Arnold, *Letters*, I, 377, 379.

54. Arnold, *Culture and Anarchy*, pp. 80–82, 97, 203, 205.

55. G. M. Trevelyan, *Life of John Bright*, pp. 361–65; Maccoby, *English Radicalism 1853–1886*, pp. 92–94. Gladstone observed to the queen that the working classes by the sixties had improved both culturally and morally (Magnus, pp. 163–64).

56. Arnold, *Letters*, I, 335.

57. Arnold, *Letters*, II, 106; review of Curtius' *History of Greece*, Vol. II, in *Pall Mall Gazette*, April 28, 1871, p. 11 (Neiman, p. 137).

58. Tawney, pp. 20, 36.

59. Morris, p. 66; Traubel, I, 232.

60. Chesterton, introduction to Arnold, *Essays, Literary and Critical*, p. xi.

Chapter V. *THE PHILISTINES*

1. Swinburne, p. 425.

2. Arnold, *Mixed Essays*, pp. 177, 287; *Culture and Anarchy*, pp. 30, 106.

3. These were, in order, John Penrose (1754–1829), John Trevenen and John Penrose of Gluvias, Thomas Trevenen of Cardynham, Thomas Trevenen Penrose and John Penrose (1778–1859), Thomas Arnold, John Buckland, Charles Thomas Penrose, and Edward Arnold. The list of course could be extended.

4. Clough, *Correspondence*, I, 238, 243, 290.

5. Arnold, *Letters to Clough*, pp. 66, 68–69.

6. Cowherd, pp. 19, 30, 39. For Lansdowne's support of legislation to remove Dissenters' disabilities see Dale, *History of English Congregationalism*, pp. 612, 615, 625.

7. Arnold, *Letters*, I, 28; II, 53.

8. Arnold, *Reports on Elementary Schools*, ed. Sandford, pp. 6–8.

9. *Ibid.*, pp. 90–91, 42–43; Connell, p. 207.

10. Arnold, *Mixed Essays*, p. 362; "The Twice-Revised Code," p. 358.

11. "The Twice-Revised Code," p. 348. (Arnold spelled the name of this group both "Mialite" and "Miallite.")

12. *Ibid.*, p. 354.

13. Arnold, "The Principle of Examination," *Daily News*, March 25, 1862, p. 6 (Neiman, pp. 36–39); *Letters*, I, 162, 164, 169.

14. Two sources of information about the relationship of the Forsters and Matthew Arnold have not been made public. They are Forster's papers and the diary Jane Arnold was known to have kept all her life. T. Wemyss Reid's *Life of Forster* is a good contemporary account but too close to the events and people concerned to be satisfactory today. In his discussion of the Revised Code, Reid does not mention the part played by Arnold. Throughout the book, in fact, the relationship is understressed, and nothing of the close social relationship, of which Arnold's letters give ample proof, is indicated. See Reid, I, 348–49. Conversely, Robert Lowe's biographer acidly notes the relationship of the two men and deduces that Forster and Arnold worked together in 1864 when Lowe resigned under the charge that he had mutilated school inspectors' reports. See Martin, II, 224.

15. Mundella had attended a Church of England school, but his family was Roman Catholic. See Armytage, *A. J. Mundella*, pp. 15–16.

16. Reid, I, 226.

17. An account of these lectures is given by F. Seebohm, who attended them, in "Mr. W. E. Forster's Early Career."

18. Yarnall, p. 253.

19. Arnold, *Letters to Clough*, pp. 114, 133–34; *Unpublished Letters*, pp. 28, 49, 50–51; *Letters*, I, 115, 130, 197, 206–7, 216.

20. Arnold, *Letters*, I, 206–7. Arnold recognized these qualities in other speeches of Forster. See also *Letters*, I, 197, 214–15, 216.

21. Moran, pp. xiv–xv; John Motley, *Complete Works* (New York, 1900), XVI, 122–23, 203; Reid, I, 359, 364; Arnold, *Letters*, II, 349, and *A French Eton*, pp. 118–21.

22. Arnold, *Popular Education of France*, pp. 75, 77.

23. Arnold, *Letters*, I, 219–20, 226.

24. Perhaps this was the meeting at Forster's that Thomas Arnold recalls as having taken place "in the sixties." He tells that when the talk turned to the subject of commercial travelers Mat-

thew Arnold remarked on "the insufferable character of 'the British bagman.' Cobden took up the matter with perfect coolness. 'I was once a commercial traveller myself,' he said, 'and while so employed I must say that I met with many excellent and intelligent men, nor do I think that as a class they deserve to be severely spoken of.' " Arnold's reply is not recorded. See Thomas Arnold (the younger), *Passages in a Wandering Life*, p. 202.

25. Armytage, "Matthew Arnold and Richard Cobden in 1864," pp. 251–53.

26. Arnold wrote that the secretary of the British and Foreign School Society was so shocked by the acrimony displayed in that campaign that "he registered a vow never to be induced to take part in a religious agitation again" ("Schools," *Reign of Queen Victoria*, II, 252).

27. Miall, pp. 50–51, 62, 65.

28. Faulkner, pp. 33–41, 116; Miall, pp. 73–87, 130–41.

29. Arnold, *Letters*, I, 227.

30. Arnold, *A French Eton*, pp. 92, 97–100, 116, 122–26, 127–28. Trilling (p. 187) notes that Arnold did not mention the economic repression to which the state had subjected the middle classes.

31. "Matthew Arnold: Poet and Essayist," *British Quarterly Review*, XLII (Oct., 1865), 243–69; Arnold, *Letters*, I, 310; Osbourn, p. 151.

32. Morley, *Life of Gladstone*, II, 149.

33. Typical uses of "Philistine" in *Essays in Criticism, First Series* appear on pp. vii, xi, 26, 27, 162–67, 193, 306.

34. Article by Louis Étienne, in *Revue des deux mondes*, April 1, 1866, quoted by Brown in "The French Reputation of Matthew Arnold," p. 230. Arnold remarks on this review in *Letters*, I, 325.

35. Arnold, *Letters*, I, 310.

36. Arnold, *Culture and Anarchy and Friendship's Garland*, pp. 317–20. It is typical of Arnold's apparent casualness in this

essay that he surrounds his remarks on English Philistines with resolutions never more to use the epithet against his countrymen (*ibid.*, pp. 318, 329).

37. *Ibid.*, pp. 348, 346–50.

38. *Ibid.*, p. 327; Arnold, *Popular Education of France*, pp. xxxiii–xxxiv; *Letters*, I, 157.

39. For the Bright and Mill references, see Elisabeth Wallace, *Goldwin Smith* (Toronto, 1957), p. 29, and Packe, p. 423. For Arnold's opinions on the American Civil War, see *Letters*, I, 130, 245, 258.

40. Arnold, *Culture and Anarchy and Friendship's Garland*, p. 327.

41. Arnold, *Letters*, I, 315–17.

42. These include letters I–VII; the remaining letters were written after *Culture and Anarchy*.

43. In the parts of *On the Study of Celtic Literature* written after "My Countrymen" Philistinism raises its head as the guilty author of Fenianism, but is not associated with any particular class. See Arnold, *On the Study of Celtic Literature*, pp. xi, 132, 136–37.

44. Arnold, *Letters*, I, 377.

45. Arnold, *Culture and Anarchy*, pp. 96, 69, 37.

46. *Ibid.*, p. 58. "Muscular Christianity," an example of non-Oxonian Anglicanism that worked to educate the workingmen of London, is relegated to the outer darkness of "machinery" (*ibid.*, p. 59).

47. *Ibid.*, pp. 52, 63, 16.

48. *Ibid.*, pp. 57, 77–82. The germ of the chapter entitled "Doing as One Likes" may be found in *Letters*, I, 376–77.

49. Arnold, *Essays in Criticism, First Series*, p. 15.

50. Arnold, *Culture and Anarchy*, p. 21. "Pharisaic self-complacency," "wild, shrieking declamation," "Hotspur shall speak for us," are examples of the enlightened utterances Arnold inspired from one Congregationalist reviewer. See "Matthew Arnold and Puritanism," *British Quarterly Review*, LII (July–Oct., 1873), 417

(noted in Robbins, *Ethical Idealism of Matthew Arnold*, p. 147).

51. Arnold, *Essays in Criticism, First Series*, p. 301. Note also Joubert's "Quiconque éteint dans l'homme un sentiment de bienveillance, le tue partiellement," quoted in Arnold, *Note-Books*, pp. 370, 387, 410.

52. Arnold, *Culture and Anarchy*, pp. 10, 11–16, 23–30, 151–54.

53. Arnold, *Letters*, I, 227.

54. *Ibid.*, II, 17.

55. Arnold, *St. Paul and Protestantism*, pp. 360–61.

56. *Ibid.*, p. 312. But see also his "A First Requisite for Church Reform," *Pall Mall Gazette*, May 30, 1870, pp. 2–3 (Neiman, pp. 169–73).

57. Sandford, ed. *Memoirs of Archbishop Temple*, I, 278.

58. Edward Baines did not join the exclusively Nonconformist committee. He had come round to thinking that state aid to education was necessary, and his organization attracted both churchmen and Dissenters who opposed those who would make all state-aided education unsectarian. Samuel Morley, another leading Congregationalist, also stood apart from his fellow Nonconformists in supporting the bill. See Hodder, pp. 335–38.

59. The expression "watchful jealousy" was used by a Mr. Winterbotham in the House as a warning to those inclined to favor the Establishment. Arnold picked it up and repeated it often as an example of Dissenters' sweet reasonableness. See Arnold, *St. Paul and Protestantism*, p. xx.

60. Dale, *History of English Congregationalism*, p. 682.

61. The quotation is Forster's. See Reid, I, 362.

62. See Buckler, "Studies in Three Arnold Problems," p. 266; Arnold, *Letters*, II, 27, 24.

63. Mrs. Humphry Ward, pp. 35–36; "Death of Mr. Forster," *Times*, April 6, 1886, p. 11.

64. Arnold, *St. Paul and Protestantism*, pp. xxxiv–xxxv; *Culture and Anarchy*, p. 31.

65. R. H. Hutton, "Mr. Arnold on St. Paul and his Creed,"

Contemporary Review, XIV (June, 1870), 332 (quoted in Robbins, *Ethical Idealism of Matthew Arnold,* p. 153); Arnold, *St. Paul and Protestantism,* pp. 376–77.

66. Hewett, p. 244.

Chapter VI. GLADSTONE, IRELAND, AND
A TIME OF CRISIS

1. Arnold, "The Nadir of Liberalism," *Nineteenth Century,* XIX (May, 1886), 662–63 (Neiman, p. 279).

2. Lynd, p. 237.

3. B. Webb, p. 41; Arnold, *Letters,* II, 166.

4. John Morley, "Home and Foreign Affairs," *Fortnightly Review,* N.S. XXVII (March, 1880), 460.

5. Roach, p. 70.

6. Arnold, *Letters,* II, 112.

7. Buckler, *Matthew Arnold's Books,* p. 133.

8. Arnold, *Mixed Essays,* pp. 386–87.

9. *Ibid.,* p. 407.

10. J. L. Hammond, p. 180; Charles Gavan Duffy, *Young Ireland* (Dublin, 1884), II, 153–54.

11. Gladstone Papers, Add. MS. 44158.

12. *Annual Register,* 1880, p. 77.

13. Whately, p. 130; Robinson, I, 314; Stanley, *Life of Thomas Arnold,* p. 323.

14. Arnold, *Letters to Clough,* p. 78.

15. Abbott and Campbell, I, 158.

16. Arnold, *Letters to Clough,* p. 78.

17. Arnold, *Mixed Essays,* pp. 316–17.

18. Arnold, *On the Study of Celtic Literature,* pp. 22–23, 180–81, i–xviii.

19. One critic feels that the book had an important influence on the Celtic revival, though its political and racial ideas could only be "a weary staleness" to the Irish (Kelleher, "Matthew Arnold and the Celtic Revival"). Stale or not, belief in the doctrine of

racial traits was widely held by nineteenth-century thinkers. See Faverty, *Matthew Arnold, the Ethnologist*.

20. Arnold wrote to his mother that the Lords stumbled into the idea (*Letters*, II, 17).

21. Arnold, *Culture and Anarchy*, pp. 11–12, 166–74, 200–201.

22. Arnold, *Letters*, II, 66–67; *Mixed Essays*, p. 269.

23. Arnold, "Roman Catholics and the State," *Works* (London, 1903), XII, 452.

24. Arnold, 1874 preface to *Higher Schools and Universities in Germany* (London, 1882), pp. i–cxxxviii; *Times*, July 31, 1879, p. 10 (Neiman, pp. 212–15); "Roman Catholics and the State"; "Irish Catholicism and British Liberalism," *Mixed Essays*, pp. 73–106; "The Irish University Question," *Times*, July 31, 1879, p. 10 (Neiman, pp. 212–15).

25. Morley, *Recollections*, I, 129.

26. Arnold, *Letters*, II, 141.

27. Rumors about mistreatment of Lansdowne Irish tenants during the famine were given new currency after this resignation and speech of Lord Lansdowne. A pamphlet written by Charles Russell attacked the management of the family estates, and the Land League singled out Lord Lansdowne as a man to crush. Income from the estates sank from £23,000 to £500, so that Lord Lansdowne had to sell some of his paintings to hold onto the house in Berkeley Square in which Matthew Arnold had worked. Lord Lansdowne, not intimidated, voted against the Carson-Redmond settlement of 1916. But when the looting, burning, and sacking of "the Troubles" came in 1922, Derain House in Kenmare was not spared. See Newton, pp. 25, 46, 50.

28. Arnold, *Mixed Essays*, pp. 299, 290, 292.

29. Arnold, *Letters*, II, 195; O'Hegarty, pp. 496–97.

30. See Holland, I, 332.

31. Arnold, *Letters*, II, 195; *Mixed Essays*, p. 268; *Letters*, II, 187–88; *Mixed Essays*, p. 288.

Ten years earlier Marx had written, "After occupying myself

with the Irish question for many years I have come to the conclusion that the decisive blow against the English ruling classes
(and it will be decisive for the workers' movement all over the
world) cannot be delivered *in England but only in Ireland*" (Marx
and Engels, p. 288).

32. Magnus, p. 297.

33. Bodleian MS. E. 10, fol. 14.

34. It is difficult to believe that Arnold would have thought the
action objectionable. Six years later, on the subject of closure, he
declared himself in favor of the most stringent form. See "Zenith
of Conservatism," *Nineteenth Century*, XXI (Jan., 1887), 151
(Neiman, pp. 315–16).

35. Arnold received Gladstone's letter of July 8, 1881, in Ireland
and replied from there. Arnold returned to London. On September
27, Gladstone asked Forster, "Is M. Arnold about to leave you?"
And on October 12, Arnold told Coleridge that he meant to write
earlier, "all the time I was in Ireland." See BM, Add. MSS. 44471,
fol. 284, and 44159, fol. 28; E. H. Coleridge, II, 306.

36. See entry from Burke in Arnold, *Note-Books*, p. 512.

37. Arnold, *Letters*, II, 165–66.

38. Arnold, *Mixed Essays*, pp. 306, 268–69.

39. A marked difference in emphasis appears in two otherwise
similar paragraphs discussing coercion, the first written in June,
1881, the second in late 1886. The earlier paragraph ends with
"redressing injustice" as its climactic phrase, the later paragraph
ends with "repressing disorder" as its climax. See *Mixed Essays*,
pp. 288–89; "Zenith of Conservatism," p. 160 (Neiman, pp.
324–25).

40. Arnold, "Up to Easter," *Nineteenth Century*, XXI (May,
1887), 632 (Neiman, p. 341).

41. E. H. Coleridge, II, 307.

42. W. E. Gladstone, "Mr. Forster and Ireland," p. 451.

43. Arnold tells this in "Zenith of Conservatism," p. 160. He
left Ireland in October, 1881, and on December 16, Forster wrote

to Gladstone that he had taken strong measures against *United Ireland* (BM, Add. MS. 44159, fol. 138).

44. Arnold, "Zenith of Conservatism," p. 159 (Neiman, p. 324); "Up to Easter," p. 632 (Neiman, p. 341).

45. Connell, p. 285.

46. Arnold, *Letters*, II, 327; "Up to Easter," p. 629 (Neiman, p. 338); *Essays in Criticism, First Series*, p. 36; "The Zenith of Conservatism," p. 148 (Neiman, p. 312).

47. Roach, p. 72.

48. Arnold, *Letters*, II, 312–13.

49. Arnold, "The Zenith of Conservatism," p. 156 (Neiman, p. 321); "On the Political Crisis" (Neiman, p. 283); *On the Study of Celtic Literature*, pp. 14–15; "The Zenith of Conservatism," p. 158 (Neiman, p. 322).

50. Goldwin Smith, p. 183; Arnold, "The Nadir of Liberalism," p. 658 (Neiman, p. 271), and "Up to Easter," p. 640 (Neiman, pp. 349–50).

51. Eversley, p. 106.

52. Arnold first mentioned the problem of merging Ulster in Celtic Ireland on January 13, 1886 (Goldwin Smith, p. 183). Churchill played his "Orange card," as he called it, in Belfast on February 22. The "Ulster will be right" phrase appeared still later in a letter he wrote to a Liberal-Unionist member. See Churchill, II, 61–65.

53. Mill, *Considerations on Representative Government*, pp. 308–19.

54. Arnold, "From Easter to August," *Nineteenth Century*, XXII (Sept., 1887), 320 (Neiman, pp. 365–66).

55. Mill, *England and Ireland*, p. 24.

56. Arnold, *Mixed Essays*, pp. 383–84.

57. Arnold, "Zenith of Conservatism," pp. 160, 161, 164; "Up to Easter," pp. 636, 643 (Neiman, pp. 325, 326, 328, 345, 352).

58. Arnold, "On the Political Crisis" (Neiman, p. 285).

59. Bagehot, *The English Constitution*, introduction to 2d ed., pp. 268–70.

60. Christie, p. 41.

61. Morley, *Life of Gladstone*, II, 139.

62. Gladstone delighted Ruskin by telling him, "I am an out-and-out *inequalitarian*" (*ibid.*, II, 190).

63. Arnold, *Letters*, II, 325; "On the Political Crisis"; "After the Elections" (Neiman, pp. 285, 288).

64. Arnold, "The Zenith of Conservatism," p. 161 (Neiman, p. 325).

65. Arnold, "Nadir of Liberalism," pp. 646–47 (Neiman, p. 263); Marx and Engels, pp. 446–48.

66. Arnold, "Zenith of Conservatism," p. 149 (Neiman, p. 314); *Letters*, II, 362.

67. Arnold, "After the Elections"; "Up to Easter," p. 637; "From Easter to August," p. 320–21, 324 (Neiman, pp. 348, 365–66, 369).

68. For Gladstone's opinion of Arnold, and in particular of Arnold's religious beliefs, see Morley, *Life of Gladstone*, II, 760–61; W. E. Gladstone, *Studies Subsidiary to the Works of Bishop Butler*, pp. 56–58, 71; W. E. H. Lecky, *Democracy and Liberty* (Edinburgh, 1899), p. xxxii; E. H. Coleridge, II, 361.

69. Arnold, *Letters*, II, 113.

70. Armytage, "Matthew Arnold and W. E. Gladstone," pp. 219–20; Arnold, *Letters to Clough*, I, 150.

71. BM, Add. MS. 44160, fols. 191–95.

72. Arnold, *Letters*, II, 207, 215–16.

73. J. L. Hammond, pp. 277, 289.

74. Reid, II, 500.

75. A full account of his last years will have to wait until the Forster papers are open to examination. That part of Forster's biography that deals with the years after 1880 "is obviously circumscribed and limited," as a friend noted, "from political exigencies" (Jeune, p. 14).

76. Arnold, *Letters*, II, 34.
77. Thompson, p. 263.
78. Young, *Daylight and Champaign*, p. 64.
79. Arnold, *Mixed Essays*, p. 407.
80. Arnold, *England and the Italian Question*, p. 30.
81. Arnold, *Civilization in the United States*, pp. 5, 43.
82. Arnold, "From Easter to August," p. 321 (Neiman, p. 367).
83. Arnold, "Zenith of Conservatism," p. 163 (Neiman, p. 328).

BIBLIOGRAPHY

The *Bibliography of Matthew Arnold* compiled by Thomas Burnett Smart (London, 1892) is still useful, although recent ascriptions have somewhat outdated Smart's work. The following list includes only those editions of works that have been consulted for this study.

WORKS OF MATTHEW ARNOLD

MATERIAL APPEARING IN BOOK FORM

A *Bible-Reading for Schools: The Great Prophecy of Israel's Restoration*, ed. and arr. by Matthew Arnold. London, Macmillan, 1872.

Civilization in the United States: First and Last Impressions of America. Boston, Cupples and Hurd, 1888.

Culture and Anarchy: An Essay in Political and Social Criticism and Friendship's Garland, Being the Conversations, Letters and Opinions of the Late Arminius, Baron Von Thunder-Ten-Tronckh, Collected and Edited with a Dedicatory Letter to Adolescens Leo, Esq., of "The Daily Telegraph." New York, Macmillan, 1883.

Culture and Anarchy, ed. and with introd. by J. Dover Wilson. Cambridge (Eng.), Cambridge University Press, 1954.

Discourses in America. London and New York, Macmillan, 1894.

England and the Italian Question, to which is appended "Matthew
  Arnold and the Italian Question" by James Fitzjames Stephen,
  ed. Merle M. Bevington. Durham, Duke University Press, 1953.
Essays in Criticism: First Series. New York, Macmillan, 1895.
Essays in Criticism: Second Series. New York, Macmillan, 1896.
Essays in Criticism: Third Series, ed. E. J. O'Brien. Boston, Ball,
  1910.
Essays, Letters, and Reviews by Matthew Arnold, coll. and ed.
  Fraser Neiman. Cambridge, Harvard University Press, 1960.
Essays, Literary and Critical, with introd. by G. K. Chesterton.
  London and New York, Everyman ed., 1906.
A *French Eton or Middle-Class Education and the State to which
  is added Schools and Universities of France*. London, Macmillan,
  1892.
*God and the Bible: A Review of Objections to "Literature and
  Dogma."* New York, Macmillan, 1924.
*Isaiah of Jerusalem in the Authorised English Version with an
  Introduction, Corrections, and Notes*, ed. Matthew Arnold. Lon-
  don, Macmillan, 1883.
Letters of an Old Playgoer, ed. and with introd. by Brander Mat-
  thews. New York, printed for the Dramatic Museum of Colum-
  bia University, 1919.
Letters, Speeches and Tracts on Irish Affairs by Edmund Burke, ed.
  Matthew Arnold. London, Macmillan, 1881.
*Literature and Dogma: An Essay Towards a Better Apprehension
  of the Bible*. London, Macmillan, 1893.
Mixed Essays, Irish Essays, and Others. New York, Macmillan,
  1924.
The Note-Books of Matthew Arnold, ed. H. F. Lowry, Karl Young,
  and W. H. Dunn. London and New York, Oxford University
  Press, 1952.
On the Study of Celtic Literature. London, Smith, Elder, 1867.
The Poetical Works of Matthew Arnold, ed. C. B. Tinker and
  H. F. Lowry. London, Oxford University Press, 1950.

*The Popular Education of France with Notices of That of Holland
and Switzerland*. London, Longmans, 1861.

Reports on Elementary Schools, 1852–1882, ed. and with introd.
by F. S. Marvin. London, Wyman, 1908.

Reports on Elementary Schools, 1852–1882, ed. Sir Francis Sandford. London and New York, Macmillan, 1889.

*St. Paul & Protestantism, with an Essay on Puritanism & the
Church of England and Last Essays on Church & Religion*.
New York, Macmillan, 1883.

"Schools," article in *Reign of Queen Victoria*, Vol. II, ed. T. H.
Ward. London, Smith, Elder, 1887.

Schools and Universities on the Continent. London, Macmillan,
1868.

*Thoughts on Education Chosen from the Writings of Matthew
Arnold*, ed. Leonard Huxley. London, Smith, Elder, 1912.

NEWSPAPER AND PERIODICAL CONTRIBUTIONS NOT REPRINTED

"Cost of Elementary Schools," letter to the *Times*, Oct. 20, 1879,
p. 6.

"Emannuel Hospital," letter to the *Pall Mall Gazette* (signed "M.
A."), April 26, 1871, p. 5.

"English at the Universities," letter to the *Pall Mall Gazette*, Jan.
7, 1887, pp. 1–2.

"George Sand," letter to the *Pall Mall Gazette*, Aug. 12, 1884,
pp. 1–2.

"Italian Art and Literature before Giotto and Dante," *Macmillan's
Magazine*, XXXIII (Jan., 1876), 228.

"A Liverpool Address," *Nineteenth Century*, XII (Nov., 1882),
710–20.

"A Speech at Westminster," *Macmillan's Magazine*, XXIX (Feb.,
1874), 361–66.

"The Twice-Revised Code," *Fraser's Magazine*, LXV (March,
1862), 347–65.

COLLECTED LETTERS

Letters of Matthew Arnold, 1848–1888, coll. and arr. by George W. E. Russell. 2 vols. London and New York, Macmillan, 1895.

Letters of Matthew Arnold to Arthur Hugh Clough, ed. and with introductory study by H. F. Lowry. London and New York, Oxford University Press, 1932.

Letters from Matthew Arnold to John Churton Collins. London, printed for private circulation, 1910.

Unpublished Letters of Matthew Arnold, ed. Arnold Whitridge. New Haven, Yale University Press, 1923.

GENERAL WORKS

Abbott, Evelyn, and Lewis Campbell. *The Life and Letters of Benjamin Jowett.* 2 vols. London, John Murray, 1897.

Allott, Kenneth. "Matthew Arnold: Two Unpublished Letters," *Notes and Queries,* CC (Aug., 1955), 356–57.

Appleman, P., W. A. Madden, and M. Wolff, eds. *1859: Entering an Age of Crisis.* Bloomington, Indiana University Press, 1959.

Arbuthnot, Alexander J. *Memories of Rugby and India,* ed. Constance, Lady Arbuthnot. London, T. Fisher Unwin, 1910.

Armytage, W. H. G. "Matthew Arnold and W. E. Gladstone: Some New Letters," *University of Toronto Quarterly,* N.S. XVIII (April, 1949), 217–26.

—— "Matthew Arnold and T. H. Huxley: Some New Letters, 1870–80," *Review of English Studies,* N.S. IV (Oct., 1953), 346–53.

—— "Matthew Arnold and a Liberal Minister, 1880–5," *Review of English Studies,* XXIII (Oct., 1947), 355–57.

—— "Matthew Arnold and Richard Cobden in 1864: Some Recently Discovered Letters," *Review of English Studies,* XXV (July, 1949), 249–54.

Armytage, W. H. G. A. J. Mundella, 1825–1897: The Liberal Background to the Labour Movement. London, Benn, 1951.

—— "George Odger (1820–1877): A Founder of the British Labour Movement," University of Toronto Quarterly, XVIII (Oct., 1948), 68–75.

Arnold, Thomas. "Early Roman History," Quarterly Review, XXXII (June, 1825), 67–92.

—— Fragment on the Church. London, B. Fellowes, 1844.

——, ed. The History of the Peloponnesian War by Thucydides. 3 vols. Oxford, J. Parker, 1st ed., 1830–35, 2d ed., 1840–42.

—— History of Rome. 3 vols. London, B. Fellowes, 1838–40.

—— Introductory Lectures on Modern History. London, B. Fellowes, 1845.

—— Miscellaneous Works. London, B. Fellowes, 1845.

—— "The Oxford Malignants and Dr. Hampden," Edinburgh Review, CXXVII (April, 1836), 225–39.

—— Sermons. 6 vols. London, Longmans, Green, 1878.

Arnold, Thomas (the younger). "Arthur Hugh Clough: A Sketch," Nineteenth Century, XLIII (Jan., 1898), 105–16.

—— Passages in a Wandering Life. London, Edward Arnold, 1900.

[Arnold, Thomas, the younger]. "Matthew Arnold (By One Who Knew Him Well)," Manchester Guardian, May 18, 1888.

Arnold, William Delafield. Oakfield: Or Fellowship in the East. London, Longmans, 1854.

Arnold, William T. "Thomas Arnold the Younger," Century Magazine, LXVI, N.S. XLIV (May, 1903), 115–28.

[Arnold-Forster, Mary]. The Right Honourable Hugh Oakeley Arnold-Forster: A Memoir by His Wife. London, Edward Arnold, 1910.

Austin, Alfred, "Matthew Arnold," National Review, XI (May, 1888), 415–19.

Ausubel, Herman. The Late Victorians: A Short History. New York, Van Nostrand, 1955.

Aydelotte, William O. "The House of Commons in the 1840's," *History*, XXXIX (Oct., 1954), 249–62.

Bagehot, Walter. *The English Constitution*. London, etc., Oxford University Press, 1929.

Baines, Edward [The Younger]. *A Letter to the Most Noble the Marquis of Lansdowne, President of the Council, on the Government Plan of Education*. London, Ward, Simpkin, Marshall, 1847.

—— *The Life of Edward Baines*. London, Longmans, 1851.

Baldwin, A. B. *The Penroses of Fledborough Parsonage: Lives, Letters, and Diary*. London, Hull [1933].

Bamford, Thomas W. *Thomas Arnold*. London, Cresset, 1961.

Barker, Ernest. *Political Thought in England*. New York and London, Butterworth, n.d.

Bell, Herbert C. F. *Lord Palmerston*. 2 vols. London and New York, Longmans, Green, 1936.

Bevington, Merle M. "Matthew Arnold and John Bright," *Publications of the Modern Language Association*, LXX (June, 1955), 543–48.

—— *The Saturday Review, 1855–1868: Representative Educated Opinion in Victorian England*. New York, Columbia University Press, 1941.

Birrell, Augustine. *In the Name of the Bodleian*. New York, C. Scribner's sons, 1905.

Bodleian Library, Oxford. Three unpublished letters.

Bonnerot, Louis. *Matthew Arnold, poète*. Paris, M. Didier, 1947.

Bosanquet, Theodora. *Harriet Martineau: An Essay in Comprehension*. London, Etchells and MacDonald, 1927.

Bowle, John. *Politics and Opinion in the Nineteenth Century: An Historical Introduction*. New York, Oxford University Press, 1954.

Bradley, George Granville. *Recollections of Arthur Penrhyn Stanley*. New York, C. Scribner's sons, 1883.

Brief Observations of the Political and Religious Sentiments of the Late Rev. Dr. Arnold, as Contained in His Life by the Rev. Arthur Penrhyn Stanley, Extracted from the Record Newspaper. London, Seeley, Burnside, and Seeley, 1845.

Briggs, Asa. *Victorian People.* London, Odhams, 1954.

Brinton, Crane. *English Political Thought in the Nineteenth Century.* Cambridge, Harvard University Press, 1949.

Brookfield, Charles and Frances. *Mrs. Brookfield and Her Circle.* New York, C. Scribner's sons, 1906.

Brown, E. K. "The French Reputation of Matthew Arnold," *Studies in English by Members of University College, Toronto,* University of Toronto Press, 1931.

—— *Matthew Arnold.* Chicago, University of Chicago Press, 1948.

—— *Studies in the Text of Matthew Arnold's Prose Works.* Paris, Impressions Pierre André, 1935.

Browning, Oscar. "Arnold and Arnoldism," *Academy: A Journal of Secondary Education,* VI (Feb., 1891), 14–18.

—— "Rugby, Arnold, and Arnoldism," *Education,* I (Dec., 1890), 309–10.

Buckler, William E. *Matthew Arnold's Books: Toward a Publishing Diary.* Geneva, Librairie E. Droz, 1958.

—— "Studies in Three Arnold Problems," *Publications of the Modern Language Association,* LXXIII (June, 1958), 260–69.

Butler, Josephine. *Recollections of George Butler.* Bristol, J. W. Arrowsmith [1892].

Campbell, R. J. *Thomas Arnold.* London, Macmillan, 1927.

Carlyle, Thomas. *Critical and Miscellaneous Essays.* 3 vols. London, Chapman and Hall, 1888.

—— "Louis-Philippe," *Examiner,* March 4, 1848, pp. 145–46.

Cecil, Algernon. *British Foreign Secretaries, 1807–1916.* London, Bell, 1927.

—— *Queen Victoria and Her Prime Ministers.* New York, Oxford University Press, 1953.

Cecil, David. *Lord Melbourne.* London, Constable, 1954.

Chambers, E. K. *Matthew Arnold: A Study*. Oxford, Clarendon Press, 1947.

Christie, O. F. *The Transition from Aristocracy*. London, Seeley, Service, 1927.

—— *The Transition to Democracy*. London, Routledge, 1934.

Church, R. W. *The Oxford Movement*. London, Macmillan, 1904.

Churchill, Winston S. *Lord Randolph Churchill*. 2 vols. New York, Macmillan, 1906.

Churton, Edward. *Memoir of Joshua Watson*. 2 vols. Oxford and London, Parker, 1861.

Clapham, John Harold. "Conservative Factors in Recent British History," *Authority and the Individual*. Cambridge, Harvard University Press, 1937.

Clough, Arthur Hugh. *A Consideration of Objections Against the Retrenchment Association*. Oxford, Francis Macpherson, 1847.

—— *The Correspondence of Arthur Hugh Clough*, ed. F. L. Mulhauser. 2 vols. Oxford, Clarendon Press, 1957.

——Letters to the *Balance* (signed "M. A. O."), Jan. 23, 1846, p. 26; Jan. 30, 1846, p. 34; Feb. 6, 1846, p. 42; Feb. 13, 1846, p. 50; March 6, 1846, p. 77; March 20, 1846, pp. 93–94.

—— *Poems and Prose Remains*. 2 vols. London, Macmillan, 1869.

Cole, G. D. H. *Socialist Thought: The Forerunners, 1789–1850*. London, Macmillan, 1953.

Cole, G. D. H., and Raymond Postgate. *The British Common People, 1746–1938*. New York, Knopf, 1939.

Coleridge, Ernest Hartley. *Life and Correspondence of John Duke Lord Coleridge, Lord Chief Justice of England*. 2 vols. London, Heinemann, 1904.

Coleridge, John Duke (Lord). "Matthew Arnold," *New Review*, I (July, 1889), 111–24; I (Aug., 1889), 217–32.

—— "Principal Shairp," *Macmillan's Magazine*, LVIII (Aug., 1888), 247–53.

Conington, John. *Miscellaneous Writings*, ed. J. A. Symonds, with a memoir by H. J. S. Smith. 2 vols. London, Longmans, Green, 1872.

Connell, W. F. *The Educational Thought and Influence of Matthew Arnold*. London, Routledge and Kegan Paul, 1950.

Coulson, Percy, ed. *Lord Goschen and His Friends (The Goschen Letters)*. London, Hutchinson, 1946.

Cowherd, Raymond. *The Politics of English Dissent*. New York, New York University Press, 1956.

Cowley, Earl. *The Paris Embassy During the Second Empire from the Papers of Earl Cowley*, ed. F. A. Wellesley. London, Butterworth, 1928.

Curgenven, John. "Theodore Walrond: Friend of Arnold and Clough," *Durham University Journal*, XLIV (March, 1952), 56–61.

Dale, R. W. *History of English Congregationalism*. London, Hodder and Stoughton, 1907.

—— "Mr. Matthew Arnold and the Nonconformists," *Contemporary Review*, XIV (July, 1870), 540–71.

Davis, H. W. Carless. *Balliol College*. London, F. E. Robinson, 1899.

Drinkwater, John. "Some Letters from Matthew Arnold to Robert Browning," *Cornhill Magazine*, N.S. LV (1923), 654–64.

Eastlake, Lady Elizabeth. *Journals and Correspondence*, ed. C. E. Smith. 2 vols. London, Murray, 1895.

Elias, Otto. *Matthew Arnolds politische Grundanschauungen*. Leipzig, Mayer and Müller, 1931.

Eliot, T. S. "Arnold and Pater," *Selected Essays, 1917–1932*. New York, Harcourt, Brace, 1932.

—— "The Second-Order Mind," *Dial*, LXIX (Dec., 1920), 586–89.

Elliot, Arthur D. *The Life of George Joachim Goschen, First Viscount Goschen*. 2 vols. London, Longmans, Green, 1911.

Ensor, R. C. K. *England, 1870–1914 (Oxford History of England)*. Oxford, Clarendon Press, 1936.

—— "Some Political and Economic Interactions in Later Victorian

England," *Transactions of the Royal Historical Society*, 4th Ser., XXXI (1949), 17–28.

Escott, T. H. S. *England: Her People, Polity, and Pursuits.* London, Chapman and Hall, 1885.

—— *Personal Forces of the Period.* London, Hurst and Blackett, 1898.

—— *Social Transformations of the Victorian Age.* London, Seeley, 1897.

—— *Society in the Country House,* Philadelphia, Jacobs [1906].

Everett, Edwin M. *The Party of Humanity: The Fortnightly Review and Its Contributors, 1865–1874.* Chapel Hill, University of North Carolina Press, 1939.

Eversley, Lord (G. Shaw Lefevre). *Gladstone and Ireland: The Irish Policy of Parliament from 1850–1894.* London, Methuen, 1912.

Faulkner, Harold Underwood. *Chartism and the Churches: A Study in Democracy.* New York, privately printed, 1916.

Faverty, Frederic E. *Matthew Arnold, the Ethnologist.* Evanston, Northwestern University Press, 1951.

Fishback, W. P. *Recollections of Lord Coleridge.* Indianapolis and Kansas City, Bowen-Merrill, 1895.

Fitzmaurice, Lord Edmond. *The Life of Granville George Leveson Gower, Second Earl Granville.* 2 vols. London, Longmans, Green, 1905.

Fletcher, Eliza. *Autobiography.* Edinburgh, Edmonston and Douglas, 1875.

Ford, George H. "The Governor Eyre Case in England," *University of Toronto Quarterly*, XVII (April, 1948), 219–33.

Forster, William E. "American Slavery, and Emancipation by the Free States," *Westminster Review*, N.S. III (Jan., 1853), 125–67.

Fortescue, Chicester. . . . *and Mr. Fortescue* (selection from the diaries 1851–62 of Chicester Fortescue, Lord Carlingford, K.P.), ed. O. W. Hewett. London, Murray, 1958.

Galton, Arthur H. "Fifteen Letters of Matthew Arnold to A.

Galton (1886–87)," *Century Guild Hobby Horse*, V (April, 1890), 47–55.

Garrod, H. W. *Poetry and the Criticism of Life*. Cambridge, Harvard University Press, 1931.

Garvin, James L. *Life of Joseph Chamberlain*. 3 vols. London, Macmillan, 1932.

Gash, Norman. *Politics in the Age of Peel*. London and New York, Longmans, Green, 1953.

Gillespie, Frances. *Labor and Politics, 1850–1867*. Durham, Duke University Press, 1927.

Gladstone, Herbert J., Viscount. *After Thirty Years*. London, Macmillan, 1928.

Gladstone, William Ewart. "Mr. Forster and Ireland," *Nineteenth Century*, XXIV (Sept., 1888), 451–64.

—— *Studies Subsidiary to the Works of Bishop Butler*. New York, Macmillan, 1896.

—— Gladstone Papers. Twenty-two letters between William E. Gladstone and Matthew Arnold. British Museum.

—— Gladstone Papers. Letters between William E. Gladstone and William E. Forster. British Museum, Add. MSS. 44157–44160.

Gooch, G. P. *History and Historians in the Nineteenth Century*. London, Longmans, Green, 1920.

Gordon, Ian A. "Three New Letters of Matthew Arnold," *Modern Language Notes*, LVI (Nov., 1941), 552–54.

Goulburn, Edward M. *The Book of Rugby School*. Rugby, Crosley and Billington, 1856.

Grant Duff, Sir Mountstuart E. *Foreign Policy*. London, Macmillan, 1880.

—— "Matthew Arnold's Writings," *Murray's Magazine*, VII (March, 1890), 289–308.

—— *Out of the Past: Some Biographical Essays*. 2 vols. London, Murray, 1903.

Greville, Charles. *The Greville Memoirs (1814–1860)*, ed. Lytton

Strachey and Roger Fulford. 6 vols. London, Macmillan, 1938.

Grisewood, Harmon, ed. *Ideas and Beliefs of the Victorians*. London, Sylvan Press, 1949.

Guedalla, Philip. *Palmerston*. New York, Putnam, 1927.

Guizot, François Pierre. *An Embassy to the Court of St. James's*. London, Richard Bentley, 1862.

Halévy, Elie. *History of the English People in the Nineteenth Century*. 6 vols. London, Benn, 1924–51.

Hammond, J. L. *Gladstone and the Irish Nation*. London, Longmans, Green, 1938.

Hammond, J. L. and Barbara. *The Age of the Chartists*. London, Longmans, Green, 1930.

Hammond, J. L., and M. R. D. Foot. *Gladstone and Liberalism*. London, English Universities Press, 1952.

Hardinge, Arthur. *The Life of Henry Howard Molyneux Herbert, Fourth Earl of Carnarvon, 1831–1890*. 3 vols. London, Oxford University Press, 1925.

Harris, Alan. "Matthew Arnold, the 'Unknown Years,'" *Nineteenth Century*, CXIII (April, 1933), 498–512.

Harrison, Frederic. *Autobiographic Memoirs*, 2 vols. London, Macmillan, 1911.

—— "Culture: A Dialogue," *Fortnightly Review*, VIII (Nov., 1867), 603–14.

Hayward, Abraham. *Selected Essays*. 2 vols. New York, Scribner and Welford, 1879.

Hearnshaw, F. J. C., ed. *The Social and Political Ideas of Some Representative Thinkers of the Victorian Age*. London, Harrap, 1933.

Hewett, Osbert Wyndham. *Strawberry Fair: A Biography of Frances, Countess of Waldegrave, 1821–1879*. London, Murray, 1956.

Hirst, Francis W. "Memories of Great Victorians," *Contemporary Review*, CLXXVIII (Aug., 1950), 89–92.

The Historical Record of the University of Oxford, 1220–1900. Oxford, Clarendon Press, 1900.

216

BIBLIOGRAPHY

A *History of Warwick*. In series *Victoria History of the Counties of England*, ed. L. F. Salzman, Arthur Doubleday, and William Page. 6 vols. London, Oxford University Press, 1904–51.

Hodder, Edwin. *The Life of Samuel Morley*. London, Hodder and Stoughton, 1887.

Holland, Bernard. *The Life of Spencer Compton, Eighth Duke of Devonshire*. 2 vols. London, Longmans, Green, 1911.

Holloway, John. *The Victorian Sage: Studies in Argument*. London, Macmillan, 1953.

Houghton, R. E. C. "Letter of Matthew Arnold," *Times Literary Supplement*, May 19, 1932, p. 368.

Houghton, Walter E. *The Victorian Frame of Mind 1830–1870*. New Haven, Yale University Press, 1957.

How, F. D. *Six Great Schoolmasters*. London, Methuen, 1904.

Hughes, Thomas. *Manliness of Christ*. London, Macmillan, 1894.

—— *Memoir of a Brother*. London, Macmillan, 1873.

—— *Tom Brown's School-Days*. New York, St Martin's Press, 1958.

—— *Vacation Rambles*. London, Macmillan, 1895.

Humboldt, Wilhelm von. *The Sphere and Duties of Government*, trans. Joseph Coulthard. London, John Chapman, 1854.

Jeune, Mary. "Recollections of Mr. Forster," *National Review*, XII (Sept., 1888), 14–23.

Jones, Howard Mumford. "Arnold, Aristocracy, and America," *American Historical Review*, XLIX (April, 1944), 393–409.

Judges, A. V., ed. *Pioneers of English Education*. London, Faber and Faber, 1952.

Jump, J. D. *Matthew Arnold*. London, Longmans, Green, 1955.

Kay-Shuttleworth, James. *Four Periods of Public Education*. London, Longmans, Green, Longman, and Roberts, 1862.

Keir, D. Lindsay. *The Constitutional History of Modern Britain, 1485–1937*. London, Adam and Charles Black, 1943.

Kelleher, John V. "Matthew Arnold and the Celtic Revival," in

Harry Levin, ed. *Perspectives of Criticism* (*Harvard Studies in Comparative Literature*, No. 20). Cambridge, Harvard University Press, 1950.

Knickerbocker, William S. *Creative Oxford*. Syracuse, Syracuse University Press, 1925.

—— "Matthew Arnold at Oxford: The Natural History of a Father and Son," *Sewanee Review*, XXXV (Oct., 1927), 399–418.

—— "Semaphore: Arnold and Clough," *Sewanee Review*, XLI (Jan.–March, 1933), 152–74.

Knight, William. *Principal Shairp and His Friends*. London, John Murray, 1888.

Lacaita, Charles. *An Italian Englishman, Sir James Lacaita, 1813–1895*. London, Grant Richards, 1933.

Lake, William Charles. "The Life and Correspondence of T. Arnold, D.D." (review), *Quarterly Review*, LXXXIV (Oct., 1844), 467–508.

—— *Memorials of William Charles Lake, Dean of Durham, 1869–1894*, ed. Katherine Lake. London, Edward Arnold, 1901.

—— "More Oxford Memories," *Good Words* (Dec., 1895), pp. 828–32.

—— "Rugby and Oxford, 1830–1850," *Good Words* (Oct., 1895), pp. 666–70.

Lansdowne, Marquis of [Henry William Perry-Fitzmaurice]. *Glanerought and the Petty-Fitzmaurices*. London and New York, Oxford University Press, 1937.

Leavis, F. R. "Arnold as Critic," in Eric Bentley, ed. *The Importance of Scrutiny*. New York, George Stewart, 1948.

Lewis, Roy, and Angus Maude. *The English Middle Classes*. London, Phoenix House, 1949.

Liddon, Henry Parry. *Life of Edward Bouverie Pusey*. 4 vols. London, Longmans, Green, 1893–97.

Lippincott, Benjamin E. *Victorian Critics of Democracy*. Minneapolis, University of Minnesota Press, 1938.

Lowe, Robert. *Speeches and Letters on Reform*. London, Bush, 1867.

Lowe, Robert Liddell. "Matthew Arnold and Percy William Bunting: Some New Letters, 1884–1887," *Studies in Bibliography*, VII (1955), 199–207.

—— "A Note on Arnold in America," *American Literature*, XXIII (May, 1951), 250–52.

—— "Two Arnold Letters," *Modern Philology*, LII (May, 1955), 262–64.

Lowell, James Russell. *Democracy: An Address Delivered in the Town Hall*. Birmingham, Boston, and New York, Riverside, 1902.

Lynd, Helen Merell. *England in the Eighteen-Eighties: Toward a Social Basis for Freedom*. New York, Oxford, 1945.

McCabe, Joseph. *Life and Letters of George Jacob Holyoake*. 2 vols. London, Watts, 1908.

Maccoby, S., ed. *The English Radical Tradition, 1763–1914*. London, Nicholas Kaye, 1952.

—— *English Radicalism, 1832–1853*. London, Allen and Unwin, 1935.

—— *English Radicalism, 1853–1886*. London, Allen and Unwin, 1938.

Mack, Edward C., and W. H. G. Armytage. *Thomas Hughes*. London, Benn, 1952.

Magnus, Philip. *Gladstone*. New York, E. P. Dutton, 1954.

Malmesbury, James Howard, Earl of. *Memoirs of an Ex-Minister*. 2 vols. London, Longmans, Green, 1884.

Martin, A. Patchett. *Life and Letters of the Right Honourable Robert Lowe, Viscount Sherbrooke*. 2 vols. London, Longmans, Green, 1893.

Martineau, Harriet. *Autobiography*. 2 vols. Boston, Houghton, Osgood, 1879.

—— *Biographical Sketches*. New York, Leypoldt and Holt, 1869.

—— A History of the Thirty Years' Peace. 4 vols. London, George Bell, 1877–78.

Marx, Karl, and Friedrich Engels. Correspondence, 1846–1895. New York, International Publishers, 1935.

"Matthew Arnold: Poet and Essayist," British Quarterly Review, XLII (Oct., 1865), 243–69.

Mayhew, Henry. London Labour and the London Poor: A Cyclopaedia of the Condition and Earnings of Those That Will Work; Those That Cannot Work; and Those That Will Not Work. 3 vols. London, Griffin, Bohn, 1861.

Miall, Arthur. Life of Edward Miall. London, Macmillan, 1884.

Middleton, R. D. Newman at Oxford. London and New York, Oxford University Press, 1950.

Mill, John Stuart. Considerations on Representative Government. New York, Harper, 1862.

—— "Endowments," Fortnightly Review, N.S. V (April, 1869), 377–90.

—— England and Ireland. London, Longmans, 1868.

—— "On the Probable Futurity of the Labouring Classes," Principles of Political Economy, II, 327–56. London, Parker, 1857.

Milnes, Richard Monckton. The Events of 1848, Especially in Their Relation to Great Britain: A Letter to the Marquis of Lansdowne. London, Ollivier, 1849.

Monypenny, William F., and George E. Buckle. The Life of Benjamin Disraeli, Earl of Beaconsfield, 2 vols. London, Murray, 1929.

Moran, Benjamin. The Journal of Benjamin Moran (1857–1865), ed. S. A. Wallace and F. E. Gillespie. 2 vols. Chicago, University of Chicago Press, 1949.

Morley, John. Life of Richard Cobden. Boston, Roberts, 1881.

—— The Life of William Ewart Gladstone. 2 vols. London, Macmillan, 1905.

Morley, John. *Recollections.* 2 vols. New York, Macmillan, 1917.

Morrah, Herbert Arthur. *The Oxford Union, 1823–1923.* London, Cassell, 1923.

Morris, William. *Hopes and Fears For Art.* New York, Longmans, Green, 1901.

Mott, Lewis Freeman. *Sainte-Beuve.* New York, D. Appleton, 1925.

Motter, T. H. V. "A New Arnold Letter and an Old Swinburne Quarrel," *Times Literary Supplement,* Aug. 31, 1933, p. 576.

Müller, F. Max. *My Autobiography.* London, Longmans, Green, 1901.

Mulvey, Helen. "Lecky: Opponent of Irish Home Rule," *Victorian Studies,* I (June, 1958), 337–51.

Myers, Frederic W. H. "Matthew Arnold," *Fortnightly Review,* XLIII (May, 1888), 719–28.

Neff, Emery. *Carlyle.* New York, Norton, 1932.

Neiman, Fraser. "Some Newly Attributed Contributions of Matthew Arnold to the *Pall Mall Gazette,*" *Modern Philology,* LV (Nov., 1957), 84–92.

[Francis Newman]. Review of *The Miscellaneous Works* of Thomas Arnold, *Prospective Review,* I, No. 3 (1845), 416–44.

Newman, John Henry. *Apologia Pro Vita Sua.* London, Longmans, Green, 1864.

—— *Elucidations of Dr. Hampden's Theological Statements.* Oxford, W. Baxter, 1836.

Newton, Thomas W. L. *Lord Lansdowne.* London, Macmillan, 1929.

Nicolson, Harold. *Sainte-Beuve.* Garden City, Doubleday, 1957.

O'Connor, James. *History of Ireland, 1798–1924.* 2 vols. London, Arnold, 1926.

O'Hegarty, P. S. *A History of Ireland Under the Union, 1801 to 1922.* London, Methuen, 1952.

Oriel College, Oxford, Library. Four unpublished letters.

Osbourn, R. V. "The British Quarterly Review," *Review of English Studies,* N.S. I (1950), 147–52.

Ostrogorski, M. *Democracy and the Organization of Political Parties.* 2 vols. New York, Macmillan, 1902.

Oswell, W. Edward. *William Cotton Oswell, Hunter and Explorer.* 2 vols. London, Heinemann, 1900.

Packe, Michael St. John. *The Life of John Stuart Mill.* London, Secker and Warburg, 1954.

Palgrave, Gwellian F. *Francis Turner Palgrave: His Journals and Memories of His Life.* London, Longmans, Green, 1899.

Palmer, Roundell. *Memorials, Part I, Family and Personal.* 2 vols. London, Macmillan, 1896.

—— *Memorials, Part II, Personal and Political.* 2 vols. London, Macmillan, 1898.

Park, Joseph H. *British Prime Ministers.* London, Oxford University Press, 1951.

—— *The English Reform Bill of 1867.* New York, Columbia University Press, 1920.

Peel, Albert. *A Hundred Eminent Congregationalists, 1530–1924.* London, 1927.

Pelling, Henry. *America and the British Left, from Bright to Bevan.* London, Adam and Charles Black, 1956.

Perry, G. G. *A History of the English Church.* 3 vols. London, Murray, 1890.

Pope-Hennessy, James. *Monckton Milnes: The Years of Promise.* London, Constable, 1949.

—— *Monckton Milnes: The Flight of Youth.* London, Constable, 1951.

Powell, H. Townsend. *Liberalism Unveiled: Or Strictures on Dr. Arnold's Sermons.* London, R. Clay, 1830.

Prothero, Rowland E. *The Life and Correspondence of Arthur Penrhyn Stanley.* 2 vols. London, Murray, 1893.

Rannie, David Watson. *Oriel College.* London, Robinson, 1900.

Redesdale, Algernon. *Memories.* 2 vols. London, Hutchinson, 1915.

Reid, T. Wemyss. *Life of the Right Hon. William Edward Forster.* 2 vols. London, Chapman and Hall, 1888.

Roach, John. "Liberalism and the Victorian Intelligentsia," *Cambridge Historical Journal*, XIII (1957), 58–81.

Robbins, William. *The Ethical Idealism of Matthew Arnold: A Study of the Nature and Sources of His Moral and Religious Ideas*. London, Heinemann, 1959.

—— "Matthew Arnold and Ireland," *University of Toronto Quarterly*, XVII (Oct., 1947), 52–67.

Robert, David. "Tory Paternalism and Social Reform in Early Victorian England," *American Historical Review*, LXIII (Jan., 1958), 323–37.

Robinson, Henry Crabb. *The Correspondence of Henry Crabb Robinson with the Wordsworth Circle* (1808–1866), ed. Edith J. Morley. 2 vols. Oxford, Clarendon Press, 1927.

Rouse, W. H. D. *A History of Rugby School*. London, Duckworth, 1898.

Rudman, Harry. *Italian Nationalism and English Letters*. New York, Columbia University Press, 1940.

The Rugby Magazine. 2 vols. London, William Pickering, 1835–36.

Rugby School Register, rev. and annot. by Godfrey A. Solly. Rugby, George Over, 1933.

Sainte-Beuve, Charles A. *Chateaubriand et son groupe littéraire sous l'Empire*. 2 vols. Paris, Calmann Lévy, 1878.

—— *Les grands écrivains français, XIXème siècle: Philosophes et essayistes*, III. Paris, Garnier Frères, 1930.

Salmon, Martha. "Frederic Harrison: The Evolution of an English Positivist, 1831–1881." Unpublished dissertation, Department of English, Columbia University, 1959.

Sand, George. *Questions politiques et sociales*. Paris, Calmann Lévy, 1879.

Sanders, Charles R. *Coleridge and the Broad Church Movement*. Durham, Duke University Press, 1942.

Sanders, Lloyd. *The Holland House Circle*. New York, Putnam, 1908.

Sandford, E. G., ed. *Memoirs of Archbishop Temple by Seven Friends.* 2 vols. London, Macmillan, 1906.

Schuyler, Robert L., and Herman Ausubel. *The Making of English History.* New York, Dryden, 1952.

Sedgwick, Henry. "The Prophet of Culture," *Macmillan's Magazine,* XVI (Aug., 1867), 271–80.

Seebohm, F. "Mr. W. E. Forster's Early Career," *Contemporary Review,* L (Sept., 1886), 305–23.

Sells, Iris. *Matthew Arnold and France: The Poet.* Cambridge, (Eng.), Cambridge University Press, 1935.

Shairp, John Campbell. *Glen Desseray and Other Poems Lyrical and Elegiac,* ed. Francis T. Palgrave. London, Macmillan, 1888.

—— *Portraits of Friends.* Boston and New York, Houghton and Mifflin, 1889.

Smellie, K. B. *A Hundred Years of English Government.* London, Gerald Duckworth, 1950.

Smith, Frank. *The Life and Work of Sir James Kay-Shuttleworth.* London, Murray, 1923.

Smith, Goldwin. *A Selection from Goldwin Smith's Correspondence,* ed. Arnold Haultain. London, T. Werner Laurie, 1913.

Smith, Henry Stooks. *The Parliaments of England from 1st George I to the Present Time.* 3 vols. London, Simpkin, Marshall, 1844–50.

Stanley, Arthur Penrhyn. *Life of Thomas Arnold, D.D., Head-Master of Rugby.* London, Murray, 1904.

—— *Letters and Verses,* ed. Rowland Prothero. London, Murray, 1895.

——, ed. *Memoirs of Edward and Catherine Stanley.* London, John Murray, 1879.

—— "Two Addresses by the Dean of Westminster, II, Arnold and Rugby (delivered in Rugby School Chapel, June 12, 1874)," *Macmillan's Magazine,* XXX (July, 1874), 279–80.

Stanley, Carlton. *Matthew Arnold.* Toronto, Toronto University Press, 1938.

Stephen, James Fitzjames. *Liberty, Equality, Fraternity.* New York, Holt and Williams, 1873.

Stephen, Leslie. *The Life of Sir James Fitzjames Stephen.* London, Smith, Elder, 1895.

—— *Studies of a Biographer.* 4 vols. New York, Putnam, 1898–1902.

Strauss, Eric. *Irish Nationalism and British Democracy.* London, Methuen, 1951.

Stuart, Andrew Godfrey. *Examination of a Tract Entitled "Brief Observations on the Political and Religious Sentiments of the Late Dr. Arnold etc."* London, Hatchard, 1845.

Swinburne, A. C. "Mr. Arnold's New Poems," *Fortnightly Review,* VIII (Oct., 1867), 414–45.

Tawney, R. H. *Equality.* New York, Harcourt, Brace, 1931.

Temple, Ruth Z. *The Critic's Alchemy.* New York, Twayne, 1953.

Thackeray, William M. *The Letters and Private Papers,* ed. G. N. Ray. 4 vols. London, Oxford University Press, 1945.

Thompson, E. P. *William Morris, Romantic to Revolutionary.* London, Lawrence and Wishart, 1955.

Thorold, Algar Labouchere. *The Life of Henry Labouchere.* London, Constable, 1913.

Ticknor, George. *Life, Letters, and Journals.* 2 vols. Boston, James Osgood, 1876.

Tillotson, Kathleen. "Dr. Arnold's Death and a Broken Engagement," *Notes and Queries,* CXCVII (Sept., 1952), 409–11.

—— "Matthew Arnold and Carlyle." Warton lecture on English poetry. *Proceedings of the British Academy,* vol. XLIII. London, 1956.

—— "Rugby 1850: Arnold, Clough, Walrond, and In Memoriam," *Review of English Studies,* N.S. IV (April, 1953), 122–40.

Tinker, C. B., and H. F. Lowry. *The Poetry of Matthew Arnold: A Commentary.* New York, Oxford University Press, 1940.

Todd, F. M. *Politics and the Poet: A Study of Wordsworth.* London, Methuen, 1957.

Traubel, Horace. *With Walt Whitman in Camden.* 3 vols. Boston, Small, Maynard, 1906.

Trevelyan, George Macaulay. *An Autobiography and Other Essays.* London, Longmans, Green, 1949.

—— *British History in the Nineteenth Century* (1782–1901). London and New York, Longmans, Green, 1922.

—— *The Life of John Bright.* Boston and New York, Houghton Mifflin, 1914.

Trevelyan, Janet Penrose. *The Life of Mrs. Humphry Ward.* New York, Dodd, Mead, 1923.

Trilling, Lionel. *Matthew Arnold.* New York, W. W. Norton, 1939.

Waagen, G. F. *Treasures of Art in Great Britain.* 3 vols. London, John Murray, 1854.

Walford, Edward. Letter to the *Times,* April 20, 1888, p. 13.

Walpole, Spencer. *The History of Twenty-Five Years.* 4 vols. London, Longmans, Green, 1904.

—— *The Life of Lord John Russell.* 2 vols. London and New York, Longmans, Green, 1891.

Ward, Mrs. Humphry. *A Writer's Recollections.* London, Collings, 1918.

Ward, Mrs. Humphry, and C. E. Montague. *William Thomas Arnold, Journalist and Historian.* Manchester, University Press, 1907.

Ward, Maisie. *Young Mr. Newman.* New York, Sheed & Ward, 1948.

Ward, Wilfred. *William George Ward and the Oxford Movement.* London, Macmillan, 1889.

Webb, Beatrice. *My Apprenticeship.* New York, Longmans, Green, 1926.

Webb, Robert K. *The British Working Class Reader, 1790–1848.* London, Allen and Unwin, 1955.

Webb, Sidney and Beatrice. *The History of Trade Unionism*. New York, Longmans, Green, 1920.

Whately, E. Jane. *Life and Correspondence of Richard Whately, D.D.* London, Longmans, Green, 1875.

Whitridge, Arnold. *Dr. Arnold of Rugby*. London, Constable, 1928.

Williams, Raymond. *Culture and Society, 1780–1950*. London, Chatto and Windus, 1958.

Wolf, Lucien. *Life of the First Marquess of Ripon*. 2 vols. London, Murray, 1921.

Woods, Margaret. "Matthew Arnold," in *Essays and Studies of the English Association*, XV, 7–19. Oxford, 1929.

Woodward, E. L. *The Age of Reform, 1815–1870* (Oxford History of England). Oxford, Clarendon Press, 1939.

—— *Three Studies in European Conservatism*. London, Constable, 1929.

Woodward, Frances J. *The Doctor's Disciples: A Study of Four Pupils of Arnold of Rugby: Stanley, Gell, Clough, William Arnold*. New York, Oxford University Press, 1954.

Wordsworth, William and Dorothy. *The Letters of William and Dorothy Wordsworth: The Later Years*, ed. Ernest de Selincourt. 3 vols. Oxford, Clarendon Press, 1939.

Wymer, Norman. *Dr. Arnold of Rugby*. London, Hale, 1953.

Yarnall, Ellis. *Wordsworth and the Coleridges with Other Memories Literary and Political*. New York, Macmillan, 1899.

Young, G. M. *Daylight and Champaign*. London, Cape, 1937.

—— *Last Essays*. London, Hart-Davis, 1950.

—— *Victorian England: Portrait of an Age*. London, Cumberlege, 1953.

INDEX

64-65, 69-70; reform and, 81-82, 115, 185*n*23; primary, 85, 87, 111, 118; compulsory, 86, 118, 135, 190*n*17; pupil-teacher system, 87; Forster Bill (1870), 87, 134-36; French, 87-88, 89-90; religion and, 90, 104, 110-11, 174; centralization, 91; Revised Code of 1862, 96, 111-12, 113; secondary, 117, 118, 123, 124, 174; Ireland and, 147, 149-50; Scotland, 161; see also Public schools; and see specific schools

Educational Review (periodical), 177*n*6

Educational Thought and Influence of Matthew Arnold, The (Connell), 185*n*23, 201*n*45

Education Department, 98, 158

Elizabeth I, queen of England, 8

Elwin, Malcolm, cited, 184*n*16

Emerson, Ralph Waldo, 37, 45

"Empedocles" (Arnold), 50

Emmanuel Hospital, 71

"Emmanuel Hospital" (Arnold), 187*n*45

Encyclopaedia Metropolitana, 11

Endowed Schools Act, 169

"Endowments" (Arnold), 187*n*45

Engels, Friedrich, quoted, 141, 167; cited, 199*n*31, 202*n*65

England: Revolution of 1688, 32; Franco-Austrian mediation offer (1859), 64, 65; balance of power and, 65, 66; aristocracy of, 67-68, 69, 76-77; Philistinism of, 123-28;

American Civil War and, 115, 116, 124, 125-26; Schleswig-Holstein dispute and, 61, 124, 126; Irish rule and, 146, 147-48, 155, 160-64, 168; Irish land rights and, 151-52; see also specific institutions, e.g., Parliament; and see specific place names

England and Ireland (Mill), 201*n*55

England and the Italian Question (Arnold), 65-66, 67-69, 93, 185*n*33, 186*nn*36, 39, 191*n*28, 203*n*80

English Constitution, The (Bagehot), 202*n*59

English Radicalism, 1832–1853 (Maccoby), 184*n*22, 192*n*55

Entering an Age of Crisis (Appleman, et al.), 185*n*30

"Equality" (Arnold), 71, 143

Equality (Tawney), 193*n*58

Erle, Sir William, 98

Escott, T. H. S., cited, 184 *nn*14, 17

Essays and Reviews, 46

Essays in Criticism: First Series (Arnold), 123, 131, 188*n*57, 189*n*13, 196*n*49, 197*n*51, 201*n*46

Essays in Criticism: Second Series (Arnold), 183*n*12, 187 *n*47

Essays in Criticism: Third Series (Arnold), 191*n*27

Essays, Letters and Reviews by Matthew Arnold (Neiman, ed.), on Oxford, 181*n*24; on property, 187*n*45; on culture, 189*nn*6, 8, 198*n*1; on school

242   INDEX

Las Cases, Emmanuel Dieu-
donné, comte de, 88
*Last Essays on Church and Re-
ligion* (Arnold), 187n46
Latin studies, 26, 31
Latitudinarians, 46
Laughton, J. K., 184n17
Lawleys, 9
Laws, *see specific* Bills and Acts
Leach, Arthur F., cited, 177n2
Leben Jesu (Strauss), 169
Lecky, W. E. H., 161-62,
202n68
Leeds, 115
Leeds Mercury (newspaper),
115, 119
Leighs, 9, 10
Leslie Stephen (Annan), 183n11
Letters, The (Smith), 184n17
Letters and Private Papers, The
(Thackeray), 184n16
*Letters of Matthew Arnold,
1848–1888* (Russell, ed.),
183nn1, 3, 4, 185nn31, 32,
186nn36, 37, 40, 191nn27,
29, 192nn40, 53, 194nn21,
23, 195n31, 196n41, 198nn3,
6; on the Decade, 182nn50-
51; on revolt of *1848*,
183nn8-9, 189n12; on Lansdowne, 185n23; on Russell,
185n26; on Palmerston,
185n29; on the lower class,
189n7, 190n16, 191n35,
199n31; on Chartist riots,
189nn10-11; on education,
190nn14, 19, 193n7, 195n29;
on Napoleon, 190n20; on
Guizot, 190n22; on Louis
Napoleon, 191n32; on George
Sand, 191n34; on Lowe,

191n37; on trade unions,
192n44; on Hyde Park riots,
192nn50, 57; on the State,
193n56; on religion, 193n57,
197nn53, 54, 62; on Forster,
194nn19, 20; on Philistinism,
195nn34, 35, 196nn44, 48;
on the Civil War, 196n39; on
trade expansion, 198n3; on
the Liberal Party, 198n6; on
Ireland, 199nn20, 22, 26, 29,
201n48; on Burke, 200n37;
on the culture of Dissenters,
201n46; on Gladstone, 202
nn63, 69, 72, 203n76
*Letters of Matthew Arnold to
Arthur Hugh Clough* (Lowry,
ed.), 181n41, 182nn50, 52,
183nn1, 4, 7, 9, 186n37, 189
nn1, 4, 10-12, 193n5, 194
n19, 198nn14, 16, 202n70
*Letters of William and Dorothy
Wordsworth: The Later Years*
(de Selincourt, ed.), 179n27
Letters to Ottilie Von Goethe
(Jameson), 184n16
Lettres au peuple (Sand), 79, 95
Libel laws, 40
Liberalism: of Thomas Arnold,
11-12, 13-14, 18-19, 22; social tension and, 32; religious,
32, 37-38; political, 38-39,
94-95; Matthew Arnold on,
73; upper class, 82; of Louis
XVIII, 89; Lowe and, 96; of
Forster, 113-14, 115; of Ar-
nold, 142-43; Irish Home
Rule and, 163, 165-66, 173;
middle class, 166; *see also*
Liberal Party; Radicalism
"Liberalism and the Victori-

nold and, 11-12, 14-16, 20;
Rugby election of 1835, 14,
178n17; Newmanism and, 36,
38; Oxonian, 39, 46; political
realignment, 42, 58, 165, 175,
184n21; Italian War, 65-66;
Anglican Church and, 71; up-
per class and, 109; Forster
and, 136; *see also* Conserva-
tism; Conservative Party
Tractarianism, 15, 35, 37-38,
44
Tract XC (Newman), 36, 37
Trade unions, 19, 97-99
Trafalgar Square, 48, 83, 102;
riots, 167
Transition from Aristocracy, The
(Christie), 184n13, 202n60
Traubel, Horace, 193n59
Treasures of Art in Great Britain
(Waagen), 184n15
Tremenheere, H. S., 85-86, 121
Trevelyan, G. O., cited, 184n16
Trevelyan, George Macaulay,
cited, 191n38, 192n55
Trevenen family, 193n3
Trilling, Lionel, quoted, 70;
cited, 187n44, 192n49, 195
n30
Trinity College, Oxford, 177n7
Trollope, Anthony, 5, 177n4
Twentieth Century (periodi-
cal), 188n60
"Twice-Revised Code, The"
(Arnold), 69, 185n24, 186
n41, 187n56, 191n36, 193
nn10-12
*Two Sermons on the Interpreta-
tion of Prophecy in the
Chapel of Rugby School*
(Thomas Arnold), 15, 178
n19

Tyler, William, 81
Tyndall, John, 166

Ulster, 160, 161, 162
Unforgotten Years (Smith), 188
n61
Unitarians, 108, 110
United Ireland (periodical), 157
United States of America: Sen-
ate election, 71; Civil War
in, 115, 116, 124, 125-26,
160-61, 163, 196n39; Arnold
in, 170; Grant as President,
174
University College, Oxford, 42,
108
*Unpublished Letters of Matthew
Arnold* (Whitridge, ed.), 185
nn31, 33; on Newman, 181
n30; on Lansdowne, 184n18,
186n37; on aristocracy, 186
n39, 187n46; on education,
190n14; on Louis Napoleon,
191n31
Upper class: Thomas Arnold's
identification with, 2-3, 20;
public-school system and, 5-
6, 9, 35; intermarriage, 10-11,
54-55; Matthew Arnold's relation to, 24, 52-53, 76-77,
79, 104, 107, 127, 140, 152;
Oxford and, 46; liberty and,
50-51; Parliament and, 57-58;
middle-class opinion and, 63,
70, 122; Italian independence
and, 65; "inaccessibility to
ideas," 67-68, 72, 74-75, 76;
decline of, 69-70, 141; inheritance rights and, 70-71; Athenian, 73; clergy and, 107-8;
Toryism and, 109; American
Civil War and, 125-26; Schles-